One Night In October

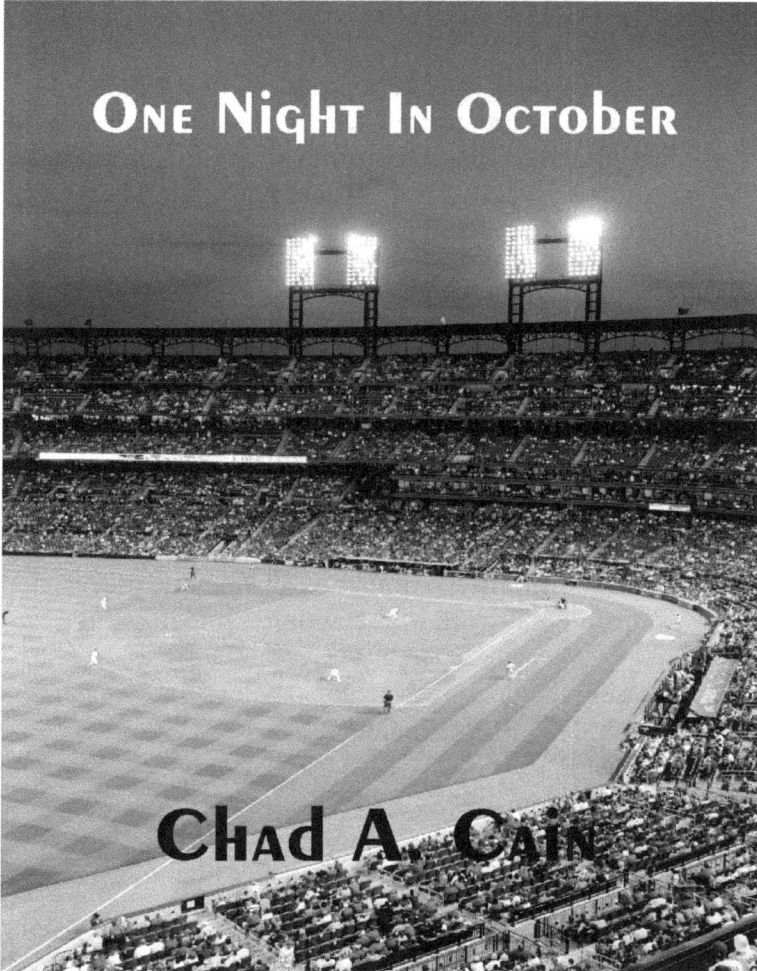

Chad A. Cain

Cover Art:
Michelle Crocker

http://mlcdesigns4you.weebly.com/

Publisher's Note:

This is a work of fiction. All names, characters, places, and events are the work of the author's imagination.

Any resemblance to real persons, places, or events is coincidental.

Solstice Publishing - www.solsticepublishing.com

ONE NIGHT IN OCTOBER

By Chad Cain

Dedication

For Robert "Hoot" Gibson, who taught me how to play golf, be a man, and love Cardinal baseball.

For Mattie Dee Cain, who taught me how to pray, read the scriptures, and love God.

And for Heather, you are my treasure and my shelter. I'll love you forever.

Prologue

I thought it was gone. When I saw the baseball fly off David Freese's bat in the bottom of the ninth of game six against the Rangers, my first thought was that it was going to leave the park. I wanted to believe it was possible, though hits like this when your team is down to their last strike in the World Series just don't happen in real life. He had just swung through the same pitch (a fastball on the outer half of the plate) on 1-1, but now I watched the ball heading toward deep right field. I had seen Freese do this a lot during the 2011 season. Hitting to the opposite field for power had become his trademark...but how could it possibly happen in this moment of desperation?

I leapt from the chair next to my father's bed. When the TV camera angle switched to Nelson Cruz in right field, my heart sank for a moment. He was going to catch it. You could tell from his reaction...he knew he was going to snag it. But then he kept drifting backward, and drifting more still. He was near the wall and jumping, but the ball caromed off the wall and rolled away. I began instinctively jumping and shouting for Lance Berkman and Albert Pujols to haul ass toward home. I nearly separated my shoulder doing the windmill along with third base coach Jose Oquendo.

Seeing the ball rolling away from Cruz, I thought perhaps there was a chance that Freese could have an inside-the-park home run. He didn't make it home, but easily slid into third and looked dazed and triumphant as he peered into the Cardinals' dugout. He had just delivered a game-tying and season-saving clutch hit for the ages. And that wasn't even his most memorable at-bat of the night!

My dad would have gladly joined me in my gleeful hysterics if this had been a typical night of baseball watching. Johnny Ray Gibson's roaring voice at one time was enough to drown out crowds at bars and raucous softball games. He had once been a physical specimen with a real gift for playing baseball and softball. He had once been the most intimidating man I had ever known. Now he lay old and withered in the house that I grew up in. He watched this game through a fog of medication and emotion. He was perfectly capable of following the action and talking about it, but he could no longer afford to expend energy on things like cheering for a game-saving hit.

He was dying, and watching the last game of his life.

I went to my father's house that night for the first time in nearly fifteen years. I went there because I knew if there was any chance of reconciliation; it would have to happen as part of watching a Cardinals game together. When they made that improbable run to the World Series in October of 2011, I took it as a sign that it was time for my return. When they came back home from Texas down three games to two, I knew I could no longer put it off. The St. Louis Cardinals were the only thing that my dad and I ever really connected on. When all else failed, we could always talk about the Cards.

That night I had a lifetime of things to say to the man, but without the Cardinals as a backdrop I would have had no idea how to begin. Most Cardinal fans will remember game six as the "Freese game" or even "the greatest World Series game ever played." I'll remember it for being the last night I ever saw my dad. I'll remember David Freese for giving us a couple of extra innings together and for giving my dad one last winner.

***

Southern Indiana, and in particular the city of Evansville, is mainly Cardinal country. I was born into the Gibson family in 1975, but I was also born into the Cardinals family. Johnny Ray was a lifelong devoted fan thanks to his dad. Had I said to him at any point that I wanted to root for the Cubs, I believe dad would have seriously considered kicking me out of his house. Thankfully I grew to love the Cards, and that was convenient because it gave me something that I could always talk to dad about without fear of an argument or, even worse, an awkward silence.

My name is Paul, which surprises me because dad probably wanted to name me Lou, Stan, or certainly Bob since Bob Gibson was his favorite player. Mom must have vetoed those in favor of a Biblical name because I can think of no famous Cardinals named Paul. My mother, Doris, was the only person who had the power to get her way when dealing with dad. He was six foot four and close to two hundred and fifty pounds of mostly muscle. Doris was about five-two and around a hundred and ten, but she never once seemed scared or intimidated by him.

Their marriage, which was still intact on the day he died, was in one sense very healthy because it was based on love. However, it could also be described as a textbook co-dependent relationship. Johnny Ray was a drinker, and as years passed he allowed it to overwhelm everything else. I found it difficult as a child to relate to the man, and nearly impossible to do so in my later years. Until the night of David Freese's heroics, I had spent the last fifteen years avoiding him entirely.

I never understood how mom could stay with him through so much turmoil. Love is of course necessary in a marriage, but there has to be more than that. One part of me admires her for "sticking it out" all these years, but there's also a large part that blames her for the manipulation and pain that dad so frequently doled out.

I suppose she was scared of raising two children, me and my sister Megan, who is six years younger, on her own. Or maybe she just got used to the version of "normal" in our lives and accepted it as good enough. I found it easier to get out when I had the chance, and I have lived with the fallout from that decision ever since.

One day in the spring of 2011, I got the usual weekly call from mom with an update on things in Evansville. I had left there to attend Southern Illinois University on a basketball scholarship in 1993 and never came back. My wife, Karen, whom I met at SIU, and I settled in a small town called O'Fallon, Illinois after college. It is a short commute to downtown St. Louis, where I work for an ad agency (of course half the reason I wanted to work there was because it was convenient for seeing lots of Cardinal games). My contact with mom consisted of weekly calls on the phone and three or four in-person visits a year, which normally involved us meeting at a restaurant or mall. I hadn't set foot in my parents' house since I left for college.

I could tell this call was different from the beginning. She called me Paul, which was a tell-tale sign because mom almost always liked to call me "Pauly." She was the only one who called me that and I secretly relished every time she said it. Her voice, which usually reflected her calm and soothing demeanor, was shaky and frightened.

"Paul. It's your mother. I...I don't know what else to say so I'll just say it. Your father has liver cancer and he's dying. We just found out today. Paul, did you hear me?"

I didn't speak for a few seconds. I had always assumed that dad would pay for his heavy drinking someday with cirrhosis or something, but it still stunned me. The man was only sixty-five.

"Uhh, my God, Mom. How are you holding up? Does Megan know yet?"

"She's here now, actually. God bless her, she's been cleaning our house for hours now. You know how she gets when there's bad news."

"But what about you?" I knew that this man had put her through hell over several decades, but I also understood that dad was the only man she had ever loved.

"I'm…I guess I'm still in shock, but I'm okay right now. I cried for about an hour after we got home. Your dad isn't really talking about it yet. Paul, I need you to do something for me." I knew what she was going to say before I heard it. I braced myself mentally.

"I need. *We* need you to come home. I know your dad wants to see you. I understand why you've stayed away and I never held it against you. But the doctor says he has six months. It's time for you to come home and see your father." She made this last point with her stern motherly tone. I hadn't heard that voice in many years and it still affected me the same way. I winced.

"Okay, mom. I promise I'll come home. I can't do it right away, though. There's too much going on with work, but I swear I'll get home as soon as I can. Okay?" This was a lie. Work was easily escapable if necessary. I just wasn't ready to face Johnny Ray…even if he was dying.

Over the next several months, I continued talking to and seeing mom as always. Dad was doing the treatments, including chemo, and feeling the effects. I assumed he would survive the treatments well considering his sheer physical power, even at his age. But mom said it was taking a dreadful toll, and there were many days when he didn't want to move out of bed. She continued to demand and then later beg me to come and see him. As summer passed into autumn, I knew that the time was drawing near.

At the beginning of September, with the Cardinals languishing ten and a half games behind in the Wild Card standings, I got word from mom that the cancer had spread to his lungs and his condition was deteriorating more rapidly. I'll admit there was a part of me that wanted him to die in pain without ever seeing his son again. I had terrible thoughts of enjoying the idea of his painful and slow death. In my heart I knew he had earned this fate through years of hard drinking and neglecting (and at times actively sabotaging) the lives of those he was supposed to love. I'm not proud of these thoughts, but in early September, they were the ones winning the debate in my mind.

That debate began to shift in late September when it became clear that something special was happening with this Cardinals team. They had chiseled that huge deficit down to just one game behind Atlanta with three to play. The Cardinals were playing a series in Houston (the worst team in the National League) and Atlanta would have to go to Philly. I began to ponder what it would be like to watch one more game with dad. Mom had been telling me he was excited about the run they were on, and I started to believe that perhaps this streak was destiny for both the team and our family.

On the night the Cards clinched the Wild Card berth, I called mom and told her I was coming to see dad soon. I now had a plan in mind: we could sit and watch a game together and at least have something to discuss. She told me she was happy, but also warned me to hurry. She didn't think he would live to see the World Series.

I knew if there was any fight left in Johnny Ray's body that he would find a way to see the Cardinals in one more World Series. I continued to drag my feet even as the Cards advanced through the playoffs with improbable wins over the Phillies (with Chris Carpenter's masterful 1-0 win clinching it in game five) and the Brewers. I knew that I would be hit by emotions and issues that I had long sought to avoid. But I also realized that I couldn't continue looking in the mirror if I didn't face him. I guess every man has to come to grips with both the lessons their father teaches them and the damage he inflicts.

On the night of October 27th, 2011, I walked into that old familiar house on Delmar Avenue and faced the father that I almost left for dead.

Top of the First

My parents lived in a working class neighborhood on the west side of Evansville known as Powell. It was, and still is, a collection of shotgun houses, bars, and Baptist churches centered around Powell Park. My parents moved into their house on Delmar shortly after I was born and, mostly due to my father, were never able to leave.

As I was growing up in the '70s and '80s, most of the families in Powell were fairly young. There were a lot of kids around my age and I spent the majority of my time on the softball fields at Powell Park or on the Centennial elementary school playground. The majority of the men in our neighborhood worked low-skill jobs in the brewery or at one of the various factories around town. Evansville has a long history as an industrial city, producing the P-47 Thunderbolt fighter as well as the LS-T ship during World War II, and there were still plenty of those jobs around in the early '80s.

My dad never had what you might call a career. He bounced around between jobs such as delivery truck driver, softball umpire, and even custodian of our church. His prospects were limited because he could never stay away from the booze. He was a whiskey man (usually Jack Daniels mixed with Double Cola or RC), but he was also loyal to our local brand of beer called Sterling. It was brewed right on the west side and was held in high regard by the men of Powell, probably more for the low price than the satisfying aftertaste. Alcohol was ever-present in our lives both at home and in public. No one ever complained about the drunk husbands (or the quietly drunk housewives) in our neighborhood because it was tradition. It was normal.

Johnny Ray carried on this tradition passed down from his dad, "Big Jim" Gibson, who had managed to make a career on the railroad as a functioning alcoholic. That's a term I didn't learn until later in life, but I think I knew the meaning very early on. I rarely saw dad without some sort of alcoholic beverage in his hand, but he was never a stumbling, slurring drunk. He didn't act like Otis from Mayberry (whom I thought was so funny watching reruns as a kid, but now not so much), he was however in a nearly constant state of "functional" drunkenness. Meeting Johnny Ray in public for the first time, you would probably have come away thinking he was a charming and well-spoken guy.

That was another aspect of my father that I didn't notice until later in life: his ability to attract people and make them laugh. At a bar or a ball game you couldn't help but notice him. He stood out because of his size, but his personality was just as big. He inspired fierce loyalty in his "drinking buddies" because he was their leader and wasn't shy about spreading his money around.

Most of the time I didn't see this side of dad. He was incredibly quiet and reserved when hanging around the house. The evenings when he did stay home, which became fewer and fewer after 1982, he would spend hours on the back porch listening to Jack Buck and Mike Shannon calling the Cardinal games on KMOX. Sometimes he would let me sit out there with him (though I had to be the beer mule).

Those were the nights I treasured because I got to hang out with dad and root for the team we both loved. Those nights were the foundation for whatever relationship we had as I grew up. Looking back, I'm glad that the games weren't on TV very often because I learned the game by listening and imagining the action as they explained it over the air. Even now, though I have the blessed Fox Sports Midwest, showing every game all year, I sometimes like to turn off the TV and simply listen to Mike and John Rooney call the action. There's just something so pure about baseball on the radio. Every fan in every city knows this feeling, and we were very lucky to have one of the best in Jack Buck for all those years. In many ways, it was the soundtrack of my childhood.

Mom never complained that dad was spending too much time sitting and listening to the ball games. I suppose she was happy to see him spend some time with his son. She was an incredibly hard worker who got very little time for herself. She worked for many years full time at Indiana Bell, the Phone Company, downtown. She started as an operator and worked her way up to a supervisor's position by the time I was born in 1975. She worked fifty or more hours a week consistently while dad found it difficult to hang onto even part-time gigs.

Most months saw mom struggling to stitch together a budget that was lean and unstable. Dad's drinking took a large chunk out of this budget. Many times this involved his directly taking cash out of her purse or straight from their checking account. Much of this money was deposited by dad at Ellis Park, the horse racing track just across the bridge in Henderson, Kentucky. She kept us going some months by relying on her sisters or neighbors to lend some money or cook a meal for us.

It didn't occur to me that any of this was wrong until I was a teenager. I knew my parents fought sometimes, but surprisingly not very often. I knew dad drank a lot, but so did a lot of dads in our area. In a tiny little world filled with people who are so similar, there is no way for a person to realize that what they're experiencing is wrong.

It wasn't until I got my first job, delivering the Evansville Press on a bike after school, at age thirteen that I was confronted with the manipulative side of dad. I was ecstatic over my first paycheck for two reasons: it was for thirty-five dollars, and it was an actual check with my name on it. I was proud of myself on that afternoon and thrilled when I found dad at home so I could share the news. I ran into the living room where dad was watching the local news with his feet propped up in his old black leather recliner.

"Dad! Check this out! My first paycheck ever! Look at that!" I was beaming when I handed the check to him. He seemed half asleep when I approached him, but awakened immediately at the sight of the check.

"Has your mom seen this yet?" She was at the back of the house in the kitchen.

"No, I wanted to show you first!"

"Okay. Here's what we need to do. I'll hang on to this for you until tomorrow and cash it at the bank. Maybe we should set up an account down there for you."

I was even more excited at this idea and I watched him fold the check and put it in the pocket of his sweatpants. Then his face turned grave and he leaned over toward me. "I wouldn't tell your mom about this right now. I'll handle these checks for you. She's got enough to worry about. Is that clear?"

I was disappointed at his suggestion because I knew mom would have hugged me and told me how proud she was. But I agreed and pedaled home faster than usual the next day after my route so I could get a look at the cash and put it in my mini-safe. Dad was in the same position watching the same local news when I got home. He looked at me when I entered the living room and seemed at first to have nothing to say to me. I knew not to be whiny or pushy with dad or he would get upset. I gave him my best "Well?" face and he responded with a grin.

I rushed over to him and he started digging into his pocket. He produced a ten and a five and placed them in my hand. I looked at the two bills for a few seconds and then back at dad. I was genuinely confused so I looked down at the fifteen dollars again. He could read my face and he grabbed my shoulder to pull me a little closer.

"Yes, it's only fifteen. I'm sorry, but there was a fee for opening a new account so I had to pay that. Plus…" He paused to find the right wording. "You're thirteen now and you're going to have to start paying your fair share around here. We've got bills to pay and we have to feed you and your sister." I'm sure he could see the absolute disappointment in my eyes. I actually agreed with what he was saying, but it was still tough to take. Then he added, "Like I said, no need to bother your mother about this. I'll handle your money for you. Bring your checks to me and I'll make sure it gets divided up the right way."

With that, he leaned back in his chair and looked at the TV, an indication that the conversation was over. I never asked him if the other twenty dollars went into my account, nor did I ever challenge him when I routinely received less than half of the amounts written on my checks. It took a few months for me to realize that he was basically stealing my money and most likely using it to fuel his nights at the bar and his weekends at the track.

Of course, this was only one of many episodes. I suppose I should be grateful that dad's abuses were always financial or emotional in nature and not physical. I have heard stories from others, mostly in my Adult Children of Alcoholics meetings, which make my dad seem like a hero in comparison. But he wasn't. He was absolutely the most self-absorbed man that I have ever encountered. How else can his decisions be explained? He took advantage of everyone he was supposed to care about and never worried about the consequences.

This was especially true concerning mom. She is a smart and hard working woman who seemed to only care about others. Her life was defined by the sacrifices that she made for her kids, her church family, and most of all, my father. He knew that mom would find a way to keep the kids fed and the house from being foreclosed on no matter what, so he could indulge his addictions as often as he needed.

There were times when mom would be wondering how she was going to keep the electricity from being shut off, while dad was lending money to his buddies so they could keep betting on the horses with him.

Even when mom tried to be smart and stash money away, always for a good reason, dad managed to find and raid it. The worst fight I ever heard them have stemmed from just such an incident. Mom had been putting away money from each of her paychecks for new carpeting that was desperately needed. She had amassed around a thousand dollars for this project and was stowing it in an envelope behind the bleach on a high shelf in the laundry room. This was theoretically the perfect hiding place since she was the only one to ever handle dirty clothes in our house. Unfortunately, dad had a nose for such schemes. He had known for weeks that mom was stashing money in the house, but had been unable to pinpoint the location.

Finally, one morning he decided to search the only place in the house that he hadn't looked. He grabbed the envelope and, in a microcosm of his entire adult life, blew the whole pile of money in one afternoon at the track. It was a defining moment for our family. That was the day that I realized my father cared more about his addictions than his family. Mom reacted with a singular fury and ordered him to leave the house immediately.

When he finally came home there was no follow up conversation. No apologies and certainly no mention of seeking counseling or even a call to her pastor. The entire episode was just buried. Mom never mentioned the missing money or her explosion again. She had learned a lesson though: find a cleverer hiding place that Johnny couldn't find.

Although mom never found the strength to leave a husband who was obviously more interested in drinking and gambling than her, two things changed after that night.

First, dad never stole cash from mom again. I'm sure he wanted to, and he always had opportunities, but that night's confrontation had branded itself on his brain. Second, he never drank in the house again.

It was his ritual to come home from a shift or from umpiring a game and grab a Sterling or Miller High Life out of the fridge. He nearly always had one either in his hand or nearby when he was at home. He also kept some Jack Daniels in the garage just in case he needed it. He never kept hard liquor in the house because mom had drawn the line at beer years ago. After mom confronted him about the money, he took the remaining beers to Phil's house, who was a bachelor, and I didn't see one in the house in all of my remaining years living there.

While getting rid of the beer seemed like a positive step, in reality it kept him away from home more often. He replaced drinking beer and whiskey at home with drinking it at Lamasco's bar, at Phil's, or at his best friend Butch's apartment. The drinking didn't stop after that night, it simply shifted venues. I also believe that mom saying those words out loud had somehow shamed him.

Looking at him as I am now, a forty year old husband and father, I don't know how he did it. I can't understand how he could carry on and not be eaten alive with guilt. I suppose staying drunk most of the time helped to dull his conscience. I vowed to myself long ago that I would not repeat his mistakes. I would instead learn how to be a good man, even if I didn't have one in my life.

Taking this path has been both incredibly difficult and gratifying. It has meant long separations from my mother and sister as I decided to stay away from Evansville as an adult. It has also meant a torturous examination of my childhood and all of its ramifications. So many people end up following their parents down the rat hole into self-destruction. I am determined to avoid committing the sins of my father.

***

When I left for college in the fall of 1993 I had a strong premonition that I wouldn't be back. I managed to find reasons for sticking around campus during holiday breaks and summers. Of course playing on the basketball team gave me plenty of excuses. I was a three year starter as a shooting guard, plus I had classes and a girlfriend to distract me from thoughts of home. I will always be grateful for that scholarship, even if I really didn't love playing the game. Baseball was my passion, though sadly I never had a talent for it. I agree with whoever said that hitting a baseball is the hardest thing to do in sports.

My only visits to Evansville during those years involved playing basketball against the UE Purple Aces. Aside from Don Mattingly, one of Evansville's few claims to fame was that their basketball team wore purple jerseys with sleeves. It was a kind of hero's welcome every time I came home to play at Roberts Stadium because I was the one kid out of our neighborhood who had "gotten out."

I kept in regular phone contact with the family during my college years. I would call a couple of times a week and talk with mom and dad separately. Mom would try to put a positive spin on the happenings around the Gibson household. I would apologize for not being there, though secretly I would be thanking God that I was hundreds of miles away. I did feel guilty for leaving Megan alone in that house, but I knew her time would come.

My talks with dad were usually short and involved three main subjects. First, how were my grades? Second, how was basketball going? Third, and most importantly, we would talk about the Cardinals.

The early to mid-nineties were lean times for the Cards and their fans. They still had Ozzie Smith, and they featured a lot of young and legitimately exciting players like Ray Lankford and Brian Jordan (the much less heralded two sport athlete). Their problem in the '90s was a constant lack of solid pitching. The Cards were competitive but always ended up well behind the Pirates in the standings.

My favorite player, Gregg Jefferies, was only with the team for the '93 and '94 seasons. He was gritty and fiery and a hell of a hitter. The first jersey that I ever bought was an authentic home Cardinals jersey with his name and number on the back. I wore it proudly, but the feeling was short-lived. He cashed in on his St. Louis success with a fat new contract from the Phillies. That was when I learned that fans are usually much more loyal to the team than the players they root for.

Our phone conversations were short but pleasant. I could tell that he genuinely missed me, if only because he needed someone around who was as passionate about baseball as he was. I'm sure he also missed the easy money from cashing my paychecks, which he did with every check I earned until the day I left for college. I missed him as well, and there were times when I thought about driving back home during a break and staying a few days. I missed my mom terribly, especially my freshman year, and she made it clear that she was very disappointed when I would tell her again that I couldn't get away. She never pushed the guilt trips too far though, because she knew why I stayed away.

***

When I arrived in Evansville on a late October afternoon in 2011, I opted to stay at a hotel on the other side of town from Powell. Walking back into my childhood home after so many years would be hard enough; the thought of sleeping in my old room or even on the couch was too much. Karen came into town with me, knowing that I needed her strength. Our son also came. Jack was six years old then (yes, named for the man who brought me so much joy on countless summer evenings growing up) and mercifully sporting the blond hair and beautiful face of his mother. Jack had never seen or spoken to his grandpa Gibson. When we arrived at the hotel I still wasn't sure if Jack would get that chance. I would have to see how things unfolded before I brought him in.

My plan was to go back home alone and face my parents and whatever else lay in the shadows of that house. I figured there was perhaps a forty to fifty percent chance that dad would see me and either turn away or just tell me to get out. But, if he didn't, and if we were able to spend an evening together in relative peace, then I would give Karen the signal to bring Jack over to see Johnny Ray. I was actually excited by this prospect, but I stayed determined not to have any expectations.

As I made the half hour drive from the hotel to their house, I flipped on the radio and caught the beginning of game six. The Rangers, whose lineup could pound the baseball from top to bottom, jumped out to a quick lead against Jaime Garcia. Josh Hamilton, who was their scariest hitter, smacked an RBI single to make it 1-0. I thought to myself that this could get out of hand early and maybe it hadn't been a good idea to make this my final game with dad. But the 2011 Cardinals never seemed to get rattled when adversity struck. They just kept plugging away and making plays. They had been counted out several times by nearly everyone, yet here they were playing at home in the World Series.

I kept myself distracted from my oncoming task by reviewing the previous five games. I thought about how amazing it was that a guy like Allen Craig, whom no one outside of Cardinal country had heard of, could produce huge late inning hits in both of the first two games played in St. Louis. His pinch-hit single in the sixth inning of game one had been the difference in a 3-2 win. He did the exact same thing the next night off the same pitcher (Alexi Ogando) in the seventh to break a scoreless tie. The Cards' bullpen blew the save that night, but I was happy to see them going to Texas with the series tied.

As I crossed over into the west side of town I passed the empty lot where the Sterling brewery used to be. Phantoms from years past flashed all around me. I refocused on the series. Game three will be remembered as the "Pujols Game." He hit three home runs that night and drove in six runs while going five for six overall. It was his crowning achievement as a member of the Cardinals (considering he pulled the ultimate Gregg Jefferies by signing a ludicrous ten year deal with the Angels later that winter). Only Babe Ruth and Reggie Jackson had hit three homers in one World Series game before. The Cards destroyed the Rangers 16-7 that night and took their fans right out of the game. I thought after that game I wouldn't see another performance as impressive as Albert's. I was wrong.

Game four was dominated by the Rangers' lefty starter Derek Holland. He blanked the Cards and evened the series once again. Game five was agonizing for Cardinals fans for a number of reasons. I squirmed in my chair most of the night under the stress of watching a close and crucial contest. Chris Carpenter pitched another great game (he may be the toughest or at least the most intense player I have ever seen) and it was tied 2-2 going into the bottom of the eighth. That's when the infamous bullpen phone incident occurred and the wrong relievers warmed up for the Cardinals.

Tony LaRussa twice called his bullpen coach and asked him to get Jason Motte, the lumberjack-looking, flame throwing closer, ready. Both times the message was not received clearly and the wrong pitchers began to get loose. How this situation could occur in the year 2011 is unfathomable, but it happened and it may have cost them the game.

The bitter taste of that game was still lingering when I pulled up in front of that faded but familiar house on Delmar Avenue. Its white aluminum siding, stained by years of dirt and grime, reminded me of how long I had been away.

While my meditation on the Cardinals' performance in the World Series had helped get me through the drive, I now realized as I walked toward the front porch door that I had no idea what I would say to dad. Mom spotted me and was already opening the door. I smiled at her and got a sudden burst of adrenaline.

I thought, *My God, I'm really here!* The rush that hit me felt good. It felt like a message confirming that I had made the right decision.

As I hugged mom and made my way inside, I could only have faith that it was.

Bottom of the First

The sights and smells of the old house overwhelmed my senses. I noticed some things hadn't changed, like the wood paneling on the walls of the front sitting room and the sky blue carpeting in the living room. But mom had managed to update a lot of the décor (no doubt thanks to her improved money hiding skills). She had maintained a fresh feel in a house that they had lived in for over thirty years. I was glad to see this, but then I was hit with a pang of nostalgia. Part of me wanted the house to look and feel exactly the same, like walking back in time. That was how I had imagined it would feel, but it didn't. Time and life had moved on without me here after all.

I spent a few minutes chatting with mom in the living room, trying to formulate a plan for when I would see *him*. She was in good spirits.

"You know your dad isn't going to know what to do with himself when he sees you here! He's so excited to see you."

Excitement was not the word to describe my feelings at that moment. My queasy stomach told me I was nervous. My sweaty and shaky hands told me I was scared. Jesus, the man is lying on his death bed, probably unable to get up on his own and I'm scared to face him. How is that possible? My initial smile disappeared and I decided it was time to be honest.

"What do you think I should say to him? I don't even know where to begin. I mean, fifteen years..." I would have rambled on but mom quieted me with her eyes. I was so grateful for her presence. There was no way I was going in to see Johnny Ray alone.

"You can start by saying hello. He's not a stranger. He's your dad. I know you're nervous, but you're doing the right thing. You're a good man, and that's why you're here. But he's a good man too. Maybe he wasn't a good father all the time, but I know how much he loves you. Just go to him and I know you'll figure it out."

This was the sort of pep talk that mom had become very good at over the years. I heard these growing up when dad had yelled at me too much, or when he didn't show up for my basketball games. The one time that it hadn't worked was on my wedding day...the last time that I had seen or spoken to my father before the night of game six.

After another couple of minutes of talking (stalling), I rose and took mom's hand. She led me down the narrow hallway, the kind that runs through nearly all shotgun-style houses, and we turned right at the doorway of the room that had been permanently off-limits to me as a child. My heartbeat, already elevated, now began a steady pounding as we reached the door. It was already open and mom stepped in front of me as we entered the room.

"Johnny Ray, look who came to see you!"

I looked past her shoulder and got my first glimpse of dad as he sat upright in bed watching the mounted flat screen on the opposite wall. My fear subsided in an instant. This wasn't my dad. It couldn't be. My dad was a wall of a man, an athlete, an intimidator. He was the guy they still told stories about (some about his ball playing and some about his fights) down at Lamasco's. The man lying in their bed did not even resemble the dad that I remembered and revered.

The first detail that struck me was his bald head. As a younger man, dad's hair had been thick and well-maintained. His bangs were always slicked back with some product and his part kept arrow straight. Now I could see the veins running through his head. I also noticed how thin his arms were in his white V-neck tee. This man had literally thrown other men through windows. He had belted four hundred and fifty foot home runs with ease. Now he looked as if he would break if I tried to pick him up.

Withered was the word that hit me repeatedly. Dad

looked withered and weak. He also looked incredibly tired. As he turned his gaze toward me, I saw the deep lines in his face. They told a story of a man who had endured large amounts of pain. Taking all of this in at once, I wondered if he would even be able to speak. Then his eyes flashed with recognition, and I saw a small grin break onto his face.

"Well! The prodigal son returns."

His voice was shockingly weak. I had heard this man roar in anger or frustration in a tone that shook your insides. His "inside voice" was equivalent to most people's "open field" voice. You always knew when Johnny Ray was in the room, or the building. I always assumed he was loud because he was the youngest of nine children. It was the same reason why he ate his meals as if it were a race. If you didn't eat fast, you didn't eat. And if you didn't yell you didn't get noticed. Now he sounded as if he had just crossed the Sahara and was still waiting for a drink. I tried to mask my horror, but it was difficult. I had heard about what cancer patients go through, but this was all too real.

I cleared my throat while he looked me over. He was still grinning slyly and I couldn't tell if it was a sign that he was happy to see me or trying to hide another emotion.

"Hey dad. Yep, been a long time, but I'm here." I paused for a few seconds and then added, "It's good to see you." With that, mom patted me on the back and then walked to the far side of the bed. I looked over at the TV (this forty-six inch Sony was a major upgrade over the twenty inch Zenith console we had in the '80s) and saw that Lance Berkman was at the plate with a runner on base and two outs. Mom was picking up a plate from the nightstand and whispering something to dad. I moved to sit down in the recliner that mom had managed to drag in next to the bed when I heard a roar emanating from the TV.

I looked up to see the ball flying toward centerfield. Berkman had delivered a big response to the Rangers' run with a two-run homer. I looked over at dad, he was smiling and pumping his fist.

"God that man can hit. I wish we'd had him all those years instead of Houston." Dad looked back at me after he said this. We both knew that Berkman had spent his career before 2011 as a Cardinal killer with a penchant for clutch hitting.

"Yeah, he's tough. I think our guys can hit Colby Lewis. I just hope Garcia can do what he did in game two." This was a rematch of game two's starters. Jaime had been fantastic in that game, throwing seven scoreless innings while dodging some bullets. Unfortunately, Lewis had been equally good and the Cards lost it 2-1.

"I'm worried about him, but Tony's not afraid to pull these guys if they're struggling. He might have a quick hook for Jaime tonight." Dad's insight was dead on. He had watched nearly every pitch of every Cardinals game since they finally got cable in 2004.

And suddenly I realized that the nerves and fear were gone. We were right back into the same type of conversations we carried on throughout my childhood. In fact, I could think of no topic outside of baseball that we had ever spent more than five minutes discussing. Thank God for Lance Berkman. He got me through those first awkward moments and now I was just settling in to watch a game with my dad. I knew there were a lot of things I needed to bring up with him that night, but the game was young and I quickly started to enjoy dad's company again.

I didn't realize that mom had already left the room. The buzz from the Berkman homer died down and we were left in silence. The TV volume was low and I thought about turning it up (I always enjoy hearing Joe Buck and Tim McCarver call a game) but didn't want to seem too eager. I also didn't want to send the wrong message to dad. I wasn't sure what I was going to accomplish, but I didn't want to blow it in the first inning. I decided to address the obvious.

"So mom tells me you're not doing well. How are you feeling?" I already knew the answer, but I couldn't think of anything better.

"Yeah, I'm dying. Cancer…it's a bitch. What can I say?" He was trying to be cavalier, but I could sense some real fear in him. He knew he didn't have long.

"Has it been hard? The chemo and all that I mean." He looked over at me when I asked this. I think it surprised him.

"Well…yes and no. The chemo just makes you feel really lousy for days. I mean you can't even get out of bed. But on the other hand, your mother has been taking good care of me." As if on cue, mom walked in the room with a pillow for dad and a glass of Nestle Quik for me. The woman knows me well.

"How's the game going fellas?" We knew that mom didn't care one bit about the game or who won, but she was enjoying watching us watch the game. She placed the pillow behind dad's head, which was resting up against the headboard.

"So far, so good mom. Thanks for the milk! It's just like I remembered." I hardly ever get chocolate milk in my house thanks to the efforts of my health-conscious wife. Apparently she wants me to live past fifty.

"You know I remember this kid drinking chocolate milk out of a sippy cup, running around here and singing Bingo at the top of his lungs!" Dad said this to mom and she laughed. I didn't expect to hear him say something like that. I had to remember that this might not be the same Johnny Ray that I had run from all those years ago. Some of my assumptions and expectations were already coming apart.

***

One of my earliest memories of dad is also one of the most dramatic. He saved my life when I was four years old, then about two weeks later he saved our dog's life. I was lying on the couch on a Saturday morning watching the Super Friends, featuring Superman, Batman, and Robin among others who gathered at the "Hall of Justice." I was alone with dad because mom was working a rare weekend shift at Indiana Bell. I could hear him in the kitchen banging around, which usually meant he was making bacon and eggs because that was really the only thing he ever cooked. He was a master of scrambling eggs and I was biding my time on the couch before a tasty breakfast.

For some reason, I decided that was the perfect moment to reach over to the end table and snag a piece of butterscotch candy. I had been told by mom not to take candy, or anything else for that matter, without asking, but on that morning I just did it. The next thing I remember is getting up from the couch and running back to the kitchen as I choked on the butterscotch. It scares me now to think of how easily I could have died right there on that flower-patterned couch, but thankfully my survival instinct kicked in.

Dad was facing away from me at the stove and I ran up and started tugging on his shirt. He brushed me off at first, telling me it wasn't ready yet. Then I started to panic. I tugged furiously at his arm and forced him to look at me. When he looked down his face changed in an instant. I'm sure my face was blue or purple at that point. His next moves were incredibly swift and confident. He picked me up and turned me upside down. Suddenly I was hanging by my ankle and being shaken violently up and down.

It only took a few shakes for the candy to come loose and fall out of my mouth. I remember seeing the yellow disc falling toward the floor, but then something caught it. Dad had swiped a saucer off the table and caught the butterscotch before it hit the linoleum floor. I sometimes wonder if I dreamed up that detail later, but I believe it is true. He wasn't much for domestic chores, but he did insist on keeping the floors clean. Perhaps he just didn't want a sticky mess on the floor, but I think now that he was challenging himself. He knew he was going to get the candy out of my throat from the moment he picked me up. The only drama for him was could he catch it before it hit the ground?

Afterward, he put me down and gave me some orange juice. I wasn't crying and when he saw that I was okay, he told me to go back and watch TV until it was time to eat. Neither of us ever mentioned this little episode to mom. I was afraid she would scold me because I should know better.

For dad, I don't believe it was a big deal for him. As I tried to refocus on how the Super Friends were going to round up this week's villains, dad was congratulating himself more for catching the piece of candy than for saving my life. Later, while we were eating, he told me to be careful if I'm going to eat candy. That was it. A life changing event for me, a blip on the radar for him.

About two weeks later, dad got another chance at being the hero. This time it involved our beagle mix, Stanley. He was named, naturally, for Stan Musial. He was my first pet and to this day still the best dog I ever had. He was lovable and incredibly cute, and dad loved that dog with all his heart. Mom was never sold on having a dog in the house (maybe because she ended up doing ninety percent of the work involved), but dad had worn her down over several years. Stanley was about three years old when his life took an unexpected turn.

Like most dogs, Stanley had a penchant for chewing on things. One evening, as we were eating supper at the kitchen table, we heard a strange noise come out of the bathroom. Normally during meal times all you could hear was the sound of dad's lips smacking together as he chewed furiously with his mouth open. This was, mom explained, another consequence of his upbringing. That night we were interrupted by a terrible yelp. Dad jumped up mid-chew and ran for the bathroom. Mom and I stayed at the table at first, not realizing what had happened.

"Oh God! Stanley!" Dad sounded frantic. I saw him carrying the dog down the hall and into the living room. Mom and I quickly joined him and saw that he had laid Stanley on his back on the coffee table. The dog wasn't moving, but his eyes were still open.

"What happened, Johnny?" Mom was as confused as I was. Dad was now rubbing Stanley's chest with his hands.

"Looked like he bit into the cord on your curling iron. I told you to keep that cord off the floor, dammit! Look at him!" I thought he was going to cry right there. I had never seen dad cry or even show concern for much of anything. I thought back to my recent choking incident and realized he was showing more concern for the dog's life than he had for mine.

The concept of CPR was not well-known in the late 1970's. That being said, dad must have seen a TV show (maybe Trapper John or Emergency!) or read an article featuring this method. After a few seconds of rubbing the dog's chest, dad commenced with chest compressions. And then, inexplicably, my father began mouth to snout resuscitation on our family dog. Mom was apparently somewhat familiar with this technique and she chimed in. "Don't push on his chest too hard. You don't want to crush his little ribs."

Dad didn't react to the commentary, he just kept on working to save his loving dog. Then, a miracle occurred. The dog started moving around and then let out a sound I have yet to hear again from any animal. Maybe it was Stanley's way of thanking dad, or perhaps he was sad for having to leave doggy heaven to return to Delmar Avenue. Then dad was hugging him and letting him lick his face (usually never allowed). After a few dazed moments, Stanley started to wag his tail and sniff dad's face. He was back from the dead.

I stood in stunned silence, still processing an event that had taken all of thirty seconds. The image of dad desperately blowing oxygen into our dog's snout wasn't something I had been expecting as we ate our beef stew. I saw that mom had tears streaming down her face. She reached for Stanley and took him in her arms. She loved him after all.

For all the happiness of that day, Stanley was never quite the same dog after that. He had lost a little something when he bit into that live cord. For instance, he would suddenly and without warning begin running around the kitchen table (dad called this "hot lapping") until he was unable to continue and then collapse in a pile of fur. He also started urinating in the house a lot more often, so much so that he became an outside dog within a year of his incident.

Dad never really answered me when I asked him later how he had known to do CPR. I think part of him was embarrassed that he had shown so much emotion over a dog. Stanley did live a pretty long life after that, but his place in the family was lost when he became an outside pet. He got attention sometimes, but as time went on he was neglected more and more. He died when I was ten or eleven and with barely a notice. Dad buried him in the backyard and that was the end of him. We never had another inside pet again.

I drank my Quik and let the memories of the house wash over me. I looked up and saw that the Cardinals were already in the field getting ready for the second inning. It had been a good opening inning for the Cards and for me. I had found my way back into dad's life just in time. Now the question was: where does the night go from here?

Top of the Second

It was obvious from the outset that Garcia did not have the same stuff going as in game two. The Rangers quickly responded to Berkman's blast with a rally in the second. Ian Kinsler drove a ball that bounced over the wall for a run-scoring ground-rule double. The game was tied 2-2 and was already shaping up to be a long and possibly wild affair. There's nothing better in baseball when you have two talented and confident teams squaring off in the playoffs. It's also agonizing for fans like me who live and die with every turn of events.

While I will never get to experience competition at the highest level, I know what pressure in the midst of a game feels like. One good trait that dad gave me was some physical ability to play sports, especially basketball. Growing up, I wanted to be like dad and play baseball the way he did. I realized early in my Pony League career that it wasn't going to happen. I just couldn't hit balls that weren't pitched straight. I guess there's no shame in that, but it lay heavy on my shoulders for years. I eventually put all of my effort into being a better basketball player.

Dad was never really excited about me playing basketball. For him it was baseball and nothing else. But he did support my decision when I quit playing baseball in eighth grade (probably to spare himself from seeing me whiff at yet another curveball). At some point during my junior year of high school, I realized that basketball could be my ticket out of dad's house and Powell. The coaches praised me for being the first one at practices and the last one to leave. The truth was I just didn't want to go home. I became a gym rat, but not because I loved the game. It was an escape and nothing more.

Thanks to my work, and inheriting some of dad's physical traits; I was six-two and a hundred and eighty pounds during my senior year, I earned a scholarship to play basketball. We won the city championship, the sectional, and the regional that year with me throwing in nearly twenty points a game. We lost in the semi-state by two points, with me missing a potential game-winning three-pointer with two seconds left. I was devastated, but looking back, I believe we overachieved as a group. Still, I sometimes wonder what might have happened if I had hit that shot. I suppose we all have those "what if" moments in our lives. I have several.

Dad never said anything positive or negative to me about the semi-state loss. Of course, by then I didn't see much of him because I kept an incredibly busy schedule on purpose. I played three sports and got involved with as many clubs as possible. It would have been a different story had I been a stud in baseball. He would have been at every game yelling for me at the top of his lungs. He would have been drunk for most of those, but at least he would have been there. Instead, I played my entire basketball career never seeing him in the stands and never hearing that coveted phrase: "I'm proud of you."

Dad was a special athlete when he was younger. He was (according to the various stories I heard so often from family and his friends) simply bigger, stronger, and faster than the other guys on the field. He was sort of the Mike Trout of Evansville during the 1960's. He hit a walk-off home run to win the city championship in 1967 as a senior. He was first team all-state that year, but his career derailed thanks to his own poor decisions and the fact that his father never supported him (he wanted Johnny to quit school and work).

Rather than get a scholarship or even go play in the minors, he left town immediately after high school to join a traveling semi-pro fast pitch softball team. Though he never said it, I believe he was running from his father. In a different situation dad might have eventually won a spot on a major league roster. He ended up as an eighteen year old playing games with men twice his age who traveled with the softball team in the summer months mostly to get a break from their wives and kids.

Fast pitch softball was extremely popular in the Midwest back then, and Evansville was a hub for such leagues. Dad's high school exploits were well known in town and he was invited to play for the Sterling Brewers in a highly competitive league with teams from five different states. The games were exciting and highly pressurized. On a Saturday night there might be as many as five hundred people in the stands cheering and jeering wildly.

Johnny Ray spent three years playing for three different teams spanning most of the calendar year. He loved the lifestyle and the competition. He was good at it and there was no real fear of failure because, as he used to say, "It was just softball." He never equated it with baseball because he thought of it as an easier game. He used to joke about it, saying, "The ball is the size of a grapefruit. Yeah, it's coming at you fast, but how can you miss it?"

He rarely missed it.

His stats during those years were ridiculous by any standard. Those leagues were high scoring, but even considering that, his numbers were impressive. The teams kept meticulous care of the scorebook for each game and I got a chance once to look through some that he had saved. I couldn't find a game in which he didn't have at least two hits and three runs driven in. He regularly contributed multiple home run games, five for five games, and even one night against Mt. Vernon in which he had six hits, including two triples and three doubles, and drove in ten runs.

He was too good for those leagues, but he didn't believe he could succeed anywhere else (or was just too afraid to try). I suppose it was inevitable that he would injure himself playing in so many games and competing with the intensity of a lunatic Pete Rose. One night while patrolling centerfield in a game in Tell City, he broke to his left to track down a ball headed for the right-centerfield gap. They say he didn't run as much as glide toward balls. He was graceful and natural in his moves and always seemed to make the catch.

As he planted his left foot to spring into a dive, something shifted (the fields they played on were more like mine fields with lines painted on them) and he felt a pop in his knee. He made the catch, of course, but he lost much more. Dad had shredded the tendons in his knee and would never again play competitive softball. Because of modern surgical methods, this kind of injury is seen more as a temporary setback by today's fans. In 1970 it meant the end of your career. It was the first of many injuries that dad would sustain, but I believe it was the most devastating.

After a couple of years, dad couldn't stay away and he found himself umpiring among the same men that he had once dominated. Though he was still young, he was respected by the guys and physically imposing enough that no one complained about his calls too much. As usual, he excelled and became the most in-demand umpire in the region. Teams knew that he was fair and accurate.

By 1980 he had achieved such a reputation that he was asked to run the entire league (he declined). In 1983 he was the first inductee into the Indiana Softball Hall of Fame. I know it isn't quite Cooperstown, but the plaque still hangs on my office wall. He tried to downplay it, but I know that he considered it the best accolade of his entire life.

One night when I was five or six (perhaps 1980 or '81) I was at Powell Park watching a game that dad was umping. Though it had lost popularity over time, fast pitch softball was still a big deal and there were at least two hundred and fifty people there that night. It was a steamy July evening. Summers in Evansville can be unbearable because of the humidity. When you walk outside the heat and moisture hit you like a wall. The air weighs on you. Your clothes stick to you. That particular evening was as sticky and uncomfortable as any.

The women were futilely fanning themselves and the men compensating for the heat with cold Sterling or Pabst Blue Ribbon. Dad was behind the plate and already soaked through by the end of the first inning. The visiting team was a collection of union warehouse workers from Carmi, Illinois who travelled to games on weekends. This bunch was rowdy from the start and were unfamiliar with dad's reputation and style. A tall, pudgy gentleman wearing the number six strolled to the plate and stood motionless as the first pitch hit the catcher's mitt like a bullet.

"Steee-riiiike!" Dad called out in his familiar tone. He was not shy about letting the folks know what his decision was. The Carmi dugout erupted with complaints about the strike zone. The batter stepped out of the box and looked back at dad. Clearly he wasn't happy with dad's perception of the previous pitch.

"Get back in the box pal," dad said in a stern but measured voice. He had seen it all and usually wasn't bothered by the whiners. The lefty huffed and then dug back in looking much more interested in hitting the ball this time. He flinched, but did not swing at the next delivery.

"Steee-riiiike two!" I sensed a bit more bravado in dad's voice on that call. The pitch had found the outside corner, but the batter acted as if it had bounced. He stepped out again and was now muttering and shaking his head. This time dad took his mask off.

"Get your ass back in that box! I'm not giving you time." He was stern but not yelling and the batter responded by pounding both cleats with his bat and then slowly edging his way back to a hitting position. The 0-2 pitch appeared to be off-speed and the batter once again flinched but just couldn't pull the trigger.

"Steeee-riiiiike three!" Dad punched him out with a

flourish. Number six threw the bat down and, though he was three or four inches shorter than dad, did his best to get into his face. The two were jawing for about thirty seconds, during which time dad continued to repeat the mantra, "Swing the bat, that's what it's for. Swing the bat, that's why you brought it up here!"

Even then I could recognize that dad was exerting a lot of effort to stay calm and handle the situation like a pro. Then number six started throwing f-bombs and dad became visibly angry for the first time. Dad was funny about the f-word. He used every other word including God's name with impunity, but something had been ingrained in him about that word.

"You're out! Get the hell off this field and into the parking lot now!" The guy continued to bark for a few more seconds and then realized he was defeated. He would spend the rest of the evening sitting in a lawn chair behind his car drinking beers out of a cooler in his trunk and cursing my father's existence.

The crowds at these games were electric. They teemed with energy generated from a combination of alcohol, working class angst, and a fierce competitive spirit. Sports were incredibly important on the west side of Evansville and especially in Powell. After the encounter with number six the crowd was absolutely primed for an explosion. Ninety percent of them knew dad and were rooting for the home team (a group sponsored by the local Rideout's Transmission).

I was sitting behind home plate and saw the Carmi players growing increasingly timid under the strain of a truly hostile environment. Boos and name calling were only the beginning. Soon bottles and threats were being launched toward their dugout. In the top of the fifth one of their guys went in for a hard slide at second and I thought a lynch mob might form. The boiling point hit when the Carmi guys had the audacity to score a run (they were down 8-0 in the seventh). When the final out was recorded on a grounder to second, the visitors were reluctant to leave the confines of their dugout.

Their compatriot, the non-swinger who had caused this situation, had already been chased off and was probably halfway back home when the last pitch was thrown. The Carmi guys did their best to keep their heads down and stay together as they attempted to walk back to the parking lot. Halfway to their cars, one of them was struck in the side of the head by a flying bottle of Sterling Light. Toward the rear of their group one of them was spun around by a drunk forty-something local and punched squarely in the nose. He melted to his knees as blood shot out of both nostrils. This was not the first time I had seen an angry crowd at Powell, but it was the first bloodshed. I saw several other Powell regulars hurrying toward the group of outsiders, sensing that a brawl could be imminent.

As the Carmi men prepared to use their bats in self-defense (since they hadn't come in much handy during the game), one voice roared over the melee and silenced them all. I knew it well and at once: it was dad. He was striding toward the Carmi team still carrying his mask in his left hand.

"That's enough!" He pointed at the visitors, "You guys get your shit and get on the road!" Now he looked around with annoyance on his face. "Everyone else just calm down! These guys might be assholes but they're not worth it. Anyone else makes a move and you answer to me!"

Coming from almost anyone else on the premises, this speech would have either been ignored or shouted down by the large number of angry drunks. Coming from Johnny Ray, it was like a papal bull. The toughs closest to the Carmi players immediately started to give way. The rest of the crowd looked around, seeming to remember whatever it was they were doing or saying before this disturbance. The visiting team was allowed to escape without further incident.

I stood at five years of age in absolute awe of my father. He was like the mayor of our neighborhood, known and respected by all. As we made the short drive home, I didn't ask him about it and he didn't speak. He apparently wasn't affected by what had just taken place. Afterward, he just sat on the back porch like always and drank a beer, reflecting on the game in the darkness. I went to bed that night with a reverence for my father that I hadn't felt before. It was a short-lived feeling, but for that night I was as proud as a son can be of his dad.

***

"Do you miss the softball games?" I asked dad, knowing that men's fast-pitch softball had been extinct in Evansville for many years by 2011.

"Not really. I mean, yeah, I miss playing, but not umpiring. Every damn one of those guys were cheats and whiners."

"But you had a real talent for that. The guys liked it when you were doing the games, didn't they?"

"Yeah, because they knew I wouldn't take any shit and just call the game. Plus, most of 'em knew me anyway. It was hard being an ump in those leagues. I saw guys get chased off the field when I was playing. You had to be a hard-ass or you wouldn't last. I just got tired of it."

In truth, the end of his softball umpiring career was not his decision. His drinking got way out of hand as the 1980's went on and eventually he was fired by the league. The fact that he was still capable of being an effective umpire even while drunk was irrelevant to the league's officials. When I think about how much talent my father had and how he squandered it, it makes me angry. I would have killed for his ability when I was in high school and college. I wouldn't have thrown away the opportunities that he did. I couldn't help myself, I had to ask.

"Dad, do you ever think about…do you ever wonder what you might have done if you had…made different choices." I tried to be as judicious as possible.

He looked at me and raised an eyebrow. I knew he may get upset, but if this night was going to amount to anything significant, I needed to start getting deeper with our conversation. It would be easy to spend the evening talking baseball and feeling good about having spent time with him before he was gone. But I wanted more, and I think he did too.

"You mean, do I have any regrets?" Dad asked.

"Yes. I guess that's exactly what I'm asking." He sat for a few moments looking at the TV but not seeing it. I was glad to see he was taking the question seriously.

"Of course I do. You think I'd be lying here at sixty-four if I hadn't lived like I did? You think you would have stayed away all these years? I know I've screwed up a lot of things. Hell, I could have joined the Evansville Triplets in 1968 if I had wanted to. They actually sent me an invitation. I turned it down. I didn't think I would have fun." He paused for a moment and sighed. "No, that's not really true. I didn't go 'cause I didn't think I could hack it. I didn't want to be embarrassed. I was the big shot in high school, but I knew the minors would be a lot tougher. That was triple A ball…one step from the majors. I didn't even try out. Yeah, I have regrets."

I had never heard about the invitation from the Triplets, and I sat stunned as I contemplated what they could have meant for him. How many guys would have killed for that opportunity? Worse, how do you live with yourself knowing that you gave away a shot at the majors?

"My God, dad. Why not just try out? At least then you would have known if you could play with those guys. That was a once in a lifetime chance!"

"Believe me, I've thought about it. I was nineteen and stupid. I wanted to do something easy and have fun doing it. I didn't have to try to be good at softball. I guess you could say I wasn't interested in challenging myself back then."

I left it alone after that. He was being incredibly open and honest in a way that I had never seen. It was like talking with a different man. I felt a great sorrow creeping up inside me. I was sad for my father because he understood what he had lost. He also knew it was too late to get any of it back. The anger that I had been storing up toward him for fifteen years was steadily rolling away and being replaced by sympathy.

Bottom of the Second

Garcia finished off the Rangers and the Cards were coming up with the score tied at two. As the Cards prepared to bat, I heard my sister Megan come in through the back door. She had been staying with our parents for a couple of weeks since dad started hospice--i.e. choosing to die at home. Though she's reached age thirty, I still see her as my kid sister. She walked into the room with us and I gave her a big hug. It had been months since we'd seen each other.

"Hey sis! Cards are tied in the second. What have you been up to?" Megan is a nominal Cards fan, but I knew she had been paying attention since the playoffs started.

"Hey you! Well, I've just been bouncing around the old homestead, helping out. How about you? You kinda look like crap. You been sleeping much?" I have always enjoyed the candor of our relationship. She was right, of course, I had been suffering from insomnia for weeks leading up to this night. She knew why.

"Hard to sleep much when the Redbirds are keeping us on edge like this every night! You sticking around for the game?"

"Sure. But I'll let you boys keep talking sports and mom and I can sit in the other room and talk about you two!" She walked over to dad and kissed him on the forehead. He just smiled at her. She did the same to me on her way out of the room. It was good to have her around again.

Megan and I were pretty different growing up. She was a brown-haired, brown-eyed clone of our mother. Even as her brother, I can say honestly that she is a beautiful woman. I joked when we were younger that she got the looks and I got the brains, but that wasn't true because she's also smarter than me. And nicer. She's just one of those people that you want to be around as much as possible.

Of course, when we were growing up I pestered her incessantly. Being a four year old girl with a ten year old brother must be rough. I made her life hell for a few years if only because I enjoyed getting a rise out of her. My specialty was scaring her, which inevitably led to my being spanked or yelled at. It was usually worth it. Her nickname for me during those years was "idiot" and her favorite phrase to hurl at me was "I hate you."

Most of my hijinks were harmless fun, and normally I made it up to her by playing Barbie. We invented a soap opera called "Beach House" and, thanks to my input, each episode ended with one or more characters being murdered. We also spent a lot of time playing board games, especially Life and Candy Land. I'm pretty sure we played ten thousand games of Candy Land and I won maybe three of those. As we grew up she found she didn't hate me as much and I didn't need to torment her all the time. As a result we grew pretty close. We had a lot of fun playing together and, whether we knew it or not, we needed each other to survive life in the Gibson house.

As years passed and I got busy with basketball and everything else in high school, our relationship changed. I became the protector (from threats both inside and outside our home) and I worried that she would end up like a lot of other young girls in our neighborhood: pregnant and out of school. I knew I wouldn't be around when she got to high school and it terrified me, but I shouldn't have worried. Megan, perhaps out of necessity, was mature beyond her years. We both saw things that kids shouldn't see.

When I found out that I was going to be playing at SIU, Megan was twelve and in sixth grade. I told her and mom about it that night while eating in the kitchen. Dad was indulging in a typical Powell evening out. "I got some news today. I have an offer to play for Southern Illinois on a basketball scholarship! My schooling is going to be paid for mom, isn't that great!" I was disappointed by their reaction. Both of them started crying.

"Why not UE? I thought UE was looking at you. What about USI?" Mom hated the idea of my leaving but she knew it was best for me. I could have played at USI, the University of Southern Indiana, a Division II school, and lived at home, but the thought of four more years in that house was unbearable.

"I know mom, I know. I'll miss you two so much, but SIU isn't that far away. It's not like I'll be across the country." Megan pushed her bowl of chili away and walked to her room, still crying. It took me off guard and I went after her.

"Megan...Megan, listen to me! You know I have to do this. You know I can't stay with dad here. He's so much harder on me than he is you. You don't understand what it's like." I knew I could reason with her because even at twelve, Megan was a sharp thinker. She went on to be a valedictorian six years later and earned her own scholarship to Indiana University where she got a business degree.

"What am I going to do around here without you? I'll be all alone. You can't do this!"

"Look, you know we'll keep in touch and you'll get to come visit me a lot. Plus, you're going into junior high soon. You're going to be busy with friends and school stuff. Trust me, soon you won't even miss me around here!"

I did my best to console her, and she finally came around to my point of view. We did our best to stay in contact during my college years, but our schedules collided and I only saw her a handful of times. In fact, the night of game six was the first time we'd been in the old house together since I left for SIU in the fall of 1993.

***

As the Cards were taking their swings, I suddenly had a strong urge to challenge Megan to a game of Life.

44

"Hey Megs!" I called out, knowing she and mom were keeping tabs on dad and mine's progress. I had been calling her "Megs" since she was two and I was still the only one she allowed to use that name. She called back with a "What is it bro?"

"When was the last time I kicked your ass in the Game of Life?"

"Uh, how about never? Why, you looking to get humiliated like the old days?" Megan shouted confidently, knowing well my terrible record against her and my sore loser streak.

"Absolutely! Whenever you're ready!"

"Okay, after the ball game if you're still up for it! I'll set it up in a little bit." I was genuinely excited when I heard this. Having her around lightened the atmosphere of the whole house. It was starting to feel like old times, except better because dad was present and sober. Never mind the circumstances, it was good to be back home.

In my burst of enthusiasm I began to think about the good times of our childhood. There had been some, though they were easily overshadowed. There had been a time early in my life, somewhat before Megan came along, when mom and dad were a loving and functional married couple. It wasn't perfect, as no marriage is, but I know there was a time when love outweighed the other stuff in our house.

I know this because I was a snooper when I was a kid. When it came to Christmas presents hidden in the house I was like McGruff the Crime Dog. I always sniffed them out. I found that I liked spying and staying hidden in small spaces (I was the opposite of claustrophobic). One evening I had holed up in my parents' closet, a place that was strictly forbidden to me, but that I was inevitably drawn to for that exact reason.

I was probably pretending to be in a bunker or something when my mom and dad walked into the bedroom. I'm not sure why I expected to be undisturbed with both of them in the house, but I was petrified when I heard them talking. I heard mom ask if he had seen me and I started chewing on my fist in fear. I just knew he would throw open the door, see me hunkered down underneath mom's dresses, and start wailing on my backside right there.

Instead, I heard him say, "I'm sure he's playing somewhere. Don't worry about him now. You relax." He was almost whispering.

The room was dark, but I could see that mom was now lying on the bed face down and dad was sitting next to her facing the headboard. At first I thought he was giving her a massage. Then my eyes refocused and I could see: he was gently scratching her legs up and down. He worked methodically up and down her leg with long strokes, then he took one of her feet and began scratching it as well. Occasionally dad would ask, "How's that feel?" or "Is that good?" Mom just groaned with approval. After a few minutes he moved himself up and started on her arms. She outstretched one of them so he could work his magic. I had never seen him do anything like this before. He was giving her a full-body scratching and she was enjoying it.

Eventually he pulled up her tank top and scratched her back as well. This went on for probably twenty minutes and, when he finished, he kissed her on the forehead and stood up. "I'm gonna head over to the bar for a little while. You okay now?"

"Yes baby, thank you. I'm just going to lay here for a while and rest my eyes." She was barely audible, it sounded like she was already half asleep. After dad left, I waited another couple of minutes to be sure and then slowly edged my way out of the closet. When I got to the bedroom door, I looked back at mom and saw that she was fully asleep. I had a strong urge to go kiss her cheek at that moment, but instead I roamed back to the safety of my room.

I now know that mom had bad arthritis (still does) and that dad's scratching her helped her to relax sometimes and take her mind off the pain. To this day it is still the sweetest gesture I have ever seen my dad give to her. I never asked mom about it, but I believe this was a regular event for them. Dad would comfort her for as long as it took, and then set off for his night of fun. One night I asked Karen if she wanted me to scratch her feet and legs to help her relax and she looked at me like I was nuts. She couldn't stand the thought of someone touching the bottom of her feet. For mom though, it must have been heavenly.

A couple of years later I was rooting around in their closet again, this time searching for possible birthday gifts (hoping to see some Star Wars logos on boxes). I came across a card that mom had tucked away in the back corner. It was an anniversary card featuring a silhouetted couple holding hands inside a large red heart. Inside I saw that dad had written a short message. I could barely read his writing; it looked like he wrote everything while riding in the trunk of a car. It said, "D- Thanks for marrying me and being the best wife ever. I can't imagine life without you! I love you baby! –J"

Dad never made any sort of statements or gestures like these in public. I don't believe I ever heard him say "I love you" to her or any of us for that matter. It wasn't his way. He made up for this by doing little things for mom like the scratchings, or keeping the kitchen clean, or taking Megan and I places so mom could have some time to herself. For mom's part she never questioned how he felt about her, but his feelings became irrelevant in later years.

Thankfully mom was an affectionate person and she routinely kissed and hugged all of us for any reason or none at all. She was the one who provided the motivation for Megan and me to excel in school and stay out of trouble in a neighborhood full of opportunities. She was also the disciplinarian. When mom felt it necessary she would call in dad as the enforcer.

When a spanking was in order she would inform dad of my crimes and leave it up to him to execute the punishment. And he was very good at his job. When I was young I got the bare hand to my butt. Later, when I became stronger, he used his leather belt to put some emphasis on whatever lesson I was supposed to be learning. I got spanked regularly, maybe once a week, until I reached junior high. That's when dad brought out the "nuclear option."

One night when I was in eighth grade, dad and I were sitting on the back porch taking in the sounds of the Redbirds when he turned to me. Normally he didn't have much to say on these evenings aside from comments about the game.

"Paul, listen to me. You're getting older now and you're a good boy. But you need to know something. Starting now, if I ever catch you drinking, even a little, I'll beat you like a man. You understand me? If I ever hear that you got a girl pregnant, same thing. I'll forget you're my son and I'll beat you like a man. Got it?"

What could I say? "Sure, dad. I got it. Don't worry about me." He scared me that night because, even though I had suffered a lot of spankings from him, he had never threatened to really hurt me. I never felt like I was physically abused, and most of the spankings were from things I knew I was doing wrong. I was kind of a little shit when I was younger, and I don't really blame them for trying to beat it out of me. I thought that would be the end of the conversation, but then dad looked back at me.

"Have you ever had liquor? Or beer? You can tell me the truth."

I had not. I was fortunate to have friends in school that weren't into that scene (at least not yet) and I had never experienced peer pressure in that regard. After I told him this he sat back and thought for a moment. Then he got up and marched through our tiny back yard and into our garage that adjoined the alley behind it. A few seconds later he emerged with a bottle. I knew what it was before I could read the label: Jack Daniels. He handed me the bottle, which was about two-thirds empty.

"Take a swig. See what you think." He was serious. I looked from him to the bottle and then back to him. I wasn't sure what he was trying to prove. "Just take a drink. It's okay. I won't tell mom!"

I went for it. I drew a healthy tug off the bottle and suddenly my mouth was filled with battery acid. What else could burn like this? I was able to swallow a small portion, but the rest ended up on the grass. "Oh my God! That's nasty! How do you drink that stuff, dad?" Now I saw his point clearly.

"I wanted you to know what alcohol tastes like. I drink it because I'm used to it, but I don't want you to get used to it. It's bad for you. Really bad. Just promise me you won't ever start on it."

It was probably one of the most sincere moments we shared together during my childhood. In fact, I'm grateful for his crude lesson because it helped me to steer clear of the party scene that so many of my basketball teammates got sucked into. As I have learned the full extent of what alcohol cost me and my family, I have continued to stay away from it.

Dad knew he had a problem. He just never had the will or desire to deal with it. Feeding the beast is much easier than trying to slay it. Part of me will never forgive him for that, but at least he cared enough to push me away from it. Mom also did her part to keep me on the straight and narrow, which I suppose is why she kept handing me over to the enforcer for my weekly whippings.

Megan, being the baby of the family, never got the level of discipline that I did. She got away with murder compared to me, but I suppose that's normal for a second child. Dad never spanked her, but didn't spend much time with her either. Megan learned to look to me for attention, and she knew that mom would force me to play with her. I'm glad she did, because we forged a solid sibling relationship that I still enjoy today.

Top of the Third

So far the game and the homecoming seemed to be going well. Dad was being receptive, though I could tell he was hurting. He shifted himself on the bed and let out a grunt in spite of his efforts to suppress any indication of pain. I spied bottles of pain pills on his nightstand and wondered if he ever considered taking an entire bottle and going to sleep forever. I knew he would never admit to me how much he was hurting. His sense of manliness would never allow it.

My seat was squeezed between the bed and a large wooden dresser. I scanned the few items sitting on it and my eyes fixed on something familiar. I reached for it and quickly realized it was an old program from Busch Stadium: a souvenir from the first, and only, Cardinals game that dad and I attended together. I couldn't believe he had kept it for all of these years. The date on the program read May 30, 1982. It was obvious that he had laid it out for me to find.

"Yes! I remember this game so vividly. What a win!" I said, flipping through the program and wondering at the names. Lonnie and Ozzie Smith, Keith Hernandez, Darrell Porter: Cardinal greats of a bygone era. Then I found the scorecard, complete down to the last play in dad's handwriting. That was the day he taught me which numbers corresponded to each position and how to keep score. It was a valuable lesson that I still make use of today. It's a skill I think all baseball fans should possess.

"Yeah, I remember it too. Big comeback that day." In fact the Cards staged two comebacks on that bright St. Louis afternoon. It was perhaps their most memorable regular season game during the 1982 season.

They were down 3-0 heading into the bottom of the ninth and lots of folks had already left the stadium. That's the constant internal debate when seeing a game in person:

stay and hope for a comeback or leave early to beat the traffic out of town. Dad was not the kind for leaving early. Even if it had been 10-0 he would have us sitting there through the final pitch. He was very much like a kid in that regard: he wanted to soak up every pitch and swing.

I had just turned seven by then and dad surprised me early that Sunday morning by coming into my room at six a.m. He wouldn't tell me where we were going, just that I needed to get dressed and be ready in fifteen minutes. I was excited and ready in five. Dad drove us in our metallic green 1974 Dodge Dart (the only vehicle they owned then) first to the gas station, and then to a little diner known as the Cross-eyed Cricket for breakfast, and then out of town heading west.

I don't remember us talking much during the breakfast or the ride over. I never asked him where we were going because I knew he wouldn't tell me. I could sense that he was excited though, and whatever it was I had a feeling I was going to like it. We mostly listened to the radio on the way to St. Louis, which was about a three hour drive from our house. Dad enjoyed the sounds of Elvis, The Doors, and even Simon and Garfunkel courtesy of the Dart's eight-track player. He hated disco and James Taylor, though I never heard him say why. The music served two purposes: it shortened the trip and mercifully filled the silence between us.

Finally, the Gateway Arch came into view.

"You see that, Paul? Know what it is?" I nodded my head. I had seen it on TV before and heard the Cardinals announcers reference it occasionally. I finally ventured a guess as to what we were doing.

"Are we going to Busch Stadium, dad?" My face must have been beaming because as soon as he looked at me he burst into laughter. Dad's laugh, like the rest of him, was big and loud and also contagious. He didn't laugh often, but when he did get tickled it was funny to watch. He shook as he laughed and his head bobbed up and down like a balloon.

"You got it, Tiger! We're going to the game today! What do you think of that?"

Tiger. That was his pet name for me that I only heard a few times in my life. I absolutely ate it up every time he used it. That moment, and that day in general, still stand as the high point of my childhood. I have attended dozens of Cardinals games since that one, and every time the arch comes into view I think back to that moment and my breath catches. It's a memory that makes my heart ache, both because there were so few moments like that with dad and because I'll never get it back. The beautiful moments float by just as fast as the mundane ones.

As we crossed the bridge over the Mississippi River my senses were overwhelmed. I had never seen a big city before. Hell, I'd never been out of Evansville before that day. The beauty of the arch, the tall buildings, the lanes filled with cars…it was all too much to take in at once. We parked in a garage a few blocks away from the stadium and started walking. My head snapped back and forth as I tried to take in the sights around me all at once.

Dad was practically dragging me by the hand as we made our way toward Busch. It was the most massive structure I had ever laid eyes on. Television really can't do justice to venues such as baseball stadiums. It was like entering Mecca. I was dazzled by the arches circling the top of it as well as its sheer magnitude. I noticed the crisscrossing stairways that led to various levels of the stadium, and then my eyes fixed on a statue standing near one of the gates.

Dad pointed at the statue and said, "That's Stan Musial. The greatest Cardinal who ever lived. That's what they do for great people…they build statues." I had heard dad tell stories about Musial before. He was old enough to remember listening to games called by Harry Carey and

Jack Buck and featuring the incredible prowess of Stan
"The Man."

We reached the base of the statue and stopped. I
read the inscription on the stone beneath the giant figure of
Stan in a batting pose. It read, "Here stands baseball's
perfect warrior...Here stands baseball's perfect knight." I
didn't understand the meaning for years after, but now I
know that it's a fitting tribute to a man who was great in
life as well as baseball.

Admittedly, having seen the statue on many
occasions since that day, I have to say it isn't particularly
well done. It doesn't resemble his face and the bat seems
too short. But, at age seven and seeing it for the first time, it
was amazing.

Dad tugged on my hand and we continued our
pilgrimage toward Busch. We walked to a ticket window
and I heard dad say, "Gimme two tickets...best you got."
He handed over the cash and then we were quickly off
toward the nearest gate.

Once inside we walked straight toward a kiosk
where a guy was yelling the word "programs!" over and
over. Dad bought one and immediately had us moving
again. We made one last stop before reaching our seats. He
walked me to a vendor who was standing behind a glass
counter. Inside it I could see baseballs, cards, and other
assorted souvenirs. Behind him was a large wall covered in
hats and T-shirts. Dad grabbed my shoulder.

"Pick yourself out a hat and a shirt. Which ones do
you like?" dad asked.

This was like Christmas morning. I was
overwhelmed. Dad just didn't do things like this. One
minute I was snoozing in my bed, the next I was whisked
away to this wondrous land where dad takes me to ball
games and buys me things. It took me a few seconds just to
process what he had said, and then another full minute
before I picked out the hat and shirt I wanted. I chose a red

adjustable hat featuring the StL logo with a mesh back, and a T-shirt featuring Fred Bird the mascot. I put them both on immediately and barely took the hat off for the next two years. It was eventually worn to the point of disintegration, my first of several Cardinal hats that became my signature look.

The shock of suddenly coming into possession of two precious new items quickly transitioned into the absolute awe of seeing the playing field for the first time. Passing through the walkways on the way to our seats, I would catch a glimpse of green and stiffen. It was so green it seemed to be glowing. We walked up a couple of flights and I started to get antsy. I wanted, no *needed*, to see that field.

When we finally found our section and turned to walk through the tunnel, my heart was pounding. We reached the end of the tunnel and stood at the railing to gaze over the entirety of the field. Once again, my senses were overwhelmed. The color of the artificial turf was a brilliant, deep green I had never seen before. The size of the field also stunned me. I thought, *How does anyone ever hit a home run here?*

We stood there for probably five minutes before continuing the search for our seats. We were in the left field upper deck, but I couldn't have cared less how close we were to the field. It was my first time in a big league ballpark and I was with my dad...does it get any better than that? I sat mesmerized for quite a while, watching first the Cardinals and then the Padres take batting practice. Seeing how hard and how far they were hitting the ball was nearly incomprehensible to me. The sound of the ball hitting those bats was like a far-away cannon.

I enjoyed the game thoroughly. I cheered, I booed, I even felt so good that I talked dad into buying me one of those big foam number ones. Ordinarily I wouldn't try to talk him into anything, but today was special. It was in many ways a holiday from our usual life and relationship.

I also learned a lot about the game that day. He explained the scoring method and how to write it correctly on the scorecard. He talked strategy with me when runners were on base. A few times he correctly predicted what would happen before the pitch came. He not only had a natural talent for the game, but he had also acquired a great knowledge of it through his years of playing and umpiring. He could easily have been a minor league manager, but then again, he could have been a lot of things if he had made them a priority.

The afternoon moved quickly and it looked like my first game was a bust. The Pads had shut our guys down for the first eight innings and took the field in the bottom of the ninth needing only three more outs for a win. It looked hopeless, but when I looked at dad, he seemed undaunted. Win or lose, he was simply enjoying the experience. I knew he had been to games before, but it had been long before I was born. That feeling of disappointment was starting to hit me, but I didn't want him to see it. I didn't want to seem unappreciative of what he had done for me.

Then something magical started to happen.

The Cardinals came to life in that ninth inning and an afternoon that seemed destined for a bitter ending turned in the span of just a few at-bats. Keith Hernandez, whom I would later root against as a member of the hated Mets, led off with a single. Another single followed from George Hendrick, and then Lonnie Smith delivered a clutch RBI double. Now the game was getting interesting. Dad and I were on our feet for the entire inning, along with everyone else in the stadium.

After a groundout, Julio Gonzalez grounded the ball to San Diego's shortstop and Lonnie Smith was caught dead between second and third base. Sometimes a game turns on a bizarre play, and this was a prime example. The shortstop flipped the ball to Luis Salazar, the Padres' third baseman. In the attempted run-down, he and Smith collided in the base path and the umpires called interference on him. At seven years old I was unfamiliar with this call and dad explained that all the runners got to move up and everyone was safe. Hendrick scored and suddenly it was 3-2 with the winning runs in scoring position. I was confused, but elated at this turn of events.

The Cards tied the game on a sacrifice fly from Tommy Herr (still my favorite Cardinal second baseman ever) and our afternoon at the ballpark got an unexpected extension. After the rally I glanced at dad. He was wearing a smile of genuine satisfaction that we rarely saw at home.

"Can't believe all those people left early! Now they're sitting in their cars listening to the game and kicking themselves I'll bet!" That rally and comment by dad are the reason I have never left a game early, even the blowouts. In baseball there are no guarantees and you never know when you're going to witness something special.

Our emotions quickly swung again in the tenth when Bruce Sutter, the Cards' future Hall of Fame closer, struggled to get outs and allowed two runs on three hits and a walk. In a blink, the Padres had regained a 5-3 lead. I couldn't believe how the game could change and then change again so quickly. I heard dad cussing under his breath…another trait I have inherited from him. Karen often scolds me for getting too emotionally involved in the games. I tell her I can't help it, and that's the truth.

When you root for a team for literally your entire life it becomes personal. Even more personal than for the players I think. Those guys only play for a team for a few years at most, and usually for several different ones. They don't have decades invested in it the way fans do. Still, I try to temper my reactions now that I have little Jack watching with me.

The crowd, which now filled less than half the seats, started to thin out even more. Most of them wagered that a second comeback was unlikely. Dad just sat back in his plastic seat and looked around. He wasn't budging, and I was glad. I didn't want the game or the day to end. I wish it had been a double-header.

In the bottom of the tenth, the first two outs came quickly. The Cards were down to their final out and I wanted to cry. Somehow, the loss was going to be more painful because of the late rally. Again, I steeled myself for fear of angering dad.

Hendrick stood in the box, and for the second inning in a row, singled to bring the tying run to the plate. Lonnie Smith, who after this game became my favorite player for two or three years, hit yet another clutch double that scored a run. I don't personally remember this, but dad told me later that I was jumping around and yelling hysterically during most of that half inning. Still, they needed another hit or the comeback would fall short.

Mike Ramsey, the Cards' utility infielder, came to the plate and delivered a base hit to tie the game and send the remaining crowd into a fit of joy. We were all primed and ready for a game winner. At seven years old, my capacity for emotional swings was at its limit. I believe all of us fans willed our guys to win that day.

The next batter was Julio Gonzalez. He was hit by a pitch and that pushed Ramsey to second with the winning run. Then there was a break as San Diego changed pitchers. While he was warming up I asked dad, "What do you think is going to happen here? You think we'll win it?" Dad knew so much about what was going on, I was hoping he would have some inside knowledge and just tell me how it would end. The suspense was too much for a kid at his first game.

Whitey Herzog, the brilliant manager who was just beginning one of the best eras in Cardinal history, made a move. He sent up Dane Iorg, a lefty, as a pinch-hitter against the Pads' right-hander. The count went to 1-1, and then I saw Iorg swing. I heard a snapping sound (he broke his bat swinging at an up and in pitch) and then saw the ball drifting over second base. The crowd held its breath as the center fielder came charging in. All at once there was an eruption of sound as the ball hit the turf. Ramsey came charging around third and there would be no stopping him. He scored, and the best game that I have ever seen in person ended in a 6-5 victory.

Dad and I were both screaming. Somewhere close by in the press box, Jack Buck was joyfully announcing "That's a winner!" to all of those faithless fans who had exited earlier. It was like a dream. Dad turned toward me with his hands facing me. I gave dad the first and only "high five" of our lives. We stood for another couple of minutes watching the players celebrate, and then began our long journey back to the Dart and reality.

Every man can point to a day or event that he feels is a defining moment in his life. May 30th, 1982 was one of those for me. I don't think I stopped smiling all the way back to Evansville, even though I slept for most of the return trip. I was exhausted from sensory and emotional overload. What a day! I asked dad as we drove back home if we could do it again sometime. He said, "Sure, kid. We'll get back over here as soon as we can."

We never made it back to another one. Our lives turned shortly after that day and I never even got around to asking him again. Little did I know, as I rested my victorious head in the Dart, that I had just experienced the peak moment of my relationship with my father.

***

I closed the program and laid it back on the dresser. "Dad, what prompted you to take me to that game back in '82? It seemed so sudden."

Without looking away from the TV he answered, "I just thought it was time that you saw a game for real. I was about that age when my dad took me to the old

Sportsman's Park. I guess I just got the urge and thought what the hell."

"That was a good day for me. One of my best days, actually. I wish we could have caught another one together." I forced myself to look right at him as I said this. We were already in uncharted territory in terms of baring personal feelings. He turned from the TV and looked me in the eyes for the first time since I had arrived.

"It was a great day for me too. Why do you think I saved the program?" I smiled when I heard this. Through all of the turmoil that occurred in the years after that day, we at least had one good shared memory to hold on to. Sometimes that's enough to keep a relationship going.

"You know, looking back, I don't think I've ever seen another game like that. Two comebacks in two consecutive innings with the game on the line? That's incredible," I said as I watched Garcia notch the third out of the inning (and his last of the night).

"Probably never see that again either. I guess I know how to pick 'em!" He chuckled a little, but then winced as the pain welled up in him. I had to keep reminding myself that he was doing well just to keep sitting up.

I decided then that things were going well enough to proceed with my plan. I walked out of the room during the commercial break and called Karen at the hotel. I told her to start getting little Jack ready for his first meeting with his grandfather.

Bottom of the Third

I came back into the bedroom as Lewis was taking his warm-up tosses. Dad looked at me inquisitively.
"What is it?" I asked.

"You know, to be honest, I didn't think you'd come back. I really never thought I'd see you here again," he said in a matter-of-fact tone. I sat back down in the recliner and chose not to address him directly. That's the beauty of having a conversation in front of a TV: it's a convenient distraction.

"Well, dad. I thought it was the right thing to do. I didn't want...I didn't want to leave things unsettled."

"So you thought you'd come here and clear your conscience, eh? Well, consider it clear. You don't have to stay here if you don't want to." He was suddenly becoming abrasive and I saw a flash of the father I had run from.

"No, dad, it's not that. I'm not here to make myself feel better. At least, not entirely. I'm here tonight because, like it or not, we have a lot of things to talk about."

"I know what happened. Your mom guilted you into this, didn't she? I know how she works. She made you think you're going to have all this regret if you don't show up and talk to the old man. Am I right?" Now something popped inside my head and I lost all sense of fear or trepidation that was ever-present in my dealings with dad.

"No goddammit, that's not it! Why do you have to be such an asshole all the time? You're my father and you're dying...I'm here because of that! I want to make things right before it's too late. Don't you see that?"

Dad's expression changed and he turned his attention back to the TV. A small grin appeared on his lips. "There's the Gibson coming out of you! I knew it was in there somewhere! Okay then, so you're staying?"

"Yeah. I'm sticking around until this game is over. I'm sorry...you bring that out of me sometimes."

"Right. Like the last time I saw you. Your wedding day." I didn't respond.

That was one of the subjects that I meant to discuss with him. I was angry, but also pleased that we were having open communication. I didn't want to play games. It was far too late for that.

"So you want to talk about things, eh? Okay. What should we talk about? How about we start with what you've been doing with yourself these last few years?" He asked. I could tell that the turn in our conversation had energized him a bit.

"All right. We can start there. What do you want to know? I've been working and watching Cardinals games and trying to be a good husband and father. That's the short answer." I wasn't sure if he was intentionally throwing me off of what I wanted to discuss.

"Tell me about Karen. I only met her what, twice? What's she like?" Fifteen years ago, he had tried to talk me out of marrying her when he didn't even know her.

"She's a lot like mom in some ways. She's a great mother. Really sweet and loving. She's generous and good natured. She's pretty much the best person I've ever met. I'm lucky to have her."

"I'm glad to hear it. A good woman makes all the difference." Then he said something that I wasn't expecting. "I never deserved her, your mom. I'm surprised she's still with me honestly. She deserves a medal or something when she gets to heaven."

Truer words have never been spoken. Mom deserved a lot of things for having put up with Johnny Ray all of those years. But she chose to stay so many times when she could have, and many would say should have, justifiably walked away. I can't imagine loving someone that much.

"Dad, I'm going to ask you something and you might get mad. But I'm asking anyway. Did you ever cheat on mom...all those nights you were out at the bars?" Only on that night could I have ever summoned the nerve to ask this. Perhaps he was too weak or too tired to get really angry, but his mood and expression remained unchanged.

"Nope. Not once. Not that I didn't have opportunities. But, you know I really never even thought about it. Those girls at the bars or the track were...a certain breed. They were all the same and none of them all that interesting. Your mother is so much more than that. No, I never cheated on her. That's the one thing I have going for me. One of the few things I'm proud of, actually." Now I felt bad for having asked, but I was relieved and heartened by the answer. "Why? You cheat on Karen?"

I laughed and shook my head. "No, no. Never. And unlike you, I don't get 'opportunities' to do so! I'm pretty happy overall. I feel lucky because I know a few guys from college whose marriages have fallen apart."

Dad was nodding his head. "Good. I'm glad to hear it. I..." He trailed off and I looked up at him. He fixed his gaze on the sheets in front of him and continued. "I'm really proud of you for everything you've done. You're a good man. Despite my best efforts, you turned out to be a good man."

I sat silent, hearing the ball game going on in the distance. In a man's life, hearing your father tell you he's proud of you is like the Holy Grail of compliments. Some kids hear it all the time growing up, or at least I had always imagined there were kids like that somewhere. My father had never uttered those words to me before that night. At some point in high school, I stopped waiting (and praying) for it and just accepted that he wasn't that kind of dad. Hearing it at age thirty-six wasn't nearly as gratifying, but it still felt very good.

"Thanks. I appreciate that. I'm just trying to do the best I can." And I do. Karen has stayed with me through my inner battles and self-serving tendencies. I never started drinking, but I did develop some bad spending habits after we got married. We were in bankruptcy within our first five years of marriage, and it was nearly all my fault. I had to learn the value of money and how to manage it. Growing up in a household where dad plays Robin Hood with the money mom brings home can skew your understanding of personal finance.

I never told mom or dad about it. Karen and I went through a year of counseling and I started attending ACA (Adult Children of Alcoholics) meetings. The work we both put in helped to save our marriage and our financial future. I still attend meetings monthly because they remind me that I still have work to do on myself.

The price of growing up in an alcoholic household can be steep, and sometimes the bill doesn't come due for many years. In addition to my spending issues, I also became a "people pleaser." I seek approval by never saying no to anyone. In high school it made me a "nice guy" and a "go-getter," but later it became crippling. I had to find the strength to stand up for myself or I would have lost my mind. Karen has been instrumental in that battle as well.

Megan is also very good at concealing her scars. Though she seemed to breeze through high school with few issues, a lifetime of warped memories finally caught up with her at IU. During her junior year she suddenly began suffering severe anxiety attacks on an almost daily basis. Though I've never seen her in the midst of one, her description of it makes me shudder. Some nights, while barely able to breathe and her heart ready to burst from her chest, Megan prayed for death.

The attacks still hit her occasionally, but medicine has helped to control it. Her bouts with depression, which shortly followed the onset of her anxiety issues, have also laid her low at times. I know of at least one occasion, about five years ago, when she truly wanted to kill herself. Thankfully, she lacked the "courage" to end it, and in recent years she seems to be keeping the demons at bay with more success.

***

We sat in silence for a couple of minutes, trying to focus on the game. The Cards didn't appear to have much going this inning. Then dad asked, "So with you working in St. Louis, I bet you get to go to a lot of games don't you?" It was his way of saying that the previous topic was now closed. Time to move on...I was willing to accommodate this time.

"Oh yes, I try to get to ten or twelve games a year. The last one I went to was right near the end of the regular season when they beat the Cubs with that ninth inning rally against Marmol."

That had been a very trying game up until the end. The Cards were still chasing the Braves in the Wild Card race and a second straight loss to their arch rivals would have been devastating. The Cards were down 1-0 in the bottom of the ninth and facing the Cubs' closer. Our guys staged a furious rally but were still one strike away from losing. Carlos Marmol walked the tying run in, and then threw a wild pitch, allowing the winning run to score. It had been no less than a season-saving comeback.

Dad grunted with approval. "I remember that one. One of the best rallies of the season. You seen many other great games there? Ever get to sit in the VIP seats?"

"Once in a while, our boss will score some tickets in those green seats right behind home plate. In fact, you've probably seen me on TV because those seats are in view of the camera." I went on to tell him about a few of the games I had seen live over the years that stuck in my mind. None of them could compare to my experience in '82, but there had been some good ones.

I was fortunate that my first year out of college coincided with the arrival of Mark McGwire from the Oakland A's. I went with three friends to the game on opening day in 1998. The hype surrounding McGwire and his possible quest to beat Maris' record of sixty-one homers had already started. He hit fifty-eight combined between Oakland and St. Louis in '97, so everyone knew it was possible.

He didn't disappoint us on that day. With the score locked at zero in the bottom of the fifth, McGwire came to the plate with the bases loaded. The buzz in the crowd was measurable. There was a collective gasp every time he swung the bat. Then he connected. The ball just sounded different coming off his bat, and it was evident immediately that the ball was gone. Grand slam. The atmosphere inside Busch at that moment could only be described as bedlam. The Cards won 6-0, with Todd Stottlemyre pitching seven impressive innings.

I wasn't able to obtain a ticket for the night that he hit number sixty-two, but I was there for sixty-one on the afternoon before. He hit a towering blast that bounced off the Stadium Club windows above left field and we all went crazy. That was in the first inning, so we got to see him bat three more times with a shot at history. Of course he didn't get it that day, but I'll never forget the crowd during those at-bats. Fifty thousand pairs of eyes focusing like lasers on one man. Groans and oohs came from everywhere with each pitch. That was probably my second favorite experience at Busch Stadium.

Dad interrupted, "What about playoff games? World Series? That's something I always wish I had done. I should have taken you back for the Series in '82." This was nearly as good as hearing him say he was proud of me. My only consolation is knowing that the experience would not have been as special. Fun, but not magical. That can only happen once.

"I would have liked that, dad." I pointed to the TV. The Cards had been retired in the third without putting up any "crooked numbers" and the players were running back to the dugout. "But at least we have HDTV now. It's almost like we're there."

"Almost," he concurred.

"Two playoff games. That's all I've seen in person." The first was against the Braves in the National League Championship Series in 1996. That was LaRussa's first season in St. Louis. He led them to their first division title since 1987 and then took on the heavily favored defending champion Atlanta Braves. The Cards lost game one in Atlanta, then played brilliant baseball for three straight games to push the champs to the brink of elimination. I was there for game four. I was still in college and it was the first game I had been to since being with dad in '82.

It was a tight, well-played game. Brian Jordan, one of the best players of the 1990's for the Cardinals, hit a home run and Dennis Eckersley (the closer that LaRussa brought with him from Oakland) finished the game to give us the 4-3 win. It was the last win of the season for that group as the Braves won three straight to clinch the pennant. Though that series was disappointing, it was the start of an amazing era of success for the franchise.

"I didn't get to go to any of the World Series games in '06. Karen and I were…having issues. I did watch them though, and I almost called you after Wainwright struck out Brandon Inge," I said.

The 2006 Cardinals were one of the most surprising world champion teams in recent memory. Their record of 83-79 barely got them into the playoffs, and no one expected much out of them. That team's run was a case of everything coming together at the right time. Chris Carpenter pitched great, David Eckstein played much bigger than his size, and the Tigers' pitchers forgot how to throw the ball to the bases correctly. The Cardinals won in five games over the hugely favored Detroit team, with Adam Wainwright, the rookie who was filling in as the closer, finishing it off. It was their first World Series title since 1982.

"I thought about you that night too. What a scrappy team! They really should have won it in '04, but '06 made up for it," dad replied. "And what about what Wainwright did to Beltran! That's still the best pitch I've ever seen to win a game."

He was referring to game seven of the NLCS in which the Mets (also heavily favored) were down 3-1 in the bottom of the ninth. Yadier Molina had just launched the most important home run of his career in the top of the ninth to give the Cards the lead. Jeff Suppan pitched his ass off in that game to keep their potent lineup in check. Wainwright came in to save it, but had problems. They loaded the bases and, with two outs, the Cardinal killer himself, Carlos Beltran, came to the plate with a chance to tie or win the series with one swing. This was the man who had destroyed Cardinal pitching in the 2004 NLCS (four homers and a .417 average) while he was with the Houston Astros.

Wainwright got ahead of him with a called strike, then he fouled the next one off to make it 0-2. Then "Waino" unfurled one of the nastiest curve balls I have ever seen and froze Beltran for strike three. The ball literally started head high and then dropped into Molina's glove at Beltran's knees. I jumped out of my chair at the same moment that Molina leaped for joy after hearing the umpire call the final strike.

"Oh no doubt! No one could have hit that pitch!" I said.

I began to realize how much I had missed talking to dad about baseball. He was so knowledgeable and passionate. There were times over the years when I was tempted to break my silence just so we could talk Cardinals for ten minutes, but I never did.

I had been applying a kind of emotional embargo on

my father for the last fifteen years. For the first few I felt justified and happy that he was out of my life. That feeling began to waver in the five or so years leading up to the night I returned. Now, seeing the man teetering on the edge of death, I felt genuine guilt. I was guilty of shutting dad out of my life. Perhaps more importantly, I was guilty of keeping him from seeing his only grandson.

Bitter pangs of regret began to roll through my mind. This reunion was going to be tougher than I thought.

Top of the Fourth

When the game returned from the commercial break, a new face was on the mound. Dad had been right as usual...LaRussa pulled Garcia after only three innings of work in favor of Fernando Salas. This had been his style during the playoffs. He was riding a hot bullpen and not allowing the starters to put the team in an early hole. Garcia had only given up two runs, but Tony obviously didn't like what he was seeing. The game would be decided by a parade of relievers from the Cards' bullpen.

Mom came in during the break and checked on us. She didn't mention the yelling that she must have heard from me a few minutes before. She filled up dad's water bottle and fluffed the pillows behind his back and head.

"Butch called earlier today. I told him you were coming to see your father and he was so happy! He said to tell you hi and welcome home," mom announced while fluffing. Butch Hanley. That was a name I hadn't heard in many years. He was a lifelong friend to dad, one of his gang of "drinking buddies" whom he had spent so much time and money with. I was somewhat surprised to hear that Butch was still alive considering his reputation.

I knew a couple of dad's friends had gone by the wayside, but good ole' Butch was still hanging in there. He was a physically impressive man, nearly as tall and wide as dad with shiny blond hair and a perpetual tan that you would swear was artificial. Standing next to each other, they were like twin towers. As a kid, I liked to think that Butch and dad could have taken on Demolition or the Legion of Doom in a tag team match.

"Wow. How's he doing?" I asked with genuine curiosity. This was a man who was known around Powell for decades as a wild man. He had brushes with death on more than one occasion, usually because of his own stupid decisions.

One night, around the time that I was born, Butch and dad were driving home after another raucous evening at Lamasco's. They were in dad's car (an old Chevy Nova) but Butch was driving because dad had imbibed a little too much. Apparently Butch had as well because he plowed the car into a utility pole and they were both nearly crushed to death when it fell down. The pole barely missed falling on the car, but the result was to put out the lights along a four block strip of Hollywood Avenue (a side street that connected with Delmar).

Dad suffered a broken arm in the crash and Butch got a concussion when his head met the steering wheel. Amazingly, neither of them were arrested. The cops in the Powell area were more than familiar with dad's bunch and some of them had even been his teammates during his softball days. In the end, Butch paid for the repairs to both the pole and dad's car. It didn't last long. Six months later dad totaled the Nova when he fell asleep at the wheel coming home from the horse track in Henderson. The car veered right off the road and into a deep ditch.

Dad said when he opened his eyes the car was in the process of rolling over while simultaneously flying toward a large aluminum drain tunnel. It ended up on its wheels and inside the tunnel. Dad somehow walked away with only a separated shoulder as a reminder of the accident.

"Butch is fine. You know he stopped drinking about ten years ago and since then he's been a different guy. He comes around and visits your dad about once a week," mom said.

"Wow again. Why did he decide to stop drinking? I mean, he was the last guy I would have picked to turn his life around out of that group!" Now mom's eyes dropped and she leaned against the bedroom door frame.

"It's not a good story. He lost his daughter. She was only twenty-two. Hit by a drunk driver one night over in

Owensboro. I've never heard him talk about it, but you know she meant everything to him," mom explained. All three of us sat silent for a minute after that.

"My God, how terrible." That was all I could muster. I had met Butch's daughter, Alison, a couple of times when we were kids. I thought of Jack, and how crushing it would be to lose him.

I began to recall more details about Butch and the other "merry men" who surrounded dad for so many years. Their lives seemed to revolve around alcohol, and their headquarters was Lamasco's Bar.

***

Sometimes when dad and the guys didn't have anyone or anywhere to leave their kids, they would bring us to the bar. It wasn't usually allowed, but the rules were relaxed for Johnny Ray and his merry men. Megan and I would sometimes spend hours in that place. We played cards or board games like Candy Land (which I never won), and sometimes just listened to the tall tales of the olden days told by a bunch of inebriated fools.

We were there perhaps once or twice a month, usually on a day when mom was working. She didn't seem to mind this arrangement; I guess she was just happy we weren't sitting at home alone.

The bartender started keeping white and chocolate milk on hand just for us. Dad made sure we ate and had milk, but for the most part we were left to our own devices. Sometimes we just listened to the tall tales of the olden days told by a bunch of inebriated fools.

One afternoon when I was around ten years old dad took us there while mom worked yet another Saturday in order to make a little extra on her paycheck. The bar was pretty quiet in the afternoons, with only the usual suspects to be found. There were a couple of guys in one corner playing darts, two younger gentlemen in black heavy metal T-shirts and ripped jeans playing pool, and three or four wrinkled patrons sitting at the bar. Seemingly all of them were smoking. The atmosphere inside Lamasco's was consistently hazy with the heavy smell of smoke and beer hovering over us. If second-hand smoke is as bad for you as they say, I probably lost ten years of my life in there.

A small color TV hung over the edge of the bar. It was muted and normally showing ESPN. There was always music playing thanks to a jukebox that seemed to only feature John Mellencamp or Bruce Springsteen music. Eventually I learned every song that was on that jukebox by heart and once in a while dad would give me a few quarters to throw into it. "Smuggler's Blues" by Glenn Frey was a favorite of mine, though I never actually saw Miami Vice until I was an adult. I'm sure there were other selections, but nearly every time we walked in that place "Hurts So Good" was either in progress or next on the rack.

A few yellowing Powell High School pennants hung around the room along with framed photos of various champion teams of Powell High history. I never came back to find out if they put my semi-state team's photo on the wall, but dad was up there in a few places. Thanks to his accomplishments as an athlete and his outgoing personality, dad had a kind of living folk hero status at the bar and generally around Powell.

Every so often a fight would break out, but mostly it was just a peaceful watering hole. I heard that it shut down about five years ago, and it actually made me a little sad to hear it. Like so many other older small businesses, Lamasco's fell victim to modernization. People don't want to go to Cheers anymore, they want a place that has fifty big screens and serves just as many varieties of microbrews.

Dad wasn't exactly Norm Peterson, but he was certainly a regular. He had a regular table and no one ever asked him what he wanted to drink. They already knew. At any given time there might have been three or four of his friends present when we arrived. Several more would come and go as the afternoon progressed. Most people in Powell considered themselves a friend of Johnny Ray Gibson, but only a few actually were.

Butch was his best friend since junior high and was around dad more than anyone else. I never saw them argue, though they would often have heated discussions involving local and professional sports. Butch was a Cubs fan (which was at least respectable in the 1980s), and he and dad would "argue" over topics such as who was the better second baseman: Ryne Sandberg or Tommy Herr. I must grudgingly side with Butch on that issue.

On that afternoon the talk was all about college football. It was the first Saturday of the season and most folks in our neighborhood were interested to see how Notre Dame would fare. Dad was only a casual fan of the sport and was more interested in catching a late season baseball game. That was especially true on that day in 1985, when the Cards were doing their best to keep the Mets at bay in the NL East.

When someone asked him what he thought of the Irish's chances against Michigan that day, dad just shook his head and smiled. "You guys know I don't give a shit either way. Notre Dame isn't doing anything special this year, that's all I'll say."

Butch replied, "Hey Johnny! I've got a hundred bucks here that say Notre Dame beats Michigan! Give me seven points!" Butch was a rabid fan of the game and had been a very respectable running back for Powell High in his day. He knew dad didn't follow the particulars of college football and, best friends or not, was hoping to cash in on dad's lack of interest. He produced two fifty dollar bills (rare currency among their group since fifties are considered unlucky by horse betters) and slapped them on the table in front of dad. Dad continued smiling as he looked up at his overconfident friend.

"You got yourself a bet, big boy! Here Chuck, you hold the money until the game is over. You all heard the man, I'm giving the big shot Notre Dame and seven points," dad proclaimed.

Chuck Simmons stuffed Butch's fifties and five twenties from dad into his shirt pocket. Chuck was another one of dad's "inner circle" and no one doubted he would keep the money safe.

Chuck, whose lean frame and pockmarked face made him look perpetually ill, was perusing the Evansville Courier (the city had two newspapers back then, the Courier came out early and the Press in late afternoon) while the other guys discussed the upcoming football game and the big bet. Chuck was the only one out of their group who was interested in politics, somewhat because he had been laid off a year ago by the local Whirlpool factory. He didn't get a chance to talk politics with the guys much, so he made the most of opportunities like this.

"You guys see this shit? The Zenith plant is shutting down next spring. Over five hundred people out of work like that! You think that bastard Reagan cares? He's running this country right into the ground! And all you guys wanna do is sit around talking football?" Chuck was a union Democrat like his father before him. Evansville had a history as a mostly blue-collar town loaded with good paying industrial jobs. By 1985 that era was just beginning to close.

"Save it, Chuck. Reagan's doing great things for this country! I'll take him over goons like Carter or Ford any day," Herm Johnston responded. Herm was the only member of dad's crew who consistently held down full-time employment. His weekdays were devoted to his plumbing career and his wife, but his weekends were spent with the boys. Herm just shook his head and looked up at the TV. He had had his fill of political talk and was now focusing on the game that would make someone a hundred dollars richer.

Dad liked betting on games that weren't of great interest to him because it gave him a reason to watch. I'm not sure the man ever watched a football game that he didn't have at least five dollars riding on. A hundred was big money for those guys. Butch must have been drunk earlier than usual to make such a proposition.

A lot of times I just sat and took in the conversations. I never minded being at the bar because there were a lot of interesting guys in there, plus it was a chance to be around dad when he was in a good mood. At home, he seemed grouchy and tired most of the time. At the bar, dad was alive. He was funny, charismatic, and full of energy.

In the middle of the second quarter of the Notre Dame-Michigan game dad's brother, my uncle Phil Gibson, walked into the bar. He bore a strong resemblance to dad with his thick, dark hair, strong jaw, and oversized ears. Phil was two years older than dad and they had a long history of conflict. On this day, it had been weeks since the two had spoken after an incident at the track. Phil was supposed to have put twenty dollars on the five horse to win in the last race of the day at Ellis. Dad, for once, chose work over fun as he had a chance to make a week's pay in one day for driving a semi to Nashville and back. Sometimes he took odd jobs like this when the price was right, but not nearly often enough.

Phil, who was most likely hammered by post time of the final race, forgot to make the bet and the five horse went off at fifteen to one and won. Dad would have won over three hundred dollars with that bet. Needless to say, any money that dad won at the track would be lost within a week or two. The more money he won, and the more he drank, the riskier he got with his wagering.

Much like at the bar, dad was a beloved customer at the track and he and the boys always got complimentary programs and box seats close to the finish line. My father was more committed to a bar and a horse track than he was to his family. I didn't yet fully understand how pathetic that was at age ten.

Phil stood in the doorway of Lamasco's and surveyed the room. He nearly always wore a tan Member's Only jacket and a solid colored button-down shirt underneath. Today it was light blue. He spotted dad and strode toward him with purpose. "Okay Johnny, I know you're still pissed at me, but I'm about to make it up to you. I got a great tip on a long shot today."

"Go on."

"I keep in touch with Steve Barron, you remember him right? He's one of the guys that walks the horses on the backside at Ellis. He's working up in New York right now and he says..." Phil explained the situation and dad half-listened as he watched the game. Uncle Phil got very excited and animated when discussing horses. He was a true junkie. After years of losing he still couldn't turn down information from an "inside man" even though most of the time the tips turned out to be bogus.

"Fine. Since you still have my twenty, put it on your long shot. And if I find out he won and you didn't make the bet...I'll break your neck!" dad looked serious. He hadn't forgotten about the five horse.

Their attention quickly turned back to the action on the TV screen. Hopes were high for the Irish that year, as they were ranked in the top fifteen and quarterbacked by the future NFL Pro Bowler Steve Beuerlein. The atmosphere inside Lamasco's was jovial during much of the first half. Both defenses played well and the score remained tight throughout the game. I enjoyed watching the guys as they reacted to the game. It was obvious from Phil's pained expression that he had money riding on this game as well.

Uncle Phil had long since been overshadowed by a

younger brother who was superior in almost every way. A lot of the guys felt sorry for Uncle Phil. He was a sucker for a bad bet and he didn't even hold his liquor well. They tolerated his presence only because he was Johnny Ray's brother.

Dad took pity and helped him out with money from time to time. Uncle Phil was still married in 1985, but shortly after that she bailed out. His gambling worsened after losing her, and for a time he was living out of his car. Though his friends saw him as a pathetic figure, and rightly so, dad never treated Uncle Phil that way. In every way except age, dad was the older brother.

I loved being around Uncle Phil when I was a kid because he was nice and always had candy in his pocket for me. He seemed to enjoy having us kids around the bar, perhaps because we were the only ones who still looked up to him.

Eventually, dad won the bet when Notre Dame failed in a late comeback attempt. The proceeds bought rounds for everyone in the bar long into the evening.

***

"I just remember Butch always being around and getting in trouble. Do you remember that Notre Dame-Michigan game when he bet you a hundred bucks the Irish would win?" I asked dad after mom had left the room.

He thought for a moment. "Doesn't ring a bell, but that sounds like him. He liked to push people just to see how they would react. He knew he couldn't get a rise out of me, but he gave me hell anyway," dad replied. He was preoccupied momentarily by what was happening on the field.

Matt Holliday and Rafael Furcal (the Cards' shortstop) had nearly collided going after a pop-up and Holliday missed the ball. The Rangers' Nelson Cruz was hustling all the way and made it safely to second. We stopped the conversation momentarily to see if Salas could work out of the jam. He didn't. Mike Napoli, who hit our pitchers about as hard as anyone in the entire playoffs, stroked a base hit and Cruz scored to put the Rangers up once again.

Dad said, "That's a tough play for Holliday with Furcal drifting toward him. Matt's got to take charge on that play and call him off."

Chalk up another profession that dad could have easily handled: color commentator. I used to dream of doing play-by-play on the radio for the Cardinals. I had a baseball board game that I would play and record myself doing the broadcast on a little tape recorder in my bedroom. If I had been granted one genie's wish on the night of game six, I would have had dad and I in the booth doing the game for Fox Sports.

Joe Buck might be the luckiest man in the world. For a time in the 1990s, Joe was on the Cardinals radio broadcasts with his dad Jack and Mike Shannon. That was a dream team. They were fun to listen to, with or without a game. In fact, some of their best moments on the air happened during the rain delays. They would bring over Harry Carey or Bob Uecker from the other press box and trade classic stories.

"You're right, but we can't have miscues like this. The Rangers are too good. Like they say, you can't give a good team more than three outs," I said, quoting one of the thousand baseball clichés I had picked up from broadcasts over the years. We continued watching for a while, but thoughts of Butch kept me distracted.

"Was Butch really as wild as everyone always said? He didn't seem so crazy to me."

"He had his moments," dad said with a smirk.

"What sort of stuff did he get into?"

"Oh Jesus, you name it. He got kicked out of high school for throwing cherry bombs in the hallway. He, uh…oh one time he got arrested in a liquor store when he smashed a guy's head with a bottle. Cut him all up. Butch said the guy spit on him and that's what started it, but who knows? Maybe he just felt like it. I swear that son of a bitch would do anything on a dare or a bet. Oh, one time he punched a horse."

My head snapped toward him. "What? You gotta be kidding me. What, like Mongo in Blazing Saddles?"

"Worse than that! We were at the track and Butch had a lot of money on this horse. Sugar Daddy…I'll never forget that horse's name. Anyway, we're sitting in the box near the finish line and Sugar Daddy is winning down the stretch. Then he just died, had nothing left in the tank. He ended up finishing way out of the money and Butch was pissed! Before I knew what was going on he's hopping over the side and running toward the track. We all stood up and yelled at him but he didn't even look back. He jumped the rail, ran out onto the track, found Sugar Daddy walking back toward the paddock, and punched that horse square in the mouth!"

Dad stopped to chuckle. This was a mistake and he immediately seized up in pain. He closed his eyes and tried to ride out the wave of pain blazing through his insides. Once it had subsided, he continued, "I'm telling you Paul I've never seen anything like it. The horse didn't fall down, but he did start jumping around and threw the jockey. Butch was cussing that horse as if it could understand what he was saying. Then he started in on the poor jockey! That guy was half of Butch's size and he just ran for his life!" Dad started to laugh again and then reined it in before it could hurt him.

"I can't believe I've never heard this story! What happened to Butch?"

"Well, after the jockey ran off Butch started walking back toward us like nothing had happened. Nobody knew what to do or say…I mean the guy just punched a horse! Right before he got back to our box two cops ran up and dragged him away. The crowd started cheering, not sure if it was for him getting arrested or him punching a lousy race horse. He was banned from the track for a while after that, but he made it back eventually."

"My God. He must have been out of his mind. What did he say about it later?"

"Nothing. He was just tired of losing I think. That horse was the last straw," dad said.

I just shook my head as I imagined that scene. I thought of how different my life was from his. Dad had seen and done things that would be inconceivable to most adults. I'm extremely grateful to have avoided following him down that path. I haven't lived a perfect life, but I've made conscious choices to try to be a responsible citizen, husband, and father.

I sometimes hear people refer to alcoholism as a disease and I just don't believe it. Dad's body didn't start producing poisonous amounts of alcohol on its own. He chose to poison himself on a daily basis. Dad didn't sleep walk his way to the horse track and blow our mortgage money month after month, he did it consciously. Why? Because of his genes? I don't believe that. Those things happened because he was a weak man who enjoyed giving in to his temptations. Dad's stories are funny, but I know they really shouldn't be. They're chapters in one long, sad story of a group of men who chose to check out from reality.

These were the sort of stinging truths that I wanted to throw at him that night. I wanted him to own up to the bare fact that his life was a failure. But as I looked at him on his deathbed, clinging to life just long enough to see one more Cardinal victory, I couldn't hate him anymore. I had fifteen years to hammer him and I had chosen silence instead. Now, in our last meeting, I didn't want it to end with me sitting in judgment. He would face that from his creator soon enough.

Instead, I would seek answers and understanding. I would choose compassion over judgment.

With Salas out of trouble and the Cards jogging back to their dugout, I prepped for the next challenge. I needed to find a way to bring up the most traumatic day in our family's history: the day my mother was attacked by an intruder.

Bottom of the Fourth

When I think back on 1982, a key year in our family's life, the first images I get are from my first game in St. Louis and the Cards' World Series run. I turned seven in April that year and I was just starting to understand the game of baseball. I was enjoying school and finally getting used to the idea of having a baby sister around. Then, when the Cards made it to the playoffs for the first time in fifteen years, dad's excitement became contagious.

He spent more time at home during the playoffs because he wanted to be able to watch the games without the goons at the bar distracting him. There's no question that 1982 was the apex of our relationship. But, when my thoughts linger on that time, other images start to creep in. I see things that no seven year old should ever have to see. I see mom on the floor of our living room in a pool of her own blood. I see a man standing over her, clinching his bloody fists and snarling like an animal.

I've done my best to block that brutal scene and dwell on the happy details of that time in my life. I spent two decades pretending it didn't happen, but those memories won't stay buried forever. They creep into your thoughts at odd times, they invade your dreams. I was forced to deal with what happened to mom and thankfully had help from my ACA friends. I knew that dad was probably still running from that day as well, even after thirty years. I knew it would be painful, and he might even get angry enough to toss me out, but it was literally now or never. I had to find out what he had experienced on that terrible November afternoon.

"Remember watching the '82 series together? That was an interesting match-up. Whitey's runners versus 'Harvey's Wallbangers.' I think the Brewers hit something like four times as many homers as the Cards did that season!" I said, knowing the best way to lead into any conversation with dad is by talking baseball.

He grunted with recognition. "Yep, the 'Suds Series.' I really didn't think our boys would pull that off. The Brewers had a lot of firepower on that team. Then again, I didn't think our boys could beat the Brewers this year. You just never know what can happen when you get into a long series," dad said.

I also had been skeptical that the Cards could beat Prince Fielder, Ryan Braun, and the rest of the potent Brewers team in the 2011 NLCS. They were the division champs and hadn't been to the World Series since '82. It seemed like it was their year, until the Cardinals stole it from them with an amazing offensive performance. David Freese walked away with the series MVP award as the Redbirds won the pennant in six games. Now they were facing another dangerous lineup in the Texas Rangers. I thought, *He's right. If the '82 Cards can pull off that win, then the 2011 Cards can do it as well. Anything is possible.*

"I remember us getting blanked in game one. But the best memory for me was game three. Remember? McGee hit two home runs that night and we went up two games to one," I said, thinking about the unique swing and face of Willie McGee. He was one of the core players (Tony LaRussa would call him a "co-signer") on that team for the rest of the decade. He won the NL MVP award in 1985 and wound up playing in three World Series with the Cards (though they lost heartbreakers in both '85 and '87).

"That guy was great! Hit for average, stole bases, and played a helluva centerfield. That series was back and forth too. I thought we had it sewn up in game four. Cards were up five to one in the seventh and looked for sure like they were going up three games to one. Then the bullpen fell apart and they lost it and the next one," dad replied.

He loved that '82 team about as much as any in his life. He probably could have given me batting averages of the players from that series.

He continued, "Game six was a big blowout for us, 13-1 I believe. But game seven was tight. Our guys did some clutch hitting to put us ahead and then Bruce Sutter closed it out. Two inning save…you don't see that anymore."

The night of game seven of the 1982 World Series was perhaps the best that I ever experienced in that house. We were watching it on TV, but as the game progressed into the late innings I got very nervous. I retreated to my room around the seventh inning and listened to the radio, preferring the familiar voices of Jack Buck and Mike Shannon to those of Joe Garagiola and Dick Enberg on NBC. Hearing Jack call the game just made me feel better, safer. It was my first experience with sports superstition. I believed that if I kept listening to the game on the radio that we would win.

I sat on the floor, staring intently at the little portable as Jack described the bottom of the ninth with the Cardinals leading 6-3. Sutter was facing Ted Simmons (the great former Cardinals catcher) and got him to ground back to the mound. The next batter was the free swinger Ben Oglivie, who grounded the ball to Tommy Herr at second. Jack exclaimed, "Nice going Tommy!" on the broadcast after he snagged the ball off the turf. One out away.

I didn't yet have a full understanding of how big or important the World Series was, but I knew it was important to dad and that was enough. I knew if they won this game they would be considered "World Champions" of baseball. Now I heard dad from the other room talking to the TV.

"Come on Bruce! Finish these guys off!" Dad wasn't quite yelling, but it was loud. I heard him stomping around, unable to stay seated during those critical moments. Now I was also pacing around my bedroom and hanging on Jack's every word.

Gorman Thomas would be the hitter. He was big and powerful, but luckily no one was on base. He could hit the ball a mile, but we would still be up by two runs. The count ran to 1-1 and Jack jokingly said, "Don't end it too quickly, Bruce." That at-bat seemed to last twenty minutes. Thomas kept fouling off pitches and hanging tough. I heard dad clap his hands a couple of times and give Bruce some encouragement that he would never hear. Finally, we both heard the words that we had been dying for.

"Sutter from the belt, to the plate. A swing and a miss, and that's a winner! That's a winner! A World Series winner for the Cardinals!" Jack shouted triumphantly from the booth in Busch Stadium. I jumped into the air and at the same moment heard dad yelling in the living room. I ran out into the hallway and into the living room. Dad looked from the TV to me and gave me the largest and purest smile I have ever seen on him. The TV broadcast was showing a huge number of fans streaming onto the field and celebrating wildly among the players.

"They did it! They actually did it. Can you believe this?" dad asked me. Of course I couldn't respond intelligently. I don't even remember what I said to him. I could barely take my eyes off the screen. The players and fans were so exultant, I hadn't seen anything like it. The people of St. Louis had been waiting fifteen years for another World Series winner. Little did we know that we would have to wait another twenty-two before the next one. We both sat and watched the post-game coverage in gleeful silence.

We both felt like champions even though we hadn't contributed anything to the Cardinals' efforts. That's one gift that dad gave me: he made it okay to be emotional about a sports team. I didn't love that '82 team the way he did because I was too young. But I learned to love later teams just as much because of his example.

After a few minutes, dad got up and walked to the

kitchen without a word. I continued watching the locker room celebration and the trophy presentation. When he didn't come back right away, I got curious and went to find him. He was slouching in a kitchen chair next to mom (who had been reading a romance novel) and sipping on a glass of champagne. I saw that he had poured mom a glass as well but she hadn't touched it yet.

He said, "I've been saving this for a championship celebration. God this tastes good." The bottle had been sitting in the back of our refrigerator for years. Mom didn't seem very happy, but she was playing along because she knew how much the Series meant to him.

"So does this mean that I can finally get the TV back? You know I've been missing some good shows thanks to these games!" Mom was half-joking. For a woman who was half the size of her husband, she exerted a huge amount of control over the television. Dad was usually content to sit outside and listen to games or be at the bar, so there wasn't much conflict about it normally.

Mom liked to watch *Dallas* and its spin-off *Knot's Landing*. I vaguely remember the night when mom watched the episode in which J.R. was shot. She didn't usually get very excited or animated about things on TV, but that night she was calling neighbors and talking about who might have done it for hours after it aired.

Much like the moment in the car with dad on our way to St. Louis, I wish I could have bottled that few minutes of time when the three of us were together in the kitchen. Dad smiled and sipped his cheap champagne as if it were Dom Perignon. Mom brushed through my hair with her fingers and teased dad about what he would have done had they lost game seven. I smiled dumbly and simply took it all in. These moments were so few and precious. I think mom understood that this was one of them, and even though it was late, she brought out some lunchmeat and Velveeta from the refrigerator and offered us a little victory snack. Nothing had ever tasted so good as bologna and cheese after a Cardinals World Series winner.

That evening in the kitchen stuck with me and, when the Cards made it back to the World Series in 2006, I made sure to have bologna and Velveeta (I was pleasantly surprised to find that they still sold it) on hand just in case. Karen seemed puzzled when my first move after watching the celebration was to the kitchen for a celebratory sandwich. She declined my offer to share in that delicious meal.

Ultimately the joy of celebration fades away and you go back to the daily tasks and routines of life. Without the Cardinals on in the evenings, dad was out with his buddies more often. Mom went back to spending her evenings tending to baby Megan and distracting herself in the realm of prime time soaps. I spent the majority of my nights alone in my room inventing games or playing old ones. It was perhaps the last period during my childhood that felt "normal." After the attack on mom, everything and everyone in my life was different.

***

The Cards had a chance for a big inning against Lewis in the bottom of the fourth. Berkman reached on an error and then Holliday walked. Two on and none out. The memories of the '82 Series were still flowing through my mind. Then I remembered why I brought it up in the first place. I needed to find a way to bring up the attack. I waited to see if Freese would add to the rally, but he rolled out to second. Berkman would later score from third on a groundout by Yadi to tie the game, but they could have had more.

Dad shook his head after the Molina RBI groundout, "Damn. They're wasting a good chance here. We're gonna need all the runs we can get tonight. They might regret this inning later on."

I nodded but didn't speak. How does one casually

bring up the most devastating event of a person's life? I decided that boldness was the best course.

"Dad, we need to talk about the attack. I know you probably don't want to and I don't blame you, but there's some things I need to know."

He continued looking at the TV as Nick Punto batted with two outs. Then he brought his hands together as if in prayer and lowered his head until his lips rested on his knuckles. He took several breaths and then finally responded in a weak tone, "You're right. I don't want to."

"Look, we've never even acknowledged it. It's time to face it. All of it." I surprised myself again with my ability to be direct with him. On some level, I think he appreciated and even respected it.

"We're having a nice time here, Paul. Watching the game, talking about old times. I've enjoyed it. Why do you have to spoil it by bringing up this shit?"

"I'm having a good time too. In fact, it's been wonderful being back here. But I'm not just here for a nice time with you, dad. I'm here to put the past to rest, to get it all settled before it's too late. I *need* to talk about this whether you want to or not. Now please, for me, just talk to me about it for a few minutes."

This was the moment. He was either going to kick me out or take my words to heart. He made me wait for his answer. Punto struck out swinging to end the fourth and a commercial started. Dad continued staring at the TV without any hint of a reply. I was about to stand up and walk out of the room when I heard him speak.

"It's just hard…thinking about that time. I've spent all these years pushing it out of my mind. What do you want me to say? It was the worst moment of my life." Dad's voice caught as the word 'life' came out of his mouth. I thought for a moment that he was going to cry. "I think about what hell she went through. What you went through. What you saw. I'll never forgive myself for not being there."

Now it was me fighting back the urge to cry. This was going to be harder than I had imagined, even though I had discussed the incident many times with Karen and the ACA gang. I allowed myself to slip back in time to that Saturday afternoon in mid-November of 1982. It rained on and off during the day so mom had me hanging out in the house. She was spending the afternoon catching up on cleaning. To my chagrin, she had me doing the same with my room.

Dad had a large stereo receiver and speaker system set up in the living room, and on cleaning days mom would turn it on and tune in to 96.1 WSTR (the "Hit Machine"). Mom was old fashioned in many ways, but when it came to her music preferences she was very modern. She loved the latest pop music of the day and I didn't mind it either. Now that I'm in my late thirties, I appreciate '80s music that much more. It's all I listen to in the car or when I'm forcing myself to run.

While picking up all of my GI Joe and Star Wars action figures (and placing them safely back into my Darth Vader case) I heard mom singing along to "Just You and I" by Eddie Rabbit and Crystal Gale. She was mopping the kitchen floor and carrying Crystal's part of the song most impressively. Mom wasn't a great singer, but she participated in the church choir and enjoyed belting out her favorites in the shower sometimes.

I loved hearing her sing because it meant she was in a good mood. It also reminded me of when I was little and mom would sing to get me to sleep. That particular song stayed with me all my life. It became the song that played during Karen and I's first dance as husband and wife in 1996. It also made it onto a lot of mix tapes that I made for her while we were dating.

Eddie and Crystal faded out and were replaced by piano sounds from another new hit. It was Joe Jackson's

"Steppin' Out." Mom didn't sing with this one, but she did start to hum as she left the kitchen floor to dry and picked up her dust rag and can of Pledge. She passed my open bedroom door on her way to the living room. I looked up in time to catch a brief smile from her. She said, "How's it coming, Pauly? I see the floor so you must be making progress!"

She didn't stop walking as she said this, so I gave her a quick "It's good, mom!" and went about my business. When she got into the living room, she turned the volume down slightly on the stereo. I could still hear Joe banging away at the keys and singing, "You babe. Steppin' ahhhowwwout. Into the night, into the light…" Mom sprayed and wiped down the furniture, enjoying the peace of a music-filled Saturday afternoon at home.

It's the song that played after Joe that will haunt me for the rest of my life. When it started playing I was busy shoving the clean clothes mom had earlier laid on my bed into the appropriate drawers in my little dresser. I knew the song, but couldn't have named it then. It was "Only the Lonely" by The Motels, a song that mom obviously knew because I heard her singing again: "We walked the loneliest mile. We smiled without any style. We kiss altogether wrong, no intention…"

It was just after mom had completed those first lyrics when we heard a banging on the front door. It didn't sound frantic or menacing, just two or three pounds with the back of a fist. I poked my head out from my room and peered down the hallway. From there I could see mom come out of the living room and look out from the window of the locked front door. She normally kept all the doors locked. Like most people she was careful, but operating under the assumption that things like break-ins and abductions won't happen to us.

Once she told me the story of Adam Walsh, the boy who was abducted at a Sears store in Florida, as a cautionary tale. Later she would force me to watch the TV movie they made about the incident, just to reinforce the point about strangers. Mom wasn't blind to the terrible things that can happen, and that's why I never understood why she opened the door.

Our house had a small rectangular screened-in porch on the right side of the front. The porch door was kept unlocked, but the door to the main house was not. The porch was purely decorative, though it was not decorated in any way. Its only memorable feature was the concrete floor, which was covered by green, artificial turf of the sort that you usually only find at miniature golf courses. Most people who visited our house (the regulars) knew to use the back door. When anyone knocked at the front it was a sign that either a salesman or a Jehovah's Witness was calling. Mom unbolted the door and swung it open.

The next few minutes of my life seemed to pass in slow motion. Even now, when I focus on those terrible moments, it doesn't feel like it really happened. It's as if I'm remembering a disturbing scene from a movie or TV drama. What hurts is knowing that I can replay it a thousand times in my mind, but I can never change the outcome. In that sense what I experienced was like a nightmare that I couldn't wake up from.

I saw mom opening the door and a man in dirty overalls and a white T-shirt standing in front of her. He wasn't as big as dad, but still towered over her. He looked to be in his forties, with dark stringy hair that was showing some gray throughout. He was sweating profusely, which combined with his outfit gave him the look of a farmer who had just come in from the fields. It couldn't have been more than fifty degrees outside, but I didn't have time to register those conflicting facts.

A second after the door opened, he was grabbing her by both arms and pushing her backward into the front room. Mom instantly began screaming, and I heard my name though I couldn't catch what she was saying. The man threw her to the floor and mom's head made a thud on the carpet. Before I could register what was happening, he was on top of her. First, he was punching her face, then she tried to roll away from him and he grabbed her legs and dragged her back toward him.

Next, he stood up and stomped on her back with a large, weathered boot. Mom stopped moving, but he continued with his assault. He kicked her several times in the ribs and legs as mom cried out in agony. The man hadn't seen me yet as only part of my head was visible from where he stood.

Before I realized it, I was screaming at the man and crying simultaneously. I had walked several steps into the hallway, though I don't remember giving my legs the command to do so. It was too much to comprehend and my brain was running my body on auto-pilot.

This intrusion seemed to startle the man and he stopped and looked up at me. His face was a twisted sneer. He wasn't quite smiling, but he looked like he was enjoying himself. I broke eye contact with him and looked down at mom. Blood was pouring from her mouth and her nose. She had a gash on her forehead that was also bleeding. She had instinctively curled herself into the fetal position and was trying to protect her shattered ribs with her arms. She looked at me in horror. She started repeating the words she had screamed when he burst in, "Go Pauly...run baby. Run to the neighbors. Get out of here Pauly now!"

"Shut up bitch! I swear I'll kill you right here in front of him if you don't shut up!" He yelled while sizing me up with his eyes.

I had no idea what to do, but the longer I stood there the more I was sure I couldn't leave her alone with this man. I didn't know what rape was at seven years old, but I believe now that was his primary goal. The fact that I was in the house had thrown him off a bit. His words hung in the air for a long time. I heard mom sobbing quietly as her face filled with blood. Somewhere, very distantly, I heard a maudlin female voice singing, "It's like I told you, only the lonely can play…"

Now the man was talking to me while keeping one boot on mom's hip. "Boy, you should do what your mom says. Get the hell out of here before you get hurt too. Go on, run out. I won't stop you." I was frozen to that spot, but not because of any brave notion. I was in shock, unable to move or speak. I just kept looking from him to mom and back to him. After a few seconds he grew angrier, "Did you hear what I said boy? Get the fuck out of here before you end up like her!" His voice was deep and gravelly.

Mom caught my eyes with hers and, though she spoke no more words, told me it was okay. I should leave now and go get help. A small spark developed in my mind and I was able to start thinking for myself again. I knew I should run next door and get the neighbors to call the police. I knew if I stayed that he would probably kill us both. Yet, I couldn't leave. Somehow I understood that if I left her, mom would not survive. Somewhere I heard the haunting ending of "Only the Lonely" fading and the opening keyboard sounds of Don Henley's "Dirty Laundry" starting up.

"Listen you little shit! You've got one more chance and then I'm coming over there. I'm gonna tear your fucking arms off. Get out now!"

With that, my body was in motion again. I turned around and walked swiftly down the hallway toward the back of the house. I still wasn't sure what to do, but I wasn't leaving. Then, thankfully, I remembered what dad had told me about a year before. He had purchased a pistol, a .38 Special revolver, and he showed it to me one day when mom was working. After briefly allowing me to hold the unloaded weapon, he put both hands on my shoulders and got eye to eye with me.

"Paul, this is not a toy and it's very dangerous. A gun is made for one purpose, and that's to hurt or kill someone. The only reason I bought one is to protect you and your mom. I'm going to keep it behind the headboard on my side of the bed. If I ever catch you or even hear that you've been playing with this gun, you won't have to worry about the gun killing you 'cause I will! Do you understand me?"

I swore to him that I would never touch the gun, but now I had to break that promise. I veered from the hallway into their bedroom and sprinted to the far side of the bed. I was terrified that he had moved it, in fact, I was sure he had hidden it elsewhere. Why would he tell me where he was keeping the gun? But it was there, and as I picked it up and looked it over, I saw that it was loaded. All at once, I realized why dad had shown it to me.

Mom cried out from the front room, and I could hear the intruder grunting and saying something to her. I held the gun in front of me with both hands and steadily made my way back down the hall. As they came back into view, I nearly dropped the gun in fear and anger. The man had ripped most of mom's clothes off and was now smacking her repeatedly across the face as he straddled her on the floor. He had unbuckled his overalls as well. I got to within ten feet of them and stopped. I pointed the revolver at his face and struggled mightily to keep it from shaking in my little hands. I was also trying my hardest not to cry.

The intruder finally noticed me and jerked himself up to a standing position in an instant. Clearly I had surprised him. He wiped his face, now smeared with her blood along with his sweat, with the back of his hand.

"What do you think you're doing with that, kid? That's not even a real gun is it?" He let out a small chuckle and took a step toward me. I stiffened, but held my ground. The gun was shaking a little, but still pointed squarely at his face. I still couldn't speak.

"Come on son, gimme the gun. You're in way over your head here. You're too young to be mixed up in something like this. Just hand it over and I promise I won't hurt you. What do you say?" He was doing his best to sound sincere to a child. I did what I had seen cops on TV as well as my dad do with guns like this. I used both thumbs to pull back the hammer.

The intruder's nonchalant demeanor disappeared. He took another step toward me and seemed to snarl at me. He bared his teeth like an animal and his dark eyes were squinted. His negotiation hadn't worked, and now he was trying to scare me into doing his will. I took another look at mom: she was naked except for her underpants and covered in blood. I refused to give in to the beast. I lowered the gun so as to aim at his midsection. I took a couple of deep breaths and mustered the power of speech.

"You leave my mom and me alone! You get out of here or I'll shoot. This is loaded...and I swear I'll shoot!" Despite my best efforts, tears began streaming down my cheeks. I didn't want to cry in front of this horrible man, but it was out of my control. I could see that he was calculating the chances of a young boy actually having the balls to fire a weapon at him.

He was clearly out of his right mind, but he wasn't completely irrational. If he had been, he might have charged and forced me to make a split-second decision. I'll never know if I was really capable of pulling the trigger, because mercifully he backed off. He put his palms out and began walking backward toward the front door. Mom had lost consciousness and lay sprawled on the red soaked carpet.

He turned his back to me and went for the door, probably hoping that I wasn't the type of kid who would shoot a man in the back. I should have done it. And now as I look back as a grown man, I wish I would have. I'd give anything to have that moment back, because I would kill him. I would unload all six shells into that bastard and then go back for more. I know that revenge is sinful and I should forgive him, but I believe I would shoot him right now if he walked in the room. But, I let the opportunity pass. He started to walk out, but then turned his head back toward me. His last words are forever seared into my mind and soul.

"This was fun." He was smiling as he said this. Then he looked down at mom's broken body and added, "Bitch is good as dead anyway." And then he left. I heard him leave through the porch door and watched as he made his way to the street. I relocked the door and then checked on mom. She was a mess. I couldn't tell if she was breathing and I got very scared.

I had taken too long to muster my courage and retrieve the gun. I had allowed that man to beat mom to death. I ran for the phone on the kitchen wall and dialed the emergency number on the orange sticker located just below the rotary numbers. Those few minutes that I sat waiting for the ambulance were the longest of my life. I sat with mom's head in my arms and cried, hoping that there was something the paramedics could do for her. From the living room, the sounds of modern '80s pop still blared from the stereo. Don Henley's voice gave way to the wailing saxophone of Men at Work's "Who Can It Be Now?"

The irony of that song didn't hit me for many years.

Incredibly, Megan had slept through the entire incident. After the paramedics and police showed up I found her still curled up in her crib. I told the police where they could probably find dad, and they brought us to St. Mark's hospital. It was my first and only ride in the back of a police car. One officer sat with Megan and me until dad showed up. He was around fifty-five with a bulging gut and a thick grey mustache. The name on his badge was Shannon, which might be why I instantly liked him. He kept talking, trying to keep my spirits up. He said things like "You know the staff here is very good" and "I'm sure your mom will be just fine." I didn't fully appreciate the effort then, but I'm glad officer Shannon was there with us.

After twenty minutes of sitting with Shannon and trying desperately not to think about mom's battered face, dad came into view with most of his bar friends in tow. I had never seen such a look of determination and desperation on a man's face. His followers' faces were grim and grey. They looked as if all of their wives had just been attacked. Dad locked eyes with me from about thirty feet away and kept the gaze until he was kneeling in front of my chair. I could see tears in his eyes, and I smelled the beer on his breath. He took a long pause and then slowly opened his mouth.

"Paul. Oh God, Paul." He put his hand on my cheek and then stroked my hair. It felt good but also strange. It was rare for him to touch me other than for an occasional spanking or a tug on my arm to pull me closer in a crowd. "You're okay. He didn't hurt you. That son of a bitch didn't hurt you."

He looked down at Megan, who was awake and in my arms, and that's when he lost control. For the first time in my life I witnessed my father crying. No, he was weeping. The tears flowed from both of us for perhaps a solid minute, then he rose to his feet and began wiping his face with a handkerchief. Butch and the boys stood a few feet away and stared at the floor. None of them knew what to say or do in such a moment. His next move was to start talking with cops and nurses and anyone else he could get information from. When they found him at Lamasco's, all the cops had told him was that his wife had been attacked. He was frantic to fill in the details.

I occupied myself by rocking Megan and trying to keep her settled. I was more than a little jealous that she was too young to know what was going on. She would never have this memory. Now I'm grateful for that fact. Once dad had milked the police and staff for answers he turned to me. I had briefly explained the events of the attack to the policemen in the car on the way to the hospital, but no one had formally asked for my side of the story. In a moment I was in a small conference room with two officers and dad. They asked me to take them through everything I could remember about the intruder and what had occurred. I recounted the story without further outbursts of emotion. I was starting to feel numb inside.

Dad sat next to me as I spoke and listened to each word with intense focus. I could see the anger in his face growing with each passing minute. After my statement was complete, the officers were both shaking their heads. "Sir, you have a brave boy here. He may have just saved his mom's life," one of them said to dad.

He nodded and looked down at me. His eyes told me he was proud of me, though he never said it out loud. I also saw something else his those eyes: fury. His body was slightly shaking, and I could tell he was trying his best not to start lashing out at everything and everyone. The two cops stood up and one of them said, "That's all we need. We'll start looking for this guy right away."

After they left, dad and I sat in silence for a minute. His eyes fluttered as he stared at the small wooden table in front of us. Then he put his right hand on my shoulder and said softly, "You did real good. I...thank God you remembered the gun." His voice trailed off as he abruptly stood up and walked out of the room. Butch, Phil, and Herm were all waiting for him in the hallway. Dad stopped and briefly described what I had just told him.

"Jesus, Johnny. Do they know who did it?" Butch asked.

"Not yet, but I do. I want you guys to stay here and watch after Paul and Megan."

"Okay, where are you going?" Phil asked.

"I'm gonna find him. And send him straight to hell."

Top of the Fifth

Fernando Salas trudged out for his second inning of work, trying to keep the game tied at three. Dad and I were both lost in our thoughts about the day our lives changed forever. I was about to speak when I saw Josh Hamilton hit a pop fly on the first pitch of the inning.

The camera switched to David Freese camping under the ball near the third base bag. Then he started shuffling his feet and moving to his left. There had already been some odd defensive plays in this game, but this was the most deflating. The ball hit inside Freese's mitt and then bounced free. Both of us groaned when we saw the ball hit the dirt.

Dad interjected, "What the hell is wrong with these guys tonight? Don't they know they have to win this or they're done? How can they not be sharp for game six of the goddamn World Series?"

I agreed by nodding, and then quickly turned the conversation back to the attack. "Okay, here's something I've always wanted to know. What did you guys do when you left the hospital that day? I never heard anything about what happened to that guy."

I had assumed as a child that the intruder had been caught and jailed, but I never asked about it because I didn't want to bring up bad memories. Even in later years, when I was grown and out of the house, I never had the nerve to bring up that day to mom. I figured she had suffered through it once and shouldn't have to relive it.

Dad still seemed hesitant to discuss the topic, but he could tell I wasn't going to let him sidetrack me all evening. "So, what exactly do you want to know?" he asked.

"I heard you tell Butch that you were going to find the guy who attacked mom and kill him. You left, and I never heard anything about it for the rest of my life. I want to know what you did. I want the truth."

Dad took a drink from his water bottle and cleared his throat. He was preparing to tell me the story. I didn't care at that moment how tired he was or how much he didn't want to discuss it, I was determined to finally get answers.

"Well, when you sat there and told me and the cops what happened, I was shocked. I was mad and confused and scared all at once. They weren't sure if your mom was going to live because of the internal bleeding, and that scared the hell out of me. Then, when you described what the guy looked like, I realized that I knew him. And then everything else just went away and I could only think about one thing—killing him."

Dad paused for another drink. He hadn't used his voice this much in a long time and it was tiring. "His name was Larry Simmons. He had been in the neighborhood for a couple of years. Just about everyone knew who he was. He lived in a little shack of a house right next to the train yard, don't know who lived with him though. As long as he had been around, he was known as kind of an idiot. He used to walk the streets during all hours of the day and night just muttering to himself, or sometimes you'd see him at a game at Powell and he'd be up in the corner of the bleachers by himself. When I figured out it was him I was surprised at first because I didn't think he was that kind of guy. I mean, he was weird, but I guess we all assumed he was harmless."

"So he had no known history of being violent before he came to our house?" I asked.

"Not that I knew of. I actually kind of felt sorry for him. Everyone did I think. No one talked to him, but then again, he never looked interested in talking with people. Someone must have been taking care of him though because he didn't work. Maybe we should have suspected him of being crazy, but what could we have done? His biggest crime before that day was talking to himself in public. We just didn't know what he was capable of."

Dad paused and rubbed his forehead. "Sorry, my head's pounding. Probably a tumor in there too for all I know!" I didn't laugh, and after a moment he continued. "But when I heard and saw what he had done, I lost it. I didn't care who he was, I was going to kill him. I had never wanted anything so badly in my life. I left the hospital feeling that one of us, either him or me, would be dead by the end of the day."

"So you weren't concerned about getting arrested, or did that not even occur to you?"

"I didn't care. I figured I would do it and then sort it out after the fact. All the cops in our neighborhood knew me and probably would be on my side anyway. But that wasn't a factor in my mind. I remember running out of the hospital and to my car. Butch and Phil were running after me, they must have made Herm stay with you kids." I nodded, remembering them yelling at Herm to stay behind as they ran down the hall chasing dad.

Dad continued, "I drove to his little shitbox and busted the front door down. No one was there and I got back into my car just as Butch and Phil were pulling up in Phil's pick-up. They were yelling for me to stop, but I blocked them out. I knew what they were trying to do, but I wasn't going to let them get in my way. I started driving the streets of our neighborhood, just hoping to get lucky. The guys followed behind me the whole time, honking and trying to get my attention. I kept ignoring them. If anything I was getting angrier as time passed. I just kept imagining the whole scene and I couldn't stop."

Dad abruptly stopped talking and closed his eyes. I could see all the emotions hitting him again, some just as fresh as nearly thirty years before. He cleared his throat again and carried on.

"It was probably fifteen or twenty minutes before I

spotted him. He was sitting on a curb on Hollywood, still covered in your mom's blood. I thought about running him down with the car, but instead I threw it into park in the middle of the street and jumped out. I popped the trunk and pulled out an old aluminum softball bat. After I closed the trunk I heard Butch's voice from behind me yelling, 'no Johnny, don't do it.'

"I looked ahead toward Larry, and I'll be damned if that son of a bitch wasn't still sitting there looking me dead in the eyes. That's when I was certain I was going to kill him."

I sat riveted next to his bed, ignoring the Ranger rally that had been ignited by Freese's error. I couldn't believe I was hearing this story for the first time.

"I started walking as fast as I could toward Larry, and he still just sat there. He had to know who I was and who it was he had just attacked, but the look on his face was just blank. I could hear the boys running from behind me, but they were going to be too late. I brought the bat back and got ready to pound him. I heard another voice, probably Phil's, screaming 'he's not worth it, please don't Johnny!' Then, I bashed him in the side of the head with my bat."

"Oh shit! You killed him! You actually did it?" I nearly grabbed him as I said this.

"Well, no, I didn't kill him. That was the only shot I got on him because Butch caught up to me and grabbed the bat away. Phil just got between me and Larry while I was trying to punch Butch and get the bat back. Now I was pissed at Butch and I really tried to hurt him, but he was quick and pretty strong. They were both yelling at me to quit and they were both standing between me and Larry.

"Larry didn't make a sound when I hit him, he just flipped over and lay face down on the pavement. I think I caught him square on his left ear and I could see a lot of blood coming out of that area. I thought maybe he was dead, but then he was squirming a little. He might have been convulsing, I'm not sure. I tried a couple of times to get through them and finish Larry off, but they were able to push me back. I finally stopped trying and my head started to clear a little.

"I saw that Larry was slowly crawling toward the curb. He was making noises, but I couldn't understand him. Then, this is the damnedest thing, I actually felt bad for a minute. I remembered that Larry wasn't a normal guy and probably retarded. You know, I hated Butch and Phil in that instant for stopping me from finishing him off, but now I thank God for it. I thought revenge would make me feel better, but it actually made the pain worse. I sat down on the sidewalk and cried again, cried hard and for a long time. Butch sat and comforted me while Phil went out in the street and flagged down the police car that was headed our way. Sure enough, the cops that showed up were two guys I knew well…and they knew about Larry. They called for an ambulance and it carted him off to St. Mark's. Butch drove me back there in my car. That's pretty much it."

"So Larry survived?" I asked. I was at least partially ashamed of myself because I enjoyed hearing about dad's revenge. I was glad that dad got at least one shot on that lunatic. The part of me that also wanted revenge would have loved to be there to see it happen.

"Yeah, he recovered. They ended up shipping him to the State Hospital because they said he was 'mentally unfit' to stand trial. He's still there right now as far as I know."

The details of his story began to sink in and they didn't feel right. The man in our house that day was certainly out of his right mind, but he was no muttering idiot. "Dad, this Larry guy, he didn't act like what you're describing when he was attacking mom. He wasn't stupid and he wasn't retarded. He was a maniac."

"Yeah, the cops told me later that there had been a

similar attack in our neighborhood about a year before that. They believed he was to blame for that one too. I guess he just picked his spots. They also told me that Larry had been knocking on doors that morning all along Delmar. And he wasn't just going door to door, he was intentionally skipping certain houses..."

"Because he knew which husbands were at home and which ones were gone somewhere!" I interrupted. Apparently Larry's habit of walking the streets was more than just for passing the time. He was casing the neighborhood and remembering which husbands worked or, in dad's case, which ones were at the bar.

"You're right. He was a lot smarter than he seemed, and I'm glad I didn't know that when I bashed his head in. I would have made sure to finish the job. You know one of the cops said that if I had hit him about an inch higher on his head, I would have caught his temple and killed him instantly. I think about that sometimes. One inch higher, and I would have gone to jail for murder."

"So we both had a chance to kill Larry that day, and neither of us did."

Dad looked over at me when he heard this. His eyes were sad and apologetic, but there were no tears. He said, "I'm sorry I wasn't here Paul. I should have been here. He would have just passed on by our house if I had been here. I've had to live with that for all these years. I should have..." I interrupted him by taking his hand. He looked down at my hand on his and then up to meet my eyes. He was visibly shaken by the gesture.

"Dad, it's not your fault. There's no way you could have known what was going to happen. You don't have to blame yourself anymore." He gave me an appreciative look, but I could see that the guilt ran deep. He had been punishing himself for almost thirty years and he wasn't going to stop now. He gave my hand a squeeze, as if to say thank you for saying that, and then pulled away.

We refocused on the game and saw that the dropped pop-up had indeed cost the Cardinals. With Hamilton at first, Michael Young drilled a pitch into the left-centerfield gap. Hamilton scored to put the Rangers back on top 4-3. Salas battled for the rest of the inning, walking a couple, but getting two big outs. Now the bases were loaded and Colby Lewis was due up.

Dad said, "If I'm managing the Rangers I'm pinch hitting right here. They've got a chance to blow the game open." Thankfully, Ron Washington, their real manager, opted to stay with Lewis and he struck out to end the threat. But another unearned run had put the Cards behind for the third time.

***

Mom stayed in the hospital for weeks and went through numerous surgeries, including several on her face. She was lucky to be alive, but would have a crooked nose and a two-inch scar on her forehead as lifelong reminders of the attack. It was three days before I was allowed to come in to see her. Her face was shrouded in bandages and her left forearm set in a splint. I cried when I saw her despite dad's instructions not to do so. She couldn't speak because her mouth was wired shut, but she squeezed my hand to let me know she loved me. Dad was different during mom's hospital stay. He didn't go to the bar or the track once. I never saw him take a drink, though his friends were around the house a lot trying to help out. It was like having five or six extra uncles, and they helped to keep my mind off the bad memories.

He took Megan and me up to see mom every day, and at home he cooked meals and cleaned. He left the laundry for mom to catch up later, mainly at her request. She didn't want him turning all his white V-necks pink. The attack sobered dad up, at least for that month or so that mom was laid up. It seemed for a time that a greater good would come out of the tragedy. Dad was shaken to his core and had recommitted himself to his family. Unfortunately, this version of Johnny Ray didn't last.

Mom came home in time for Christmas and it was a joyous celebration. Dad cooked a big meal for us and mom got to enjoy real food. It was exactly the type of festive and relaxed family gathering that I've been chasing ever since.

That night, mom came into my room and tucked me in as usual. She kissed my forehead softly and said, "Pauly, I'm so proud of you for what you did for me. You saved my life, I know it. I love you so much. You're a good boy." Tears were streaming down her face. They were welling up in my eyes too.

"I just wanted to stop him from hurting you. I'm sorry I pulled the gun out. I swear I won't touch it again!" I said, remembering mom's many lectures about that gun. She giggled.

"You did exactly the right thing. You did what a man does. He protects his family. If your dad had been here, he would have done the same thing. He couldn't be prouder of you for what you did for me…for all of us." She wiped tears from her cheeks and then mine.

"Mom, what did he say to you? Why did you open the door for him?"

She paused for a moment, perhaps surprised by the question.

She answered, "He told me he was a friend of your dad's and that his car was stalled on our street. He said he just needed to make a quick phone call and he'd be out in no time. I don't know why I trusted him, but he looked familiar. I knew I had seen him around, so I guess that's why I believed him. It was a stupid mistake. Pauly, don't you ever open a door for someone unless you're absolutely positive that you know them and can trust them. Promise me."

"I promise, mom. I won't ever do that."

"Okay, good. Now you get to sleep. I love you," she

said and then kissed me on the cheek. Those were the kisses that made everything okay for a while.

"How much do you love me?" I asked as part of an almost nightly ritual mom had started when I was very young.

"Up to the sky and back...that's how much! Good night, baby." With that, she walked to the door and turned to give me one last look. The scar on her forehead was prominent in the light of my bedroom. It ran vertically between her hairline and her left eye. Over the years it would become less noticeable, but still ever present. She gave me a quick wink and then shut off the light and closed the door.

I slept well that night, but sometimes I would see Larry Simmons' face in my dreams and awaken crying or even screaming. Those nightmares tapered off over the years, but every so often I still get a night when my brain takes me back to our front room where mom lies bloodied and broken, and that monster snarls at me with his inhuman face. Some memories are like burning embers that can never quite be extinguished. Once in a while they flare up to remind you that they're still active.

Christmas came and went and mom got back to work early in January of '83. We all started to fall back into our normal routines, and that included dad. At first he seemed hesitant to leave mom and us kids alone. He would bang around in the garage or even sit and watch mom's shows with her at night (a fact that I believe annoyed her at least a little). But, as time passed, he felt comfortable enough to go back to his friends at Lamasco's.

The first night that he went back, after at least six weeks of sobriety, Butch brought him in through the back door at three in the morning. Dad was so drunk that he could barely stand. The noise woke me up and I peeked down the hall to see Butch guiding dad into their bedroom. I had never seen dad look that way. Normally you couldn't tell the difference between drunk dad and sober dad unless you were in range of his breath. It didn't take him long to get his tolerance for alcohol back.

As winter turned to spring I got excited because it was almost time for baseball season. The month of March is in many ways the greatest month for a baseball fan. There is genuine hope for fans of all teams and, after a long winter, it's refreshing to see the boys back on the diamond. That spring was particularly exciting for Cardinals fans because they were coming off their victory in the World Series. Most of the team was coming back intact, and I couldn't wait to hear Jack and Mike calling those familiar names over the air.

But in the midst of my anticipation, I became aware that dad was spending less and less time at home. There were many days that he would already be gone to the bar or track by the time I got home from school, and he would stay gone until well after I went to bed. By the time the real baseball season began in early April, I rarely saw dad outside of a Saturday afternoon (hanging out with him at the bar) or a Sunday when he would take us out to eat.

I ended up spending most evenings during that season (and several that followed) listening to the games alone in my room while playing or doing homework. Jack and Mike became my surrogate fathers, their voices giving me nightly comfort and stability.

The post-attack stay-at-home dad that I had thoroughly enjoyed was now permanently displaced by a part-time father who had become a full-time drunk. Mom seemed not to notice, at least she didn't openly complain. Sometimes he would come in after my bedtime and I would hear the muffled sounds of an argument. I couldn't understand why dad stayed away so much after mom's recovery.

As we sat through the commercial break following Lewis's strikeout, I took the opportunity to address it. "Do you remember the time after mom got back home from the hospital? You took really good care of us when she was recovering, but after she got home and started working, you stayed away. I mean, you were gone way more than even before the attack. What was going on?"

Dad may have felt like he was on trial at this point, but so be it. He had a lot of things to answer for, and only one night to face it all.

"I don't know what you're talking about," he said flatly. It was the first time during our conversation when I felt that he was lying.

"You were completely MIA after mom healed up and started working again! Why? If anything I'd think you would want to spend more time at home with the woman you almost lost," I said. We had covered enough ground already that I no longer felt hesitant or fearful about my tone.

"Don't push me, Paul. We've gone far enough on this topic, I think. Just watch the game."

"Why are you avoiding this? Just tell me. Why did you stay away so much after the attack?"

"I don't want to talk about it!" dad said with as much authority as he could still muster.

"What was it? You got tired of hanging out at home? Couldn't stomach the domestic life? Mom wouldn't let you drink in the house? What?" Dad's face changed and I could see that he was genuinely angry at me.

"No goddammit that's not it! You can't possibly understand what it was like." He stopped and looked into my eyes. "How would you feel if Karen was nearly killed in your home because you weren't there to stop it? Huh? You'd feel like shit, like a failure as a man. That's what I was going through. It got to a point where every time I looked at her, or you, all I could think about was that bastard and what he did to her. And what he could have done to you and Megan. It was guilt. I felt guilty for not being there and it was unbearable."

"But dad, you realize that by staying away from us so much, it only made things worse. You can't make up for not being here by not being here even more! That doesn't make sense."

"Yes, I see that now. It was just so damn painful being here, thinking about that day. I couldn't stand it, so I stayed away."

"What about now? How often do you think about the attack?" I asked.

"Are you kidding? I think about it every day. Every time I walk into the living room and pass by the front door, it hits me. Maybe that'll be one good thing about dying...I won't have to think about it anymore."

His words hit me hard. I hadn't considered how the attack affected him, and a flicker of pity flashed within me. Just the thought of Karen enduring such an attack made me wince.

I understood how dad might have felt, but it didn't excuse him. A man has to face those demons and overcome them, especially when young kids are involved. Dad never had the courage to turn and face them.

A sad truth descended on me in that moment: the entirety of dad's sins, all the damage he had done to his family and himself, was entirely fueled by weakness and cowardice. And now, at the end of his life, perhaps he was also coming to that realization.

Bottom of the Fifth

J ohn Jay, one of the many young Cardinals, who have recently risen through their minor league system, came in to pinch-hit for Salas. We couldn't have known then that the ball game had yet to reach its halfway point. Dad's words about feeling guilty were still lingering in the air as Jay took his swings. I was unsure of where next to take the conversation. Dad looked tired, even a bit weary. I wondered how much longer we would be able to continue watching the game. Just then he surprised me by reengaging.

"That day ruined everything for us. I wasn't the same, and neither was your mom. I wasted a lot of time wishing I could go back, but I should have been busy trying to make things better. I guess I just didn't know how," he said.

"I don't blame you for not knowing how to handle it. That's something no one could have prepared us for. But you chose to check out instead of stepping up for us. Things didn't have to go the way they did," I said. I was facing him, but he focused his eyes on the TV.

"You just don't know what it was like here in the neighborhood after that day. Everybody, hell, even Butch and the guys, looked at me differently. It was like I was less of a man because my wife got beat up. It could have happened to any of those assholes, but they didn't think about that."

"Did any of them ever say that to you? I can't believe that's true," I asked.

"No, of course not. They knew I would pound the first guy who brought it up. I never talked to any of them about the attack. It just went away, but it was always in their minds. Always in my mind."

They knew this because he did beat up a man just a few months after the attack. It happened outside of

Lamasco's one night as their group was leaving. A guy in his early twenties, who perhaps was not yet acquainted with the unwritten rules of Powell, let slip that dad was "that dude whose wife got beat to shit." Before Butch and Herm were able to pull him off the kid, dad managed to break his nose, jaw, and collarbone. It was just another Powell bar fight so no one got arrested or even questioned about the incident.

Johnny Ray never lost a fight in his life, except his last one against cancer.

Life got harder for all of us in the years after the attack. Mom went back to work, but her carefree spirit and sense of humor never fully returned. She got sick a lot more. In fact, in all the years since the attack I can't say that she's experienced a full week of feeling completely healthy. She always seems to have a touch of a bug, or irregular bowels, or migraine headaches. Perhaps the psychological toll somehow manifested itself in physical ways.

Dad's behavior certainly didn't help. His work life, which was spotty even before the attack, became a complete casualty. His umpiring gig, which had been his steadiest form of work, began to collapse as his performances grew worse. He had once been the most respected and requested umpire in Indiana, but after the attack he turned apathetic.

He would show up at games late and very drunk, and his calls behind the plate became sloppy and inconsistent. He lost the respect of the players as well as his ability to control and call a good game. By the end of 1984 he was virtually out of the game altogether, and the league made it official by firing and banning him. The one job that dad loved and was genuinely good at was lost because of his own recklessness. His Softball Hall of Fame plaque got thrown in the garbage, but I fished it out and hid it in my closet. I was proud of what he had accomplished in the sport, even if he chose to throw away those accolades.

Dad still found ways of bringing in money, though in ever smaller quantities. He took occasional truck driving jobs with several local companies, including the brewery, Ray's Electronics, and Dan's Cleaners. Amazingly, he managed to pull off these delivery runs fully drunk, but with no accidents to speak of. Still, these businesses called on him less frequently over time as his personality soured. By the end of the '80s, it was rare for dad to be seen working at all.

The pressure of taking care of all the family's needs fell squarely on mom, who took it on with incredible strength. She was very good at her job at Indiana Bell and won several promotions during that decade. By the time dad's income flat-lined, hers had improved enough to at least keep us in the house. I never heard her complain about this arrangement, and though she rarely felt good she never called in sick. Mom had a soldier's mentality about working, knowing that she was the last and only barrier between her kids and the streets.

There were only a couple of instances when I thought mom might actually get tired of dad's lifestyle and leave him. The first time came in the fall of 1985, after dad lost his delivery job with Sterling when they found he was drinking too much of their product while on the road. It was a Saturday night and mom took Megan and me to visit dad's sister Pauline. They grew to be like sisters over the years, perhaps because they both knew what it was like to deal with Johnny Ray.

Pauline had a son two years older than me named Philip, and we got along well when forced to play together because we shared a love for the Transformers. Philip and I would combine our collection of robots and have huge "battles" in his bedroom for hours.

On this night we were all going to the west side drive-in to see a double feature. This was a rare treat for us.

We probably only went to the drive-in three or four times during my entire childhood. Those were exciting evenings for a kid: watching movies in the car and eating delicious fried food. It's a shame that drive-ins have mostly died out.

That night we were seeing *Back to the Future* followed by *The Goonies*. Many kids ignored the films being displayed on those giant screens backdropped by miles of Southern Indiana cornfields. They preferred to play on the small but well-equipped playground located at the base of the main screen. Though I had intended to join them, I remained transfixed by both stories. I soaked them in from the backseat of Aunt Pauline's Mustang. Unlike most kids who were asleep or begging to leave by the end of the second feature, I was locked in until the final scene when One Eyed Willie's pirate ship floated out into the Pacific.

Between movies, Philip got out and went to the bathroom while I stayed in the car pondering the possibility of time travel in a DeLorean. I heard mom and Pauline chatting about the movie, but then the subject quickly shifted. Pauline, who was older than dad by several years, was fiercely defensive about her brother with everyone except my mother. She knew what mom was dealing with and went out of her way to help us with a night out, a meal, or just a sympathetic ear.

She asked, "So Doris, how's it going with Johnny?"

Mom sighed. "He lost another job this week. Sterling this time. I don't think he's going to bring in any money this month, and I don't think he cares!"

"Oh honey, I can help tide you over a little if you need to pay a bill or something. Don't hesitate." Pauline was exceptionally generous to us. I think she felt somewhat responsible for dad's actions, though there's nothing she could have done.

"Thank you Pauline, you're such an angel. Really, I can't imagine what I'd do without you sometimes. I don't know…we can't go on like this for much longer. Johnny's getting worse with the drinking. He's not umpiring anymore, he's lost his best driving jobs. I feel like he's giving up on us."

Mom started to cry and Pauline handed her a napkin. Mom had forgotten I was in the car for a moment. She looked back at me and said, "Oh Pauly, you don't need to hear any of this. Why don't you run up to the concession stand and get some ice cream. Here's a dollar. Don't you worry about anything! That's my job!"

I jumped out and got myself a chocolate soft-serve cone. I was fully aware of dad's descent and I was worried. I worried about our money, about mom, about our future, about a lot of things that a ten year old shouldn't have to think about. Thankfully, I was able to put all of that aside and picture myself as one of the Goonies. I may never have enjoyed two movies more in my life. It was truly an escape. Later, while lying in bed, my mind was a whirlwind. A flying car, a freak with uneven eyes yelling, "hey you guys," and my mother crying over her drunk husband all took turns at the forefront. I understood that if things continued as they were, my parents were going to split.

But something happened in October of 1985 that brought dad back to the house, at least temporarily. The Cardinals were back in the playoffs for the first time since their title run three years earlier. They were up against the NL West champion Dodgers.

Just like in '82, dad preferred watching these games in his own home and away from the noise of the bar. It was a refreshing change to have him around, and it took me back to the good times before the attack on mom. I was thrilled to see the Cards rebound from a couple of tough years, and even more excited to be watching them with dad.

The series started rough for the Redbirds. They dropped both games in Los Angeles, with Fernando Valenzuela shutting them down in game one. They rebounded in St. Louis, winning the next two and setting up a critical game five at home. However, before game four my favorite player at the time, Vince Coleman, was struck by what has to be the most bizarre injury in sports history. His foot was caught by an automatic rolling tarp on the field at Busch, and he was knocked out for the rest of the playoffs. It was ironic that perhaps the fastest man in baseball was injured by a tarp travelling perhaps one mile per hour. It was also a devastating loss at the worst possible time.

Game five was a Monday afternoon affair, and dad picked me up from school early so I wouldn't miss the first couple of innings. They were facing Valenzuela again, but this time they managed to put two runs up on him in the first. Willie McGee and Ozzie Smith, both walked to lead off the inning, and Tommy Herr made the Dodgers pay with a two-run double. The rally faded after that, and Valenzuela settled in to keep the score close. The game was tied at two after Bill Madlock hit a two-run homer off of Bob Forsch. It stayed that way until the bottom of the ninth.

Just as in '82, I retreated from the moment into the sanctuary of my bedroom. I needed to hear Jack Buck's voice. I just knew that they would find a way to win if I stayed in my room and let Jack call the action. Dad stayed in his chair and shook his head when I left the room. But, deep inside, he appreciated my superstition and was actually proud of it. He had raised a true Cardinal fan.

McGee started the inning with a pop-up to the third baseman. That was disappointing because Willie was the MVP of the league and the "table setter" for the entire offense. It would be Smith, batting against the righty Tom Niedenfuer.

Ozzie worked the count to 2-2 batting from the left side. I didn't know it at the time, but Ozzie had never hit a home run while batting left-handed. Then I heard Jack's voice spark to life and deliver one of the all-time great calls: "Smith corks one into right down the line! It may go! Go crazy, folks! Go crazy! It's a home run! And the Cardinals have won the game by the score of three to two on a home run by The Wizard! Go crazy!"

I went running into the living room, experiencing a strong déjà vu sensation, and saw Ozzie's teammates pounding on him with joy at home plate. Dad was still seated, and I realized that he hadn't yelled as was customary for him when the Cards did something great. He just had a big smile on his face. He looked at me and the smile broadened.

"That's incredible. I can't believe Ozzie just did that!" He said, watching the celebration.

"He really is a wizard!" I shouted.

"Well, all this really means is they still have one more to win before they get to the real series! They'll have to win in L.A. and that won't be easy. Don't get too excited just yet."

Dad, as always, put things into perspective. It didn't dampen my spirits though, and when Wednesday came I couldn't wait until game time. Once again he took me out of school early (mom never learned of these little vacations) so we could watch the first pitch together. I was his form of superstition. He wanted me around like a lucky rabbit's foot.

Orel Hershiser, who would lead the Dodgers to a World Series championship three years later, pitched game six against the Cards' Joaquin Andujar. Hershiser had the better of it for the first six innings. It was 4-1 Dodgers heading into the top of the seventh, and looking like a game seven would be necessary. But the Cards rallied to tie it up with a two-run single from McGee and then a triple by Smith off of Niedenfuer.

I stayed in the living room with dad for the first eight innings just as I always had, but then felt the bedroom and the comfort of the radio calling to me. Dad smiled when the eighth inning ended and said, "Go on Paul, I know you can't stand to watch when the game is on the line. Go listen to Jack and bring us home another winner!" I loved him for understanding and for believing. The Cards needed some magic; they were down 5-4 with three outs left.

Cesar Cedeno struck out against Niedenfuer to open the ninth, but Willie got the rally going with a base hit. He stole second, putting the tying run in scoring position. Ozzie drew a walk, and then it was up to Herr. He got down 0-2 and then grounded to the first baseman, whose only play was to toss to the pitcher covering first.

Jack Clark, the Cards only legitimate power threat, stepped to the plate with the game on the line. Niedenfuer had struck him out swinging in the seventh and, with another solid hitter in Andy Van Slyke on deck, he decided to pitch to Clark even with first base open. I paced my room, on edge, but not panicking. I knew that they still had a chance in game seven if they lost this one.

Clark dug in with the shadows covering home plate in the late afternoon, and my heart leaped when I heard Jack's next words. "Swing and a long one into left field! Adios! Goodbye! And maybe that's a winner! A three-run homer by Clark, and the Cardinals lead by the score of seven to five, and they may go to the World Series on that one!" I ran into the living room to see the replay as dad clapped and laughed in his chair.

Clark had drilled the first pitch deep into the left field bleachers. Pedro Guerrero, the left fielder for the Dodgers, who later played for the Cards, threw his glove to the ground in disgust as Clark's bomb sailed over the wall. It was indeed the game and pennant winner. This time I stayed in the room and watched with dad as Ken Dayley came in to pitch and retired the Dodgers in order. The stunned Los Angeles crowd watched while the Cardinals danced and mobbed each other on their field.

Dad stood up and looked at me. "This calls for a celebration. Get your jacket and your sister. We're going for pizza!" We went a couple of miles down Broadway Avenue to a little family owned place called Parkway Pizza. They were known in Powell as having incredible thin crust pizza and the best soft-serve in town.

Everything felt different that evening, like the bad times of the last three years were finally fading away. I allowed myself to forget the doubt and disappointment lurking under the surface and simply have fun. The pizza was perfection (mushrooms and pepperoni with extra cheese) and was topped off by a bottle of Ski, a regional soft-drink that locals would call heaven's answer to Mountain Dew. I nearly made myself sick from eating so much, but I couldn't help it. Everything just tasted better. Dad stood talking with the owner about the ball game and the upcoming World Series. The knowledge of more games to come with dad was the best part of that night.

* * *

Most Cardinals fans of a certain age would agree that the 1985 World Series was the "one that got away." They faced the Kansas City Royals, the team that Whitey Herzog had managed before coming to St. Louis. The series could not have started better from our perspective. Dad and I watched happily as John Tudor pitched a masterful game one. After game two, I thought it was in the bag. The Cards were down 2-0 heading into the ninth after being flummoxed all evening by the crafty left-hander Charlie Liebrandt.

As usual, I retreated to my room, and on cue the Redbirds staged an amazing rally. The biggest blow came with the bases loaded, two outs, and the Cards down a run. Terry Pendleton, the third baseman who went on to even bigger success later with Atlanta, delivered a bases clearing double to put St. Louis up 4-2. They held on and headed home with two road wins under their belt.

I reveled in the prospect of enjoying another World Series celebration with dad. After game two I allowed myself to believe that it was destiny. They couldn't possibly lose four out of five, with three of those at home, could they? I was even surer after game four, when John Tudor again dominated the Royals lineup and put the Cards one win away from the title. Unfortunately, they missed their chance to clinch it at home, and went back to KC needing only to split the final two games.

Game six featured a great match-up between the Cards righty Danny Cox and the Royals' Liebrandt. My anxiety grew exponentially as each scoreless inning passed. It became clear that just one run would be enough to win. The Cards finally got their chance in the top of the eighth when they pinch-hit for Cox with men at first and second and two out. They sent the little known or used Brian Harper to the plate for a once-in-a-career chance. He battled Liebrandt's array of darting pitches until he finally sent one looping toward centerfield. Pendleton scampered around the bases and scored to make it 1-0. They were six outs away from a championship.

When the bottom of the ninth came around, dad looked at me and grinned. I knew what he was thinking, but I surprised him. "I'm staying to watch this time, dad! I want to see it happen instead of just listening!"

I don't know what I was thinking, and to this day I still feel partially responsible for the chain of events that occurred after I made that decision. Dad cocked his head and gave me a funny look, but didn't protest. I know part of him wanted me to go to my room and listen because it was our ritual. But the rational part of him knew that it didn't matter how we watched or listened, or if we watched at all. The game was out of our control, though no fan really wants to believe that.

I rubbed the bill of my red Cardinals hat (now showing a lot of wear after three years of continual usage) for luck and stood beside dad in his chair. I hoped that foregoing Jack's call would be worth it in order to see the final out and the beginning of the celebration. Instead, I bore witness to one of the biggest letdowns of my life. Jorge Orta was first up facing the Cards' hard throwing closer Todd Worrell. Todd got him down 0-2, but couldn't put him away.

He hit a chopper toward Jack Clark at first base. Worrell flashed toward the bag and had to hurry because Orta was flying down the line. Clark flipped the ball to the stretching Worrell, who managed to put his foot squarely on the bag and catch the ball in his mitt with Orta's foot still hovering above.

He was out, but then he wasn't.

We both sat in disbelief as the umpire emphatically signaled safe. Worrell turned toward the ump with an incredulous look. The play had been fast (a "bang-bang" play as they say), but it was an easy call. Dad leapt from his chair.

"What? What? That's…oh my God! Terrible call! Terrible call! Jesus Christ, I don't believe this!" He continued on for a full minute as replay after replay showed how right he was. The ball was clearly in Worrell's glove before Orta's foot hit the bag, but Don Denkinger (the star-crossed umpire whose name would forever after live in infamy) had positioned himself in foul territory behind Worrell and couldn't have seen when the ball was in the glove.

Of course it was only one play, one runner. No one would remember it if Worrell had settled down and struck out the next three batters. But the blown call instantly shifted the feel and momentum of the game and the series. I should have realized that I had been terribly wrong not to listen to the ninth in my room. I stayed to watch the carnage unfold.

The Royals capitalized on their sudden good fortune

as the next batter, Steve Balboni, singled to left. A passed ball and an intentional walk followed, and the Royals had the bases loaded with one out. The Cardinals were a double play grounder away from winning the series. They were also one more base hit away from facing a game seven. The next batter was one whom I should have instantly recognized but did not.

Dane Iorg, the man who had sent me home happy from my first live game in Busch Stadium, was up with a chance to beat his old team. He took the first pitch for a ball, and then smashed the second one into right field for a hit. Kaufman Stadium exploded as the Royals capped an unlikely comeback and kept their dream alive.

Dad and I sat stunned for a few seconds. This wasn't the ending I had envisioned. I thought by now we'd be on our way to Dairy Queen for a late night celebration treat, or at least in the kitchen enjoying some bologna and cheese.

I felt empty at that moment, but everything looks a little different after you've seen your mother attacked and left for dead. I didn't cry, nor have I ever cried because of a sporting event. I take that back, I still get teary-eyed every time I see a replay of the end of the 1980 USA Hockey win over the Soviets. That aside, I have never cried because my team lost. There have been nights, such as that one, when I've wanted to. The joy, elation, sadness, and anger that a fan feels for their team is real and needs to be expressed. No one should have to make apologies for their reactions to sports.

When the Cards lost game six, I lost it with them. I didn't sleep well that night, and I worried that they would have trouble bouncing back after being so close to winning.

Dad didn't say a word after the loss. He grabbed his jacket and slammed the back door on his way out. He stayed out for the rest of that Saturday night, knowing that he wouldn't sleep even if he wanted to. They would play game seven the next night, and both of us had a bad feeling. Our only consolation was that John Tudor had been excellent throughout the playoffs. He was up against a young and talented Bret Saberhagen, so it figured to be a low scoring night.

I elected to spend the entire game listening in my room…taking no chances. The Royals picked up two runs in the second, and then three more in the third. Down 5-0, I still believed a rally was possible. I turned my cap around and paced around my room, hoping for Jack and Mike to describe a comeback. It only got worse.

KC blew it open in the fifth with six more runs, and it might as well have been a hundred. The Cards were clearly deflated from an agonizing game six and never recovered. The Royals were champions.

Dad emitted no sound, though I knew he was suffering as I was. He accepted the Cards' fate with quiet resignation. I think he knew what would unfold before the game ever started. He walked out of the house sometime during the decisive fifth inning, needing the comfort that only a few beers and Jack Daniels could offer. I listened to every pitch of that game, not because I thought the Cards could come back, but because I knew I wouldn't hear Jack and Mike's soothing voices again for many months. Win or lose, I always hated to see the baseball season end.

For dad and me, it was the end of a very good couple of weeks. I mourned the end of the Cards' run because it meant no more evenings hanging out discussing strategy and numbers. It would be twenty-six years before we would watch another World Series game together.

Seeing the Cards retired in order by Colby Lewis, I wondered if this year's team would bring us that same feeling of missed opportunity and emptiness. I studied the visage of dad, or the sad shell that he had become, and then did something I had never done during a sporting event. I said a silent prayer for God to let the Cardinals win game six, just in case dad wasn't around for the last one.

Top of the Sixth

Lance Lynn, another in the seemingly endless stream of young power arms in the Cardinal organization, ascended the mound to start the sixth inning. Dad rubbed his eyes and took a deep breath. The game and the conversation were taking their toll on him, but he was fighting. He had been preparing himself for this night since the moment mom told him I was coming over.

He said, "You hungry? Your mom's got a lot of stuff in the fridge. She stocked up after she heard you were coming. Go on, I don't think the Rangers are going to do much against Lynn."

I realized after he spoke that I was indeed famished. I hadn't eaten much in three days because of the anxiety of facing dad. Now my body relaxed and let me know it was okay to resume normal eating. My stomach grumbled as if in agreement with my mind.

I took his advice and walked to the kitchen. Mom and Megan were sitting at the table with an old photo album, remembering and laughing. Mom immediately went into "mom mode" and went to the refrigerator. "What would you like? I've got some lunch meat and some chicken salad, or I could cook you some eggs."

I smiled in appreciation. "How about all of the above? I'm starving!"

"Let's start with the chicken salad. That still one of your favorites?"

"Of course. And add some pickles if you have them!" I said, knowing that this sandwich would not be as tasty as the ones she made when I was a kid. Mom sometimes liked to make her own chicken (and occasionally tuna) salad, and it was incredible. This was store bought, but it would do the trick. I sat down next to Megan and she laid her head on my shoulder.

"Mom, did you ever think you'd have both your

kiddos back in the house, hanging out in the kitchen like the old days?" Megan asked as mom feverishly produced my sandwich.

"Oh, I had faith that this would happen, but it took longer than I thought. I'm just glad to see it. You know your dad couldn't be happier to have both of you running around here."

"Mom, I'm glad to be here too. I'm sorry it took me so long to get back," I said.

"Yeah, really! What happened? You lose the address?" Megan said while poking me in the side. She loves to give me grief.

"And here you go! One chicken salad sandwich with extra pickle, some bar-b-cue Grippo's chips, and a Ski on the rocks! Enjoy." My eyes widened as she laid the plate in front of me. Like Ski, Grippo's are a regional treat not found near St. Louis. I hadn't tasted them in years and I inhaled the meal like I was Chevy Chase emerging from the Arizona desert in *National Lampoon's Vacation*. Wiping my mouth, I let out a small but satisfied belch.

"Oh my God! That was amazing! Thank you, thank you!" I leaned over and kissed mom squarely on her forehead. She smiled and grabbed my plate. Her motherly instincts were still very much intact.

"Now let's see, what do we have that's sweet around here? I believe we have a package of Oreos somewhere," mom said, glancing back at me from the sink.

"This night just keeps getting better! Hit me!" I said. I nudged Megan. "Hey, guess what? Eddie lives!" She took a second to process this, then a huge smile came across her face.

"That's right! Eddie Wilson and his gang of Cruisers! But he doesn't go by Eddie you know...he's Joe West now."

Megan was referring to the only videotape that existed in our house when we were growing up: *Eddie and the Cruisers 2: Eddie Lives*. I believe it was purchased at a garage sale for a quarter. The movie was more about the music than the acting, but we didn't care. At one time we could have reenacted the entire plot from memory. I still keep the soundtrack on my iPod. Megan and I traded quotes from Eddie and his bandmates for a minute or two, but then I was distracted by the Oreos and milk.

I began to think of the many family meals and conversations that had taken place at that table. It was oval shaped with an ugly solid tan finish, and probably older than me. Mom had logged countless hours standing at that stove and sink. She enjoyed cooking, though not so much the cleaning up. Dad helped with that part sometimes, but Megan and I both took turns as dishwashers and table clearers. We were forever claiming that it was the other one's turn to wash and/or dry the dishes.

Mom spent a lot of years pretending to be satisfied with the status quo. Even after the attack, she went right back to being the bread winner and caregiver. Dad was free to resume his life of doing whatever the hell he wanted. After the '85 Series he withdrew even more from our daily lives. I hit twelve years of age in '87 and mom started allowing me to watch Megan alone in the house (naturally with all doors bolted and curtains drawn). It was shortly after my birthday that year when dad found mom's thousand dollar stash and gambled/gave it away in one day. In fact, I was a witness to the deed.

***

Once or twice a year dad would let me tag along with him and the boys to Ellis Park. It was an old Kentucky horse track with a huge grandstand and the musty smell of many racing seasons gone by.

Early on I knew this day was special because dad gave me a twenty dollar bill and told me to buy him a program. When I came back with it, he told me to keep the change. Later in the day he gave me another twenty to bet on any horse I wanted. I picked one in the fifth race named Grendel's Apex (he was 15-1 on the board, but I didn't care since he had a cool name). I bet the horse to place and, naturally, he came in third. Thus my first lesson in horse betting was learned: the best bet is not betting at all.

I stood next to dad as he placed his bets. Normally he would bet ten dollars to win or five to win and place on a horse. That day he was betting all sorts of exotics like two dollar exacta boxes and even some Pick Fours. He was also being generous with his buddies. Phil, his brother who was the definition of a degenerate gambler, got a hundred from dad early and then came back for another fifty later in the afternoon.

Phil would bet on anything if there was action. He nearly lived at the track, staying longer than even dad, Butch, and the rest of the gang. On a day with nine races, most of the guys would be out of money or just ready to go by the end of the sixth. Phil never missed a race, and stayed after to talk with jockeys, mutuel clerks, and anyone else whom he thought he could squeeze information from.

The fourth race was the most important for dad. He had an early Pick Four going and he needed the six or the seven horse to win this one. Both horses were 5-1 shots, and dad was very confident that one of them would win. We sat in their usual box, which was shaded by the grandstand and had a perfect view of the stretch run. Dad stood up as the horses came around the final turn in the fourth race. His seven horse was winning and the six wasn't far behind. He started shouting, "Get it baby! Get it baby!"

His cadence got louder and faster as they neared the end. I got excited because it looked like the seven was going to pull it off. Then I saw a flash of yellow, the four horse, giving a determined run and gaining ground. The four passed him about ten feet from the finish post.

Dad threw his rolled up program toward the track.

He was as angry as I had ever seen him aside from the day of mom's attack. "Goddamn bastards! Cheats! What a bunch of bullshit! Twenty-one to one? What a goddamn joke!" He slumped back into his chair and Butch turned to him.

"Yeah, thought you had that one sewn up. That four had no business winning."

I stayed silent and still, looking to avoid the wrath of Johnny Ray. He stayed somber for only another minute, then seemed to spring back to life. "Well, hell. It's still early! Come on boy, let's go get another program and figure out who's going to win this next one!"

He did indeed hit the exacta in the next race, but a string of unexpected (by him at least) results followed and dad's demeanor steadily grew more sullen. Between his bad bets, "loans" to Phil and some other guys, and many rounds of beer, dad had managed to waste nearly all of the money that mom had diligently put away out of so many paychecks.

Three days later, when mom cashed her check and went to add another twenty to her growing carpet fund, panic hit her when she couldn't find the envelope. Her realization was immediate.

I was playing with some Transformers in my bedroom that evening when I heard the fracas begin. As I was busy transforming Optimus Prime from robot to truck mode I heard mom's footsteps pounding toward my bedroom door. This was always cause for fear as it usually meant I had made a mess or done something to make my little sister cry. These footfalls were just as brisk and purposeful, but they passed quickly by my door on their way to the living room where I knew dad was probably slumped in his chair watching Magnum or perhaps Simon and Simon.

I didn't need to put my ear to the door to hear what came next. "Where is it Johnny? There was a thousand dollars in there and we need it! Tell me what you did with it!" I could tell from her voice that she was in tears and shaking.

"I don't have it. I don't have any idea what you're talking about." His first and only defense was always denial. His voice was calm. He had prepared himself days in advance for this inevitable conversation.

"You...do you know what you've done? How are we ever going to fix anything in this house if you just throw it away every chance you get? Look at me Johnny! You have a problem!"

This was the first time mom had ever directly addressed what both of them had known to be true for years. Even as a child, I realized that this could be a turning point. She might actually leave him. I was scared but I also knew that something needed to change.

Dad sat silent. He probably didn't know how to respond to mom's blunt statement. Of course he had a problem and he knew it. But he was too weak or selfish to ever look inward and honestly attempt to change. That would have been hard work and unpleasant, and dad's life was all about easy and fun.

"Just get out! I can't even look at you right now! Go to your drunk buddies and do what you do best!"

She was shouting desperately. It was like nothing I had ever heard from her before and it scared me so badly that I immediately abandoned the robot battle in front of me and crawled into bed. For a kid, there's no retreat better than the bed. The sheets and blanket can form a barrier and make you safe; at least that's what you tell yourself. I could hear Megan crying in her room and, for once, my natural instinct to torment her gave way to sympathy. I wanted to comfort her, but I was too afraid to walk outside my room.

I heard mom pass by, whimpering as she went to compose herself in the bathroom. After a moment I heard her in Megan's room saying everything was fine and to go to sleep. Dad didn't move for a couple of minutes. I think he was genuinely stunned by what he had just heard. Then, I heard him get up. He grabbed his keys and walked out the front door. There was no slamming or shattering of glass.

He had only one course of action to take and that was to do exactly what mom had told him. He drove away and I didn't see him for several days after that. Mom said later that he was staying with his brother Phil.

Of course, it was only after I heard mom confront him about it that I realized why he had been such a high roller on that day. I actually tried to give mom the nineteen dollars that dad let me keep from the program I bought, but she refused to take it. She told me to hide it somewhere safe, and I did.

After their encounter regarding the thousand dollars, nothing changed immediately. Dad wasn't around much anyway, except an evening here and there when I could still listen to a game with him. But those nights were fewer and fewer as his drinking became more of a priority. Then one Saturday morning I woke up and walked into the living room to catch some Looney Tunes or perhaps the Smurfs on TV. I found dad sprawled out on the couch, still wearing his dark brown slacks and brown wingtips (he owned many pairs of these in various colors and styles). My cartoon time was ruined because I was scared to wake him up. He continued to sleep on the couch each night for a few weeks, until one evening when mom sat both of us kids down at the kitchen table.

"Kids, I know you've noticed that your dad and I are…having some problems. I don't know what to say except that sometimes this happens with married people. It doesn't mean we're breaking up, but we need to spend some time apart. I'm taking you guys and we're going to live with Aunt Pauline for a little while. I want you both to go to your rooms and pull out some clothes, socks, and underwear and bring them to my room. We're leaving tonight."

She didn't take time for more explanation, she simply turned toward the refrigerator and prepared to create our meal. I was numb throughout the process of gathering my clothes, but not distraught. I had known for a while that things were bad and that this was a possibility. Still, I was scared and I knew Megan would be as well. I went to her room and tried to help get her essentials together. Instead of shirts and pants, Megan was gathering a pile of dolls and My Little Ponies to take with her.

"Need any help?" I asked.

"No. I don't know which dolls to leave behind. Do you think mom will let me bring all of these?"

"I doubt it. You better just pick a couple of your favorites and leave the rest for now. We're not going to be gone that long anyway," I said, trying to sound confident. I knew there was a real chance that this was the end of their marriage. And if mom did try to divorce him, I had no idea how dad might react.

Megan started to say something else, but then she was crying. Although most of my childhood was devoted to teasing and tormenting her, at that moment my only thought was to take away her fear and make her smile. I did this by taking two of her dolls and acting out a quick scene from our Beach House saga. She was laughing in no time, and within the hour we were throwing our bags into the trunk of Pauline's Mustang. Our only vehicle at the moment was a used Colt Vista (a precursor to the minivan), and dad had taken it for the evening. Mom would have to rely on Pauline for a ride to work or take the city bus. She didn't care, it was a worthwhile sacrifice to get herself and her kids out of that house.

I didn't wonder until much later why mom chose to leave with us rather than just asking dad to stay elsewhere. Perhaps she didn't want to risk a major confrontation. I believe she left because it would force dad to live in an empty house full of reminders of the departed family. If dad left, mom must have feared that he might not come back or maybe fall into a tailspin that would only make things worse. In any case, it was a necessary move if their marriage was to survive.

As I walked out the back door with my suitcase in hand, I spotted a letter that mom had left on the kitchen table. It read: "Johnny, I'm taking the kids to your sister's house. We won't be coming back until things change. I hope that you'll think about what you've been doing to me and your children. I can't do this anymore. I'm sorry. You can come see the kids when you want, but they're staying with me. –Doris"

Conflicting emotions clashed in my mind after I read the note. I was upset that our home life had come to this. I obviously didn't want to leave our home to go live in Pauline's damp and musty basement. But I also felt a pride in mom for having the courage to take this drastic step. I hadn't realized how unhappy she was because mom was very good at putting on an act. Now she would force dad to make a decision, and if he chose not to change, then she would boldly move forward as a single mother.

The next day mom kept us out of school so we could get situated in our new subterranean home. Megan and I were glad to see more of Aunt Pauline and her electrician husband Sal. They were generous people who laughed easily and made marriage look effortless. I often wondered what it would be like to have a dad like Sal, who went to all of Philip's Pony League games and was always home at night for supper. I sometimes envied Philip because his parents had money and they were a real family. I never wished for a different father, just for mine to be more interested in our lives.

At around noon, as Megan and I played Chutes and Ladders (another game that I'm pretty sure I never won) in the basement, we heard a loud knocking at the front door.

Mom was upstairs talking with Pauline in the kitchen, and they quieted abruptly. They knew dad had arrived. I crawled up the stairs to try to get a listen. Mom and Pauline walked together to the front door and opened it.

I heard dad's voice first and he sounded frantic. "Doris how? Why did you do this? Are the kids here? Can I see them? Doris, let's talk about this."

"The kids are here and they're fine. We can talk, but we're not coming home today. Or tomorrow. You're out of control and I'm not dealing with it anymore!" Mom sounded angry but under control. She had prepped herself for this conversation. I heard the front door close and movement as mom and dad sat down in the living room while Pauline retreated back to the kitchen.

"What's going on here, baby? Why are you doing this to me?"

When mom next spoke, her scoffing tone was evident. "To you! To you! All you do is go to that bar and get drunk, and then you go to the track and gamble and get more drunk, and then you go back to Butch's and drink some more. Then you want to come back home and pretend everything is just fine. That thousand dollars you took was so we could get some decent flooring in that house! You just threw it away didn't you? We're never going to get anywhere with you acting like this, and you're getting worse!" Mom wanted to continue but she broke down. She wept for over a minute as dad sat in silence. He was looking in a mirror for the first time in years.

"I...I know I have a problem. I know I do. I should be working. I should be at home more. I know it. It's just...hard," dad said, sounding sincere. It was refreshing to hear him admit that he was wrong, but it wasn't an apology.

"Johnny, you know I love you. But that's not enough anymore. The kids need a father, a real father. And I need a partner. Right now you're neither. I...I just want you to take some time and think about what you need to do. And then I want to see you make some changes. Then, if you're willing to do that, we'll talk about coming home. Okay?" This was followed by another long silence.

"Yeah. I hear you. I love you too. I, uh. I'm gonna go now. Tell the kids I'll see them soon and that I love them. Will you do that?" dad asked. He sounded defeated and dumbstruck, which was completely foreign to me. Dad's voice was always confident and sometimes brash, but now he sounded like a different man.

"Yeah, Johnny. I'll tell them. Like I said, you can see them anytime you want. I'm not going to stand in your way. They miss you...a lot. Especially Pauly."

I choked up a bit when I heard this. It occurred to me that I had sorely missed dad as he was before mom was attacked.

I heard the door close when dad left, and then mom was crying again and much harder than before. I heard Pauline reassuring mom that she was making the right decision. Now we would all have to wait to see how dad would react.

Life resumed a modicum of normalcy after their encounter. Megan and I had school to attend to and mom had her work. In the evenings I would play catch with Philip or watch TV with Megan. Thankfully the '80s were a golden age for sitcoms and we got to enjoy classics like Cheers, Family Ties, and The Cosby Show. It was a little thing, but having those lovable characters to count on each week helped to ease our burden. I especially loved Family Ties because of the character of Steven Keaton. He was a loving, compassionate father, something I craved in my own life. Even now, when I catch an episode on Netflix or late night TV, I feel a pang of jealousy because Alex got a great dad and I didn't.

We stayed with Pauline and Sal for nearly six months, and in that time we only saw dad twice. He would call once a week and talk to both Megan and me for a few minutes on the phone, and then mom would get on and give him the update on all that had transpired. My phone time with dad consisted of telling him about school (ten percent), and discussing what was happening with the Cardinals (ninety percent).

In October of '87 the Cards once again crowned NL East champs and were facing the San Francisco Giants in the League Championship Series. I ended up watching them at Pauline's house, and without dad. I knew he would be watching these games at home, and part of me desperately wanted to be sitting in the chair opposite his and rooting the Redbirds into the World Series the way we had in years past. But I never told mom this, because ultimately I was on her side and didn't want her to think I preferred to live with dad.

The Cardinals took seven games, but they finally got past the Giants and won their third trip to the Series in six years. John Tudor and Danny Cox were brilliant in games six and seven, shutting out the Giants for eighteen straight innings en route to another National League pennant.

I could never have understood how spoiled I was as a young sports fan. In the '90s, when they only made it to the postseason once, I learned to better appreciate the great seasons. This time they would be facing the Minnesota Twins, whose best weapon was the crazy Metrodome environment. The Twins had the best home record in baseball in the "baggy dome." No one wanted to play there, but the Cards had to in the first two and last two games of the series.

I watched all seven games with Sal and Philip, whose allegiance to the Cardinals did not run nearly as deep as dad or I. They wanted the Cards to win, but they were dispassionate observers at best. I was used to watching games with a man who lived and died with each pitch, swing, and managerial decision. It wasn't nearly as fun, but I could hear dad's voice in my head criticizing calls and explaining Herzog's decisions. As expected, the Cards dropped the first two games in Minnesota, but bounced back with three straight wins at Busch Stadium. Just like in '85, the Redbirds hit the road needing only one more win to secure the World Series trophy.

Dad called and asked to speak to me before the start of game seven in Minnesota. He seemed upbeat, though the Twins had scored a combined twenty-nine runs in their three home games. Danny Cox was going to have to be at his best, and that still may not be enough. He also told me that I should have a radio handy in case the game was close going into the ninth.

I was waiting for him to ask me if I wanted to watch the game with him, but he never did. Perhaps he remembered our experience in '85, when the Cards lost the final two in KC. Before we got off the phone dad said, "Remember Paul, win or lose this was a great season. They can't win everything every year, even though we want them to. I'm sorry we can't watch this one together, but I promise opening day next year you'll be here to listen with me. Okay?"

I said okay and hoped that when we next caught a game together that he would be sober. The Cards got out to a 2-0 lead early in game seven, but couldn't get anything else across against Frank Viola. The Twins chipped away and eventually took a 4-2 lead. As dad had prescribed, I retreated to the basement for the final frame to see if Jack and Mike could bring us a rally.

Jeff Reardon came on to close the game and the series for the Twins. He retired Tommy Herr, Curt Ford, and Willie McGee in order and the celebration began in the dome. Twice in three years I had seen my team come within one win of becoming champions, only to be undone by two consecutive road losses. In retrospect the '85 loss was much harder considering how close they came to winning game six. But in that moment, the feeling was just as bitter, the heartbreak just as painful.

The loss compounded what had already been a difficult year for all of us. I lay awake in the basement that night contemplating another upcoming winter without baseball, and without dad. We had already been living there almost four months, and there was no sign that mom was ready to bring us back home. She never gave us updates on what dad was doing, or if he was trying to get himself together. She just kept telling us that she "needed more time" and "he's not ready yet." She was waiting for a sign, or some kind of proof that dad was willing to recommit himself to us. Only God knew how long that would take, if it ever happened.

***

As the three of us sat at the kitchen table after my chicken salad feast, I got a text from Karen: "Almost ready to go here. Still okay to come over with Jack?"

I replied back, "Still good. Get here ASAP, he's very tired." Megan looked at me as I hovered over my iPhone.

"That Karen? Is she coming over with the boy?"

"You got it. They should be here in forty-five minutes or an hour."

"Yay! So exciting! I'm glad dad is going to get to meet little Jack! I haven't seen him in a few months myself," Megan said. She is a good aunt. I knew that somewhere in the house, she had already stashed a present for him, even though it wasn't his birthday or Christmas. She always had something for him every time she saw him.

"Yeah, it's good for Jack too. One day when I tell him all our family stories he'll be able to remember dad and this house." Mom stayed silent during this exchange. I knew she was especially happy about Jack's meeting with his grandpa. She had been talking about it since the day he was born. "Speaking of family stories, mom. I wanted to ask you something."

"Oh boy, here we go. What do you want to talk about?" Mom said, rolling her eyes.

"Well, I want to know about the time when you and dad were separated. I mean, I think we all knew why you wanted to get away, but what happened to make you come back? I've never heard you say anything about that time," I said.

Mom huffed and looked at me. "Is it really necessary to bring that up right now? You know I don't care to talk about that."

"What can I say? I'm on a roll tonight. It's 'uncomfortable topic night' at the Gibson house. Why turn back now?" Mom frowned anytime she thought I was being a wise-ass.

"You know why I took you guys to Pauline's. I didn't know what to do, but I knew things couldn't stay the same. It was a tough decision, and I cried a lot during those months. Your dad had to learn that we needed more from him," mom said, staring at the table.

"Okay, but then at Christmas that year suddenly we were back home with not a word spoken about why. I think Megan and I were both happy to be back in our own beds, but I'll admit it was a surprise."

"Your dad used those six months to figure some things out. At first he didn't change anything. In fact, he got worse for the first month or so. A couple of times he came to Pauline's late at night trying to get in to see you kids, but she and I both refused to let him in. He was stone drunk and there was no way I was going to let you two see him like that. I thought he had given up. I thought for sure he was going to end up dead or get someone else killed what with all the drunk driving he was doing. Once Butch even came over and talked to me. He said your dad was miserable and I had to do something. I told him I had given that man enough. He needed to do this on his own.

"But then, things started to get better. He would call me in the evenings and he sounded sober, or at least not as drunk as usual. He started telling me how much he loved me and missed me. I hadn't heard him say those things in a long time. Still, I told him that wasn't enough. He had to prove he was getting better. Then one night he told me he had gotten his driving job back with Ray's TV. And he was looking into umpiring some high school baseball games. I was happy, but I told him we'd have to wait and see. That went on for a couple more months. He wanted me to come over and have dinner with him one night, and I told him I wasn't ready for that yet. I just wasn't sold yet...I needed something else.

"That's when Charlene Jackson called from church. She was the pastor's secretary back then and a good friend. She told me that Johnny had been in to visit with the pastor on several occasions just to talk about things. My jaw dropped. Your dad in a church...and of his own free will no less! I decided then to give the dinner idea a chance. This was just after Thanksgiving. I probably told you guys I was going to a church meeting or something. I didn't want to get your hopes up.

"So I came here for dinner, trying to keep my expectations low. Kids, you've never seen your father dressed up like this. He had on a dinner jacket with the patches on the elbows...probably borrowed because I know he didn't own one. He had the house absolutely spotless. He had dinner on the stove, we had a meatloaf that was a little overcooked, and some canned vegetables. But he did his best, he was really trying. And the best part was that he was completely sober. Not a drop of liquor in him. He said he had been dry for almost three weeks. I couldn't believe it. We had a good talk, and I told him at the end that I would need to think and pray about all of it. I wanted to cry, I was so proud of him.

"After another couple of weeks of talking and seeing how great he was doing, I decided it was time to bring you guys back home. That was our best Christmas. He was clean, you guys were back home. We were happy." Mom trailed off and tears welled in her eyes. I squeezed her shoulder and then rubbed her back. She was right. That was a great Christmas because, for once, we had a sober father who was actually involved, mom seemed happier than ever, and Megan and I were showered with gifts.

That was the year I got an electric football game (plug it in, set up the players, and then watch them move randomly all over the field…perhaps the dumbest game I played as a kid), a new bike, and a huge load of baseball cards. Megan got anything and everything Barbie related. It was like a dream, and by that I mean it was fleeting and forgotten over time. That Christmas was an aberration rather than a new beginning.

Mom continued, "He did really great for a while. We had real money for once. You guys had a real father. I had an actual husband. He just couldn't keep it together."

Megan chimed in, "That's what I've always struggled with, mom. If you were willing to leave him once, why didn't you do it again when things got bad?" I was inwardly ecstatic to hear Megan ask this. I didn't want to be the one to ask, but there would never be a better time to bring it up.

Mom shook her head and looked up at Megan. "Because I love him. I didn't want to leave him, I just wanted to him to be a better man. I knew he loved me, and I knew he would do anything for you two. Don't think I didn't consider it. I did. I prayed about it and rolled it over for years. I just couldn't do it."

She looked as if she wanted to say more, but then paused. We both had to respect her answer, though I wanted to scream that real love shows in action and not just words. I wanted to berate her for putting up with things that no wife or mother should. Instead, I sat nodding in agreement along with Megan.

She continued, "That man lying in there. He's done a lot of things that I know he regrets. He's hurt you two probably more than I know. He's wasted a lot of years, and now he's dying because of his own foolish choices. But if it was me lying in that bed, he'd trade places with me in a heartbeat. He'd do it for both of you too. Don't you ever doubt it. He's your father and he loves you." I had never heard mom defend him so passionately.

"Excuse me," she said as she pushed herself away from the table. She headed for the bathroom and shut the door. Megan looked at me and we both were at a loss.

"Wow." That was all Megan got out. I took a breath and then turned to look down the hallway.

"Maybe I should get back in there. Not sure how much longer he can hold out tonight. He might need to sleep soon," I said while standing and stretching. Dad was still propped up and awake when I came in and I saw that the Rangers had indeed gone quietly in their half of the sixth inning. The Cards had already started their at-bats in the bottom half.

Dad didn't speak as I returned to my seat next to the bed. Now I was feeling a bit groggy. After a filling meal and so much emotional conversation, I felt drained again. I tried to give myself a little mental pep talk, knowing that the roller coaster was far from over. We still had a lot of unpleasantness to discuss, but I was now more concerned with Jack's impending arrival. I couldn't wait to see how dad would react to seeing his first (and only) grandchild.

Bottom of the Sixth

Pujols had already struck out looking for the first out when I got back to the bedroom. Frustrated, I was already counting the outs in my mind: eleven more outs are all we have to give. Dad's face was hard to read. He had a pained look about him, but that was mostly from his battle with what was happening inside his body. He was fighting to stay awake and alive to see his grandson and see the Cardinals win one more World Series. I truly believe that if the Cards had failed to make the Series, dad would have passed away before that night.

"You know, I was talking with mom in the kitchen just now. She told me about how you got sober and changed some things in your life so we would come back home. What do you remember about that time?" What I really wanted to ask was if that had all been an act just to dupe mom into coming back home.

"Jesus, boy, you just won't quit tonight with the questions will ya?" he asked. I snickered.

"Well, it's not like we've got a lot of time here. Why the hell not talk about these things? I've been in the dark my whole life and I want to hear it from you before you're gone. Is that okay?"

"I suppose I don't have a choice. You wouldn't leave if I threw you out anyway would ya?"

"You're right, I wouldn't. But I don't think you want me to leave," I said and gave him a big smile. I know a lot of people who don't want to know the truth about their family. They operate willingly in oblivion, never really knowing their parents or siblings. It would have been easy to let dad die without making him dredge up these memories, but how could I let him?

"Well, I did go sober for a while. A few months at least, I don't remember for sure. And yeah, I did it because I wanted you guys back home. I thought I could just let the old life go and start fresh, and it worked for a while. I even started working part-time at the church as a janitor. And you know something? I liked that job. I was good at it and I liked hearing from people about how clean the sanctuary was. I took pride in that, as much as I ever did as an umpire. I think that's what kept me going as long as I did without drinking."

"Mom said you talked with the pastor sometimes."

"Oh yeah, old Reverend Marne was a great guy. I never thought I would set foot in a church...always thought of guys like Marne as crooks and liars. I thought the whole church thing was just to bilk people out of their money every Sunday. But when I got desperate, when I really thought I was going to lose your mom for good, I went to see him.

"Marne didn't try to preach at me, and he never asked me for money. He just quoted a couple of scriptures about what marriage is supposed to be like. He really made me think about what it means to be a husband. That's when I stopped drinking and started looking for work again. I had a new mission, and that was to win you guys back. And it worked...I owe that man a lot!"

The Reverend Eugene Marne, long time pastor of Powell Southern Baptist Church, was seemingly a miracle worker when it came to dealing with my father. Marne was extraordinarily patient and persistent with dad because he said Johnny Ray was "one of the most passionate men I ever knew."

"And you even started coming to church with us sometimes. I remember the congregation just staring in shock when you walked in holding mom's hand!"

"Yeah, that's half the reason I did it: the shock value! I guess I felt like I owed it to your mother, and to Marne, to make an effort. And it wasn't so bad. I hated the singing, but I did enjoy hearing the reverend's messages. He always made sense to me. Sometimes I felt like he was preaching directly to me!"

In fact, he probably was. Marne made it his personal mission to get dad saved and baptized. It would be the final jewel in his heavenly crown.

"He was a good preacher. And he finally got to you, didn't he?"

Dad gave a small laugh. "Yeah, he wore me down. After one of our face to face meetings I told him he could sign me up for a baptism and he almost choked right there in his office! He asked me if I had committed my life to Christ and I said yes as much as I could. I'm not sure why I agreed to do it, I didn't really want to get dunked in front of the whole church. Marne just had a way of making me feel at ease about all that stuff."

Dad's baptism most likely still stands as the most heavily attended church service in the history of Powell. The balcony, normally not even used for Sunday morning services, was overloaded with people primed to witness a miracle. There were dozens of folks standing at the back of the sanctuary as well. Everyone wanted to see Johnny Ray, poster boy for the rough men of Powell, who lived for booze and softball, commit himself to Jesus. Even Butch, Phil, Herm, and Chuck, his band of enablers, showed themselves for this event.

The baptismal pool was located in an elevated position just behind the pulpit. A huge stained-glass window featuring a cross and Bible stood behind the pool. When Reverend Marne emerged from behind a wall with dad trailing behind him, the place erupted in applause and cheers. Dad was wearing a white robe that had been donned by hundreds of local folks before him in the same ritual. Reverend Marne raised his right hand and silenced the crowd in an instant. His face was beaming with a huge smile as he faced the congregation. He was used to looking out at a tempered audience, but this bunch was more like a crowd from the Friday night fights held at the downtown

Coliseum.

"My friends, I've waited a long time for this day to come!" Marne announced.

Before he could continue, the sanctuary exploded with more cheering and some laughs from the people who knew how true that statement was. He calmed them again with his upheld hand. He turned to dad, who looked shell-shocked. The reverend placed his hand on dad's left shoulder as if to steady and reassure him all at once.

"Johnny, have you accepted Jesus Christ as your Lord and Savior?" The crowd leaned in, still not believing this was happening. I half expected dad to suddenly turn to the audience and say "Ahh, just kidding guys!" Instead, he looked the reverend directly in the eyes as he responded.

"Yes, I have." More applause. A few women, including mom, cried into their tissues.

"Upon your profession of faith and in accordance with the Lord's command, I baptize you, Johnny Ray Gibson, in the name of the Father, Son, and Holy Spirit."

As he finished the sentence, Reverend Marne placed one hand on dad's back and the other on his shoulder. Dad slowly leaned back and immersed himself in forgiveness. A second later, he emerged from the water as Marne concluded the traditional remarks. "Buried in the likeness of His death, and raised in the likeness of His resurrection. God bless you Johnny!"

This time the crowd went crazy and the standing ovation lasted for well over a minute. Dad patted the reverend on the back (the closest he came to hugging another man) and immediately made his way out of the pool. I'll admit, I still couldn't believe it happened in the weeks and months that followed.

Dad spent the better part of 1988 as a sober, employed family man. We listened to a lot of games during that baseball season, though the Cardinals never got on track and finished twenty-five games behind the Mets. It was still great to listen with him, even if we heard a lot of losing. As the year moved into fall, I began to notice the smell of beer on his breath. He started going out for an evening every once in a while, and staying out later and later. By the end of the year we were hearing mom and dad arguing again over a multitude of issues. The old Johnny Ray was creeping back into our lives.

"So, you already know my next question. Why did you relapse? Was the whole getting saved business just to please mom or was it sincere?" Dad grimaced and shifted on the bed when I asked this. He muttered something under his breath. "I didn't catch that. What?"

"I said I'm about goddamn tired of being interrogated in my own house, in my own bed no less!"

"This isn't an interrogation, and you don't have to talk to me if you don't want to. I'm sorry if I'm making you mad, but let's be real. This is possibly the last time I'm ever going to be face to face with you. Now, do you want me to leave or shall we keep going?"

I was fifty-fifty on what he would say. I'm sure from his perspective, it was like an extended episode of "This Is Your Life." I waited for a long minute and noticed that the Cardinals had a rally in progress. Lance Berkman managed an infield single after Albert's strikeout, then Matt Holliday reached first on a botched play by the Rangers' first baseman. Freese was up with two on and only one out.

Dad said, "Big at-bat right here. If Freese gets on this could be a big inning."

We silently agreed to table the previous discussion until after the rally. Freese worked a walk and not only loaded the bases, but knocked Colby Lewis out of the game. With Yadi Molina coming up, Texas brought their lanky right-hander Alexei Ogando into the game. Ogando had been extremely effective throughout the season, but he was facing a tough out in Molina. When Yadi's career began with St. Louis he was all defense, as many catchers are. But he has evolved into an offensive threat who rarely strikes out.

"Anything in the air would be good. No grounders…it's a sure double play if he hits it at someone," I said, knowing that Molina is the opposite of Vince Coleman on the bases.

"You're right. I think he's going to make something happen here," dad replied.

I didn't remember him being quite so optimistic about games when I was younger. He was still every bit as perceptive though. Molina took advantage of Ogando's initial wildness and took a walk to make the score 4-4. Now it was Nick Punto at the plate with a great chance to give the Cards another lead. He took a strike and then took the second pitch, which was followed by the Rangers' catcher suddenly firing the ball toward third base. The camera changed and we watched Holliday get tagged out. Rally killer. Both of us reacted at the same time.

"How? How do you let yourself get picked off in this spot? What kind of…" dad would have continued but he had allowed himself to get too worked up and the pain hit him again. He continued shaking his head while letting out an involuntary hum.

"Unbelievable. That's a killer!" I added. The feeling worsened when Ogando threw a wild pitch that would have allowed Holliday to score easily. Punto walked to reload the bases, but they were on with two outs. Jon Jay stepped in and promptly grounded back to the mound, ending the inning with minimal damage done. Another opportunity lost.

"You still hanging in there, dad?"

"Fine. I'm fine. It's just…I can't stand plays like that. I can't help it, its fundamentals."

"Looked like he hurt himself on the slide. Hope he's okay. They need him," I said.

The rally had not only tied the game, but it provided me with a chance to reset our conversation. "Okay, I'm sorry for questioning your conversion. I shouldn't have done that. But you have to admit that after a while, things slipped again. I just wanted to know what happened because you were doing so well for so long." I hoped that my rephrasing would soften his response.

"And you want the truth?"

"Of course."

"Well, a lot of things happened. It wasn't like I woke up one day and decided to be a drunk again. You know how the Baptists use the word 'backsliding'? That's pretty much what happened with me. I just gradually fell back into the old habits. One thing was, and I'm ashamed to admit this, I was bored. I never had a life where it was just work, home, family all the time. There wasn't any action. No juice. I didn't feel alive and I wasn't having fun.

"Don't get me wrong, there were lots of times I enjoyed being around you kids and your mom. But I wasn't used to it being all the time and it...got old. Like I said, I'm not proud of it. After a while I needed a taste of the old life."

A part of me regretted asking for the truth. It's a hard thing to hear your father say he got bored with being around you.

"Couldn't you have found a happy medium? Hang out a little with the guys and some with us at home? Did it have to be all or nothing?"

"Look, I can't give you what you want. I can't explain all my decisions and actions to you. I know I wasn't a good father or husband. I know I could have done things differently. If I could I would change some things, but it's over now. I'm lying here with no time left and you want me to go back and relive every goddamn bad choice I ever made."

"That's not the point! I'm not trying to rub your

face in it. I'm just trying to understand. You know, I left here a long time ago and spent a lot of years trying not to think about you. Trying to pretend my childhood happened to someone else. But I'm here now and it's because, in spite of everything, I still love you dad. That's why I'm here."

I bit my lower lip to keep my tears at bay. I thought I had been mentally and spiritually prepared for this night, but it's impossible to know what thoughts and feelings will emerge when trolling the depths of the past. A moment passed as I awaited his reaction.

"Well, I love you too son. I hope you know that. I never meant to run you off." I smiled when he said this. It didn't make up for anything that had happened, but it felt very good. We sat in silence for another minute, then he retrieved his train of thought.

"There was one big thing that happened that helped to knock me off the wagon. When your Uncle Phil died in the winter of '89, that's when I really lost my grip."

***

Uncle Phil's death was a memory I had long suppressed. In fact, I hadn't even heard his name in probably twenty years. It was a sudden and devastating loss for dad. I cried and mourned for a time because he was my favorite uncle and a genuinely nice man. Sadly, I only saw him in the midst of his addictions.

"That's right…the fire. I haven't thought about that for a long time."

"Phil got in too deep with some bad people on the backside. He didn't understand what he was into until it was too late," dad explained.

The "backside" is the general term for the clusters of stables, barns, and dormitories located on the opposite side of the horse track from the grandstand. From what I gathered during odd conversations, the backside was sort of its own small town. Hundreds of trainers, jockeys, horsemen, and various other workers made up the population. Though many came and went with the seasons from one track to another, most of them knew each other to some degree.

The backside was also sometimes known to be a dangerous place, especially for outsiders. It had a kind of "Wild West" atmosphere where people settled their own scores without involving authorities. Once in a while we'd hear a rumor about someone being raped or beaten on the backside, but no one ever seemed surprised.

Uncle Phil, always looking for a better way to earn easy money at the track, befriended a couple of "hot walkers." These were the men who worked intimately with the horses and knew things that the betting public didn't. Everyone knew (or assumed) that some races were fixed ahead of time and the jockeys made the outcome happen the way they, or someone more powerful, wanted it. Phil decided he would find a way inside that world and lay his hands on some precious information.

Dad never showed any indication that this was a bad idea. Usually he just chuckled and shook his head whenever Phil had a new idea about how to make money. In fact, that was most people's reaction to nearly anything Phil said.

The guys were at Ellis one afternoon for a full day of live racing, and it was one of those rare occasions when dad asked if I wanted to join them. I loved going to the track because dad was generous with his money and, at age fourteen, I enjoyed seeing the pretty girls in their shorts and sleeveless shirts. That day was blazing hot and sunny, and I won thirty-six dollars on an exacta box in the first race. It was the highlight of my betting life (both then and now).

Dad and I were in the usual box seats with Butch, Phil, and Chuck. At one point, I witnessed Phil standing beside the mutuels line talking with two Hispanic looking men. It was obvious from their dress that they were from the backside (both wearing dirty jeans and one sporting a dingy cowboy hat).

The conversation went on for several minutes, and at one point the exchange got very heated. Dad took notice of this as well but stayed in his seat. It became clear that Phil was being threatened. He threw up his hands and gave a "calm down, everything is fine" gesture to the two men. The episode ended with the one in the hat putting his finger in Phil's face, and then violently turning and storming away with his partner. No one mentioned the incident when Phil came back to our group. He looked concerned, but not scared, and I wrote it off as just one more example of his tendency to piss people off.

The rest of the afternoon passed in the usual fashion: betting and drinking. They talked horses and sports with other guys, they flirted with the younger female clerks, and they continued to drink. By the end of the seventh race, Butch indicated that he was out of money and ready to leave. Normally this was the cue for all (except Phil) to start heading for the gates.

But this time dad didn't move. He said, "I think I'm going to bet the late daily double here and stick around for the last two races. I really like the two in this next race."

This made Butch reconsider and he told dad to put twenty extra on the double and he would pay his share later. Dad was always making bets for the other guys, so I didn't realize that this one had a larger purpose. He didn't want to leave Phil alone.

Just then an old track buddy of dad's walked up and started chatting up the whole bunch. It was Denny Garrett, a man who had done everything from driving a semi, to owning and training horses, to being the mayor of a small Illinois town. He was the kind of guy who had something to say about any topic, even if he knew nothing about it. He was intelligent, but his thick South Midland accent (prevalent in the tri-state area of southern Illinois, Indiana, and Kentucky) made him seem less so.

"Well Johnny, havin' any luck today? These motherfuckers are killing me. I can't figure these ponies out here. I've always had more luck on the harness tracks myself."

"Not bad today, Denny. I like this two horse in the eighth for what it's worth. I heard you were opening up a bar somewhere over in Carmi. That true?"

"Mount Carmel actually. Yeah, I figure what the fuck. Give it a shot. I made some money off some oil wells over there so I'm lookin' to blow it now!" Denny said and let out a wheezy smoker's laugh.

Denny almost always had a lit Swisher Sweet cigar either in his mouth or between his fingers. I smoked them myself for a time in my twenties. A good cigar can be as delicious and satisfying as any food, but I gave them up at Karen's behest. The heavy aroma of a cigar now makes me think of old Denny. He and dad continued to chat for a few minutes, and then I caught something of interest.

"Hey, I saw your brother earlier with those two Mexican lookin' fuckers. Didn't look too good. You don't think he's into 'em for money do ya Johnny?"

"I saw them too. I don't know, but I'll keep my eyes open. Thanks Denny."

We watched the last two races (dad's two horse stumbled out of the gate and never got into it), and then started to make our way out of the grandstand. I noticed dad looking around and staying close to Phil as we walked. Phil drove a well-worn white Chrysler K-Car, and I was the first to spot it and the two young but rough looking "backsiders" standing in front of it. These weren't the same guys Phil had encountered earlier, but they looked equally upset. The white one wore blue flannel in spite of the blazing heat, and he was brandishing a tire iron. The other one, a Hispanic, had no visible weapons, but looked eager to hurt someone.

Butch noticed that our group had veered toward Phil's car. "Hey, what are you idiots doing? My car's over here." Just then he noticed the crew standing guard around Phil's sad little vehicle.

There were five of us with me included, but dad stopped and looked back at me before we made it to the K-Car. "You stay right here and don't move. Whatever happens, you don't move. Got it?" I nodded and froze. I removed my Cardinals cap and wiped the sweat from my brow while inching closer so I could make out what was being said.

Butch spoke first, "Gentlemen, what seems to be the problem? You've camped yourselves around our friend's car and we don't appreciate it." It was a diplomatic approach, much different from what dad would have probably led with. The Hispanic pulled a cigarette out of his mouth, dropped it on the pavement, and took a step forward.

"Oh, no problem. We just have a little business to discuss with your friend here." He gestured toward Uncle Phil.

"Okay, consider us his business associates and just tell us what this is about," Butch responded.

"Friend, I don't think you want to be associated with him. He's got debts to pay…and he hasn't been paying. Perhaps you'd like to vouch for him?" Butch and dad looked at Phil, who seemed to be shrinking as they stood there. We all knew that Phil was a compulsive gambler, they all were to some degree, but this was the first time any of them had heard about unpaid debts.

"How much?" Butch asked. Tire iron man used his free hand to lift a small pad of paper from his front pocket.

"Thirty-eight thousand seven hundred and twenty-two dollars as of this morning."

Dad finally broke his silence, "Jesus Christ, Phil! Thirty-eight thousand! From what? Who are these guys?

What the hell have you been doing?" Phil's head lowered and he said something inaudible.

"Phil has already been given three months extra to pay, and he has failed. That's why we're here," their apparent leader said. Even at fourteen I knew what he meant. Phil was in trouble and had no chance of paying off that much debt.

Dad addressed the group, "Okay, so what are his options? How long does he have? We can try to help him out, but you've gotta give us some time."

It was clear that Phil did not owe these men that much money. They were speaking for someone, probably one of the many horse owners who descended on Ellis each summer, who possessed far more power and funding than they could ever manage.

"We can give him one more week, but no more. What can I tell you gentlemen? Your friend here borrowed a lot of money from the wrong man and he knew the consequences of failing to reimburse."

The leader handed a card to dad and it appeared they were going to leave in peace. I heard a click and before anyone could react, the Hispanic man had produced a switchblade and buried it in Phil's right rear tire. "I'm afraid he'll have to find another way home today," he added and with that the two men quickly departed.

My mind raced as we drove toward home. I realized that dad had probably just saved Phil's life by sticking around longer than usual. I was worried for him, but dad's presence made me believe that he would not be harmed.

Butch dropped me at home and the rest of the guys met at Phil's house to discuss what to do. It seemed clear to me that Phil had only one real choice: leave town. That was also the advice that dad and his friends gave him that evening. They had no way of helping him pay off that amount, and not much interest in getting into a war with a dangerous man. How Phil could allow himself to get in so deep was beyond any of their comprehension. Later dad told me to forget what I had seen and heard that day, and that I shouldn't worry about things I can't control.

A week passed, and then two. Dad didn't talk about the incident and I didn't dare ask. We hadn't seen or heard from Phil, but that wasn't unusual. It seemed that the incident had blown over.

I started high school in August of '89 and forgot all about that day in the parking lot. Like most freshmen, I was focused on surviving the first semester in a huge school full of strange older kids. I had homework and basketball to keep me occupied, as well as Cardinal baseball. 1989 wasn't a bad year for the Redbirds. They finished with a winning record, but in third place in the division. Months passed quickly and I finished my first semester at Powell High with good grades and a starting position on the JV basketball team.

One night shortly after New Years' we got a call around midnight. The ringing awoke all of us, and dad stumbled into the kitchen to answer it since there was no phone jack in their bedroom. On the tenth ring (dad preferred no answering machine) he answered in a groggy voice, "Yeah? Oh my God! Yeah, I'll be there in a few minutes!" He sounded panicked. I sprung out of bed and into the hallway. He saw me in the darkness of the house and stopped. "Paul, put on some pants and get your jacket. I might need you."

It took us both just a minute to gather ourselves and then we were in the freezing cold of our Pontiac Bonneville (we never kept the same car for more than two years due to wrecks and dad's penchant for trading). We flew down Delmar and made a turn onto Barker Avenue. A few minutes later we saw the flashing red and blue lights of police cars and fire trucks. Then we saw the flames.

Phil's ragged rent house was fully engulfed, and

firefighters were struggling to keep the flames from catching the houses that were close on either side. Dad parked the car and immediately ran to the first policeman he saw. He was an older officer who knew dad well. "Where's Phil? Is he inside?"

"Johnny, we don't know. The house was like this when we all arrived. The firefighters haven't been able to get in there yet. The neighbors called it in. They said…"

Before he could finish, dad was stomping toward the house. First a cop and then a fireman tried to stop him, but dad was bigger, stronger, and more determined. He shoved them out of his way and kicked in the flaming front door. I expected to see fire shoot out through the open doorway, but none did. Dad ran into the house before anyone else could get near him. I think I screamed, but I'm not sure now. I know I was terrified. A moment later I noticed Butch standing next to me. I told him dad had gone inside and he gave me an unbelieving glance.

It seemed then that dad was in that house for a long time, much longer than a human could survive. In reality it was probably two minutes or less. Butch put his arm around me and told me how tough dad was and that he would be fine. I wanted to believe him, but the house was ablaze and the roof seemed ready to collapse. Three firefighters had followed dad into the house, and soon they emerged from the front entrance.

Dad was still nowhere to be found. I felt a panic creep into my mind: what if he died in there? I had an image of dad's funeral, and for a second I wondered what songs they would play.

Those thoughts abruptly halted when I spotted dad's massive frame in the doorway. He was empty-handed. He stumbled out and fell to one knee in the front yard. A paramedic ran up and gave him oxygen. He took just a few breaths from the mask and rose to his feet. His face and clothes were covered in black soot. I noticed his sleeves on both arms were burned off to the elbow and his bare arms were badly burned. He didn't seem to notice. His eyes stared vacantly into the street as he walked past us toward his car. I started to cry as I realized what had happened. Phil was dead inside, and dad had failed to rescue him.

"Jesus, Johnny! Was he in there? Did you see him?" Butch asked, marveling at dad's condition and the fact that he was still standing. Dad didn't speak for a while. He leaned against the Bonneville and stared at the blazing house. Then I heard him whisper Phil's name. Finally, after several minutes, dad focused on us and looked at Butch.

"I told him to stay gone. I told him to keep his ass down south. What the hell was he doing back here?" Dad said shaking his head.

"So he was in there," Butch replied.

"I found him in his bed. He was tied to the bedpost...and his throat was slashed. He was probably already dead when they lit the fire. Christ, I hope he was already dead."

"Oh Johnny, I'm...I don't know what to say. I'm sorry. I..." Butch stopped. He welled up, but did not openly cry.

Apparently Phil had followed their advice and gone south to live for a few months. Maybe he thought the whole situation had blown over, or he was out of money and had to come back home. He had made the stupid mistake of renting the same house, and they had been waiting for him to return. I don't want to think about what they put him through before they cut his throat. The fire concealed any evidence of who had been there or what was done to Uncle Phil. Dad never mentioned the two men we had encountered to the police. He knew they would have long since moved on to another track.

Dad was very quiet in the weeks after that night, and some evenings he never left the refuge of their bedroom. Then, as time passed, his typical lifestyle resumed. He worked a little at the church, hung out with the guys at the bar, and spent some rare evenings at home. Dad swore me to secrecy about Phil's demise. Mom, and the rest of the neighborhood, was led to believe that he fell asleep with a lit cigarette. We never talked about it again.

I believe the way Phil died shook dad to his core. How could it not? Dad was a stoic man, aside from the occasional emotional outburst during a ball game, and it was difficult to tell sometimes what he was thinking or feeling. His newfound faith in the Almighty took a major hit that night. I'm not sure he ever fully recovered it.

After a while his attendance at church reverted back to his pre-baptismal days. His meetings with the pastor, so instrumental in helping him get his life back, also stopped. Within a year of Phil's death, he had even quit his church custodial job. It was as if he was holding a grudge against God and didn't want to be associated with Him, even for a paycheck. Though I didn't realize it then, nothing was ever the same after Phil's death.

Dad couldn't shake those images that only he carried, and it slowly consumed him from the inside out.

Top of the Seventh

Lance Lynn started his second inning of work, and things didn't go well. I was caught up thinking about Phil when a crack of the bat made me raise my head. Adrian Beltre crushed the second pitch he saw deep to right centerfield. After the Cardinals spent twenty minutes staging a game-tying rally in which the ball never left the infield, Beltre put the Rangers ahead once again in a blink. Dad let out a hiss and turned to me.

"You see what I'm saying? The Cardinals keep throwing away their chances and they're gonna get beat. These guys have too many big guns."

I agreed. It had been a frustrating night. But the 2011 Cardinals would have had it no other way. They had put their fans through more agonizing losses during the regular season than I could ever remember. Blown saves, one-run losses, missed opportunities…yet here they were in the World Series.

I said, "I'm not worried. We've been in worse predicaments than this and come back. Still a lot of game left to play."

As if to quell my rare bout of optimism in the face of adversity, Nelson Cruz swatted a 1-2 pitch from Lynn toward the left field seats. It was a bomb that ended up in the third deck. Beltre and Cruz had gone back-to-back to start the seventh, and now the Rangers had a 6-4 lead. We sat stunned, and suddenly my faith in the endless heart of this Cardinals team was in doubt. I regrouped after watching the replays.

"We've got to find a way to hold them at six runs. We'll come back, but the bullpen has to hold the rest of the way."

Dad nodded. "I'm not sure they can. This Rangers lineup is tough. Maybe it's their year," he said as the visage of Nolan Ryan, owner and most well-known face of the

Rangers, was shown on the screen sporting a cautious smile. Perhaps he could sense that this might be the inning that secures their first ever World Series trophy.

Though my spirits were dampened by the sudden turn of events, I attempted to bring us back to the real reason I was there. I knew dad was finished with talking about Phil, and there was no reason to pick at the subject anymore. I was more interested in recalling what came next: dad's "backslide." First, I checked my phone for the time and any other messages from Karen. I thought it must be only a few minutes more before she would be rolling in with Jack.

"Dad, why did you quit going to church? You really seemed to be enjoying it, I thought you had a good relationship with Reverend Marne." He sniffed and didn't answer right away. He was noticeably weaker and paler than at the beginning of the game.

"Well, for one thing I didn't need everyone patting me on the back telling me how sorry they were about Phil. I hate that shit."

"Is that it?"

"No. I was mad. Really mad. I was mad at Phil for being so stupid. I was mad at myself for not having stopped him before things got out of hand. And, yeah, I was mad at God. I mean, I just get on board with the church thing, I get dipped in front of the whole damn town, and then He lets my brother get murdered like that. It didn't make sense to me."

Part of me didn't blame him for feeling that way. But, as I've learned, playing the "why me" game isn't very constructive. Bad things, even terrible things, are going to happen in this life. To me, the people who blame God are just spinning their wheels.

I thought about making this argument to dad, but he was in no mood or shape for that kind of debate. "What about now? Do you still have faith? Do you ever pray?"

"You mean, do I think I'm still saved even though I stopped going to church and started drinking again?"

"Yes."

"Well, your mother says the Baptist credo is 'once saved, always saved.' So if you go by that then I suppose I am. You know I was serious about it when I accepted Jesus, that's why I agreed to take a bath in front of God and everyone. But I guess you could say I'm still pissed at Him, so no I don't pray or read the Bible or any of that. I've had all the church I'm gonna have."

***

I turned fifteen in 1990, the spring after Phil's murder. That fall, as a sophomore, I won a starting position as the shooting guard on our varsity team. From that point I consumed myself with school work and practices, so much that I was able to successfully block out the image of Phil's burning house and the pain of knowing that dad had fallen completely back into his old life. I still kept the tradition of listening to Cardinal games alive while doing homework in my room, but the days of dad and I listening together were over.

It was a new era both in our house and in the Cardinals organization. In the midst of a miserable first half in 1990, Whitey Herzog resigned as the manager. The names and faces I had grown to love during the '80s: Coleman, McGee, VanSlyke, Pendleton, Tudor, and many others, were replaced by a crop of young talents like Bernard Gilkey, Ray Lankford, Brian Jordan, Felix Jose, and Tom Pagnozzi. They were an exciting group to follow, but would prove incapable of producing the type of success I had come to expect.

Dad suffered a number of mishaps during that time, fueled in large part by his accelerated drinking. Having quit his custodial job, he once again convinced Ray Welsh to hire him for his Electronics business. But, instead of just making deliveries, dad was also given the task of setting up

TV antennas and hooking up home theatre systems. He seemed to enjoy it, but it didn't last long. One day, on the roof of the widowed Martha Simpkins (another of mom's church pals), dad was replacing her antenna with a new, more powerful one. He somehow managed to slide off her roof and land on the sidewalk running between her house and the neighbors'. While he was lucky to be alive, he shattered his hip and suffered yet another concussion.

Months later, with dad healed, but now permanently fired by Ray, dad resumed working as an umpire at the high school level. We heard no complaints for a time, and I even watched once as he called a game involving Powell High. But, before the end of the 1991 season, dad was fired and banned for life. He apparently got into the face of a kid who questioned one of his strike calls. Dad put his finger into the kid's chest and told him to sit down. When the kid's coach came out to defend his player, the conflict exploded as dad nearly knocked him back into his dugout with one punch to his jaw. Dad walked off the field that day and never again put on an umpire's uniform.

That incident was a clear sign that dad had fallen into a dark place. He had encountered a lot of angry and brazen softball players in his time as an ump, and managed to keep his cool every time. One pimple-faced kid turns and gives a questioning look about a borderline pitch, and suddenly he's out of control.

A lot of the kids at school knew the stories about my dad, and to their credit they were mostly sympathetic or at least apathetic about it. I didn't talk about him to my friends, and I made sure to only bring a date home when I knew dad was out. He didn't meet a single girlfriend of mine during my high school years.

It was during basketball season, when I had plenty of things to distract me from dad's increasingly tumultuous presence, that I thought of him most. Like any son, I wanted him to come to my games and root for me. I wanted to hear him cheering and see him high-fiving the other fathers when Powell won a big game. I wanted him to tell me the next day at the kitchen table how great I had played and how proud he was of me.

And every time we took the floor and I saw mom sitting with Pauline and Megan, but with no sign of dad, I felt my heart sink a little. On one hand, I was thankful that he wasn't coming to the games because his behavior had turned erratic, but I would have jumped out of my shoes at the first sight of him in the crowd.

At a friend's house one night I watched the film *Hoosiers.* A few of our varsity players were staying over and watching inspirational movies in preparation for our upcoming sectional games. I had to excuse myself halfway through the movie because I could no longer contain my emotions.

I completely identified with the character of Everett, who was dealing with his alcoholic father Shooter. In the darkness of the house none of the others could tell I had been crying when I came out of the bathroom. I struggled to contain tears again at the end when Jimmy hit the game-winner to give tiny Hickory (Milan High School in real life) the 1952 Indiana state championship. I sat silently as the credits rolled and Chip Wells, the senior captain on our team, looked at me.

"Are you okay man? Haven't you ever seen that movie before?"

"First time." That was all I could get out for fear of letting out a sob. I blame mom for making me into a crier. My whole life I've been crying at movies and trying to hide it. The end of *Glory*, when the 54th Massachusetts regiment heroically charges Fort Wagner, gets me every time. When I saw *Saving Private Ryan* for the first time I was alone in the theatre with a few much older couples. I sat through the credits and a few minutes after to collect myself because I was openly sobbing after the old man Ryan asked his wife if he had lived a good life.

The worst, however, was my first encounter with the film *Field of Dreams.* I was in college and dating Karen when she rented the movie thinking I would like it. While I had heard of the movie and knew the basic plot, I had never watched it. With Karen curled around my arm we watched in the confines of her dorm room.

I struggled mightily to contain the tears when Ray Kinsella asked his dead father if he wanted to have a catch. I thought I was doing a pretty good job of covering up, but Karen noticed my body shaking. She looked at me and saw the tears streaming down. Something in her eyes hit me hard, and I buried my face in her shoulder. We had only been dating a few months at the time, and she had no knowledge of my father or our history. I wept for a few minutes while Karen gently rocked us back and forth. After that I told her some of the story of Johnny Ray. The way she comforted me that night, the sweetness of her kisses, the kindness in her eyes...I fell in love with Karen that night.

***

At some point in high school I started to accept the idea that dad was a lost cause. I began to prepare for the possibility that we would never have the relationship that I really wanted. Time seemed to speed up when I reached high school, and suddenly I was a senior.

I was excited because our basketball team had a chance for a special season. We had a great mix of juniors and seniors who were talented and loved playing together. I was also taking a lot of advanced classes and participating in groups like Student Council and Business Professionals of America. On top of that, I had my first serious girlfriend. Stephanie was a sophomore soccer player who I met through mutual friends. She was a beautiful blonde, short with an athletic build. She had probably the best legs I've ever seen on a woman.

Some days I was so busy attending to all of these interests that I barely had time to think. That was the whole point. I buried my anger and disappointment under a mountain of responsibilities. Actually, I've been doing that my entire life. These are the things that I learned through the ACA meetings. Like so many others who grew up in an alcoholic household, I became a people-pleaser. I drew my happiness from the acceptance of others and by committing myself to many different activities.

I also possessed an overdeveloped sense of loyalty. I was afraid of letting anyone down, and I rarely said no to them. Even when I went away to college, and I knew the relationship with Stephanie couldn't last, I allowed it to continue out of a fear of hurting her. We carried on for a few more months, and finally it came down to her saying goodbye because I couldn't.

In ACA I learned the three rules that children of alcoholics live by: don't trust, don't feel, and don't talk. I lived by those even though I didn't know about them at the time. Karen was the first person that I allowed myself to really care for, and whom I could openly talk to about anything. That night in the dorm room opened the door to a lifelong, loving relationship with her. Thank God she chose *Field of Dreams* that night instead of her first choice, *Pretty Woman*.

My senior year was a dream scenario for a lot of high school kids. I was the captain of the basketball team, Vice President of Student Council, a fully accepted member of the "jock" clique, and carrying a 3.9 GPA while taking a load of college prep classes. I also managed to squeeze in a part time job working maintenance for the Silver Tower Apartments.

From a distance I must have looked like one of those annoyingly perfect characters from a teen movie. What no one realized was that I was compensating for a huge hole in my heart. Over the summer of '92, dad moved from worthless drunk to neighborhood pariah. Kids at school knew the stories about dad, but I was a master of ducking and deflecting any questions about him. Those stories drove me to want to succeed even more to make up for all of his failings.

In August of '92, as my senior year was beginning, the Cardinals were in the midst of celebrating their one hundredth season with a young team that was talented but light on pitching. They drew the nickname "Cardiac Cards" that year because they staged a number of late inning rallies. They were hosting the Atlanta Braves for a weekend series, and I went to a friend's house to watch the Saturday night game on TBS (we still didn't have cable). That was also the night that dad was thrown in jail.

The night looked to be a bust for me early as the Cardinals fell behind 9-0 by the fourth inning. Rheal Cormier, our starting pitcher, got bombed for eight runs in less than three innings. I thought about taking off early and heading home to finish some homework (unusual for me on a Saturday night), but something told me to stick around.

My persistence paid off, and the Cards began an impressive comeback. They continued to chip away at the normally dominant John Smoltz, and were in striking distance (down 11-9) in the bottom of the eighth. Felix Jose, the only real source of power on that team, blasted a game-tying home run. Later, Luis Alicea delivered a clutch RBI base hit to put them ahead for good at 12-11. I jumped onto my friend's coffee table and screamed as Brian Jordan scored the go-ahead run.

Two miles away, at our house, two of our classmates were also screaming. Dad came home early from the bar that evening (sometimes he would slip into the house and try to coax mom into a conjugal visit), and was walking from the garage toward the back door when he heard rustling and giggling coming from the front. Though dad was a large man, he was agile on his feet and managed to creep up on the two teenagers who were toilet-papering the one large Bradford pear tree in our front yard.

One of them was busy flinging a roll into the tree, while the other was preparing to hit the three bushes in front of our living room window. Dad grabbed the one near the bushes by the back of the neck and, without a word, threw him into the trunk of the pear tree. The other kid reacted slowly. He didn't see dad coming at him on a moonless evening. Dad took the second kid by the front of his shirt and lifted him into the air. According to their statements to the police afterward, dad said, "You little bastards. You picked the wrong house for this shit!"

Dad then proceeded to throw the kid straight down onto the grass. He turned to the first kid, still writhing on the ground after hitting the trunk squarely, and walked to him. He grabbed the kid's collar and dragged him toward his counterpart who hadn't moved since being planted in the turf. Dad grabbed his collar with his free hand and began to drag both boys into the street.

According to a witness who drove up just as dad was hauling them off his property, dad slammed their heads together once and then turned, walking back to the house. He left the boys lying unconscious and bleeding in the middle of Delmar Avenue. The witness, a man named Perkins, who lived nearby but had never had any contact with dad, was so shaken that he left his car and ran to a neighbor's house to call the police.

When the cops showed up, dad was camped at the kitchen table as if awaiting their arrival. The two officers, both younger and unfamiliar with dad's reputation, insisted that he come to the station for questioning. He cooperated, and after the police took his statement and spoke with the teenagers' parents, he was taken into custody. Both the boys were sixteen years old and though I knew who they were, we weren't friends. I couldn't imagine why they had chosen our house to pull such a stupid prank. Most of the other local folks either liked Johnny Ray too much or feared him enough not to mess with him or his property.

Though bail was set at only a hundred dollars, mom refused to pay it and let dad spend the night in jail. I didn't find out until I came home the next morning to get ready for church. Instead, we made a trip to the police station. The boys, who said later they thought they were toilet papering Missy Knapp's house (a girl one of them had a crush on), were released from the hospital on that Sunday as well. Both had cuts and bruises, but remarkably that was the extent of the damage.

That fact, along with the reality that they were trespassing on private property, helped to shield dad from any major charges. None of that was yet known on that Sunday morning, and mom was left contemplating the possibility of her husband doing real jail time. When the three of us arrived at the station, mom sent me back to speak to him because she couldn't face him. Though I was hesitant, I agreed for her sake.

The officers led me through a series of doors until we approached what was commonly called the "drunk tank." In Powell on a Saturday night, the drunk tank might have as many as a dozen men taking up residence. By nine o'clock on Sunday morning, there were only four men lounging in a cell that was very reminiscent of what I had seen on TV.

The concrete block walls were painted a hideous slime green, and long benches lined each of the three walls. Two more benches in the middle of the cell ran perpendicular to the bars through which I spoke to my father. As I approached, he was seated with his head between his hands on one of the inner benches.

The escorting officer announced in a purposely too-loud voice, "Gibson! You got a visitor!" Dad looked up and we made eye contact. He looked terrible. His face was grey, which made his bloodshot eyes stand out even more.

It was clear he hadn't slept at all. I saw appreciation in those eyes, probably because he was glad it was me and not mom seeing him like this.

"Hey dad, mom sent me to see how you're doing. You okay?" He rose and walked to the bars just in front of me.

"Is your mom here?"

"Yeah, she's with Megan out in the lobby. She said she didn't want to see you."

"Those little bastards are lucky I didn't kill 'em. Did you see what they were doing to our yard? Who the hell were they anyway?" He had no remorse at all in his voice or demeanor.

"Just a couple of punks from school. It sounds like they were trying to prank some girl and just got the wrong house."

"You bet your ass they had the wrong house! Well, any word on when I'm getting out of here? Did your mom post bail?"

"Um, she's not going to do that. She said you're going to get whatever's coming to you this time. She's pretty upset dad."

He turned and let out a long sigh, and then paced around the cell for a minute.

"Okay Paul, would you do me a favor? Just tell her that I'm sorry. I lost my cool and I probably took it a little too far. And tell her I love her. Would you do that for me?"

"Yeah, dad. I'll let her know. Anything else?" I said this with some sarcasm. I felt a real sense of disgust flowing through me during that exchange. Part of me was hoping for serious charges so he could have a few months or even a year to dry out. Dad ended up staying in jail for another three days and then was brought before a judge.

Fortunately the judge was another of dad's old acquaintances from his softball days, and he went easy on him. One year probation and time served. Dad celebrated, naturally, with the guys at Lamasco's. For our family it was just one more reminder that the man who had once committed his life to Christ was never coming back.

There were others. Though dad's bad decisions never seemed to stick to him, they nearly always had consequences for those he was supposed to love. As I grew older, his shadow grew heavier and my need to escape grew stronger.

In my job at Silver Tower, which I worked all year except during basketball season, I learned a lot about making repairs and doing basic home maintenance. It was enjoyable because the manager, Kevin Builtman, was a very nice man and didn't mind accommodating my schedule. But dad also got to know Kevin. When I started working there, dad would come in sometimes just to have chats with him about how I was doing.

Dad would also show up every other Saturday morning to pick up my paycheck for me. This wasn't a favor, it was his way of making sure he got his tribute. On payday weekends dad would get my check, then come back and pick me up from the house. We would go to the nearby Royal Foods grocery store where the manager was happy to cash the check for us. I signed the check, the cash would go to dad, and then we would walk back to the car. He would give me "my share," drop me back at the house, and then begin enjoying his weekend funded by my labor.

I never protested because there was no point. I accepted this arrangement as a part of life, and I consoled myself with the knowledge that things would be different once I left for college. I tried to square it in my mind by pretending I was paying my dues. But being taken advantage of by your own father is a far greater burden than the loss of money. It eats away at your heart and makes you start looking around for an exit.

I found my exit through basketball. Dad and I both knew when I left home on a bus in the fall of 1993 that I wouldn't be coming back. He didn't wait around to say goodbye on the morning I left. He made sure to be out of the house early, which he never did otherwise at that stage of his life. I took it as a sign that I was doing the right thing.

***

I looked up and realized that the Rangers were still batting in the top of the seventh. Derek Holland, their pitcher, had reached second base after a failed sacrifice bunt attempt and then a wild pitch by Octavio Dotel. Dotel had come to the Cardinals in a mid-season trade and did nice work throughout the playoffs. He was especially good during the NLCS as the antidote to the Brewers' slugger Ryan Braun. But now, facing Ian Kinsler with two outs, he was unable to wriggle out of trouble.

Kinsler laced a single to center and Holland came around to give the Rangers a 7-4 lead. I slumped back in the recliner. I saw dad shaking his head from the corner of my eye. Neither of us said a word, but we were both thinking the same thing: the series was slipping away. After treating us to a season full of difficult-to-watch losses, it seemed our boys had saved the most painful one for last.

Just before Elvis Andrus struck out swinging to end that devastating inning, I got a text from Karen saying they had arrived. It was perfect timing. It would take introducing Jack to his grandpa to get my mind off what appeared to be certain defeat for the Cardinals.

Bottom of the Seventh

I left the bedroom and headed for the front door. My heart began to churn just as it had when I first walked into the house earlier that evening. I opened the door just as Karen and Jack were walking through the porch entrance. I smiled when I saw how Karen had dressed him. He was wearing his red Cardinals T-shirt with Pujols' name and number five on the back (his favorite player).

It occurred to me that I may be having a difficult conversation with him in a few months because Albert was going to be a free agent. Jack was also sporting his navy blue Cardinals cap, which he wore most of the time, including while he slept. He ran to me across the ruffled green, artificial turf and wrapped his arms around my left leg. The feeling I get from those moments is pure joy.

"Hey buddy! Have you been watching the game?" I asked, kneeling to his level.

"Yeah, but they're not doing very good. We need a rally!" He had heard me say that during countless games.

"You're right, pal. Still time for a comeback. Did your mom tell you who you're going to meet here tonight?"

"My grandpa Johnny!" He said, sounding genuinely excited about it. All Jack had ever been told about my father was that he was sick a lot, so we had to stay away. There's no explaining alcoholism to a five year old.

"That's right! And he's excited to meet you!"

They both entered the front room where mom and Megan greeted them with hugs and kisses. Another surge of positive energy ran through me. There hadn't been this much love and happy vibes in that house in a long time. As skeptical as I had been coming tonight, I was now just as convinced that I had made the right choice.

After Jack had endured the shower of adoration, I picked him up and carried him back toward dad's room. I could hear that the game had resumed with the good guys in need of runs.

"Are you ready to see your grandpa?" He looked a bit apprehensive.

"Yeah. Is he a big Cardinals fan like us?" He knew the answer to this, but he just needed the reassurance. Like me, he would use baseball as a way of connecting with Johnny Ray.

"Actually, he's the biggest Cardinals fan in the world! I've never met anyone who loves them more than he does. You'll see." With that, Jack's smile returned. He has the cutest big dimples that came from Karen's side. His slightly oversized ears and deeply set dark eyes come from me.

We turned and entered the bedroom. Dad looked up at us while taking a sip of water. I've never seen a more dramatic transformation in a person's face. A huge smile broke out, and his eyes gleamed as they once had when I was a kid. It had been many years since I had seen dad sober and happy at the same time. He carefully put the glass on his nightstand, never breaking his gaze on Jack. Dad was completely transfixed.

"Dad, I'd like you to meet your grandson Jack. Jack, this is your grandpa Johnny."

Dad used what strength he had remaining to pull himself completely upright in the bed. I slowly bent to let Jack down, not knowing if he would be willing to leave the safety of my arms. When his shoes touched the carpet I let him go, and Jack steadied himself. He was studying dad's face just as dad was studying his. For a long moment the only sound in the room was that of Joe Buck's voice from the broadcast. It appeared the Cardinals rally was not going to start in the seventh. The first two batters had already been retired.

Finally, dad spoke. "Well hello Jack! You know you look just like your daddy did when he was your age! Except he didn't have those adorable dimples! And I see

you're a Cardinals fan! Who's your favorite player?"
Without a word, Jack turned and let him see the back of his
T-shirt. "Oh, Albert. Good choice. He's a great player isn't
he?"

"Yeah, he hits a lot of home runs. He hit three in
one game the other night!"

And just that simply, Jack had established basically
the same relationship with Johnny Ray as I had. For dad, it
must have seemed like traveling back in time. Dad was
nodding in agreement as he looked up at me.

"Paul, you've got a beautiful kid here. I'm glad to
see you're raising him right!" I didn't answer him right
away, I just smiled. I could see that they were becoming
fast friends. Dad reached out to Jack with his huge paw of a
right hand, and Jack slowly raised his to meet the invitation
for a shake. "And he's got a good handshake too!"

"Daddy says that men always greet each other with
a handshake," Jack said.

Dad's face broke again into a glowing smile. The
knowledge that I had subconsciously been punishing my
father by keeping him from his only grandson would hit me
later with crushing effects. In the moment, I chose to focus
on the beauty of seeing two generations of Gibson men
discovering each other.

"You're a smart boy, you know that? I'll bet you
already know how to count and say your ABC's and
everything!" Dad said, still perusing every feature of Jack's
face.

"I can say the ABC's front ways and back ways,
and I can count to a hundred!"

"Wow! That is impressive! Paul, you've got a
genius on your hands here!"

"Yep, he was the only kid in his preschool class
who could count that high. Karen is really good about
working with him on that stuff. I just fill his head with
baseball jargon!" I said.

Dad nodded again. "Hey, that's important too. A boy needs to know the game. Jack, do you like to play baseball?"

Jack answered quickly, "Yeah! I played tee-ball this year and it was fun! I played third base most of the time."

Naturally I was still keeping one eye on the ball game. Jack hadn't noticed that Pujols was batting, perhaps for the final time as a Cardinal. He grounded the ball to short and the seventh inning ended quietly. They went 1-2-3 against Holland. Three runs down and six outs left. I pushed away my growing despair over the game. I wanted to savor this meeting, for it would be a once in a lifetime occasion.

Mom slipped into the room and stood next to me. Karen and Megan had begun a conversation in the front room and were probably still there. Though they don't get much face to face time, they're constantly communicating through Facebook or texts. Karen has an amazing relationship with my sister and mother, as if she were born into our family. But she has no love for dad and I knew she had no intention of even peeking her head in to say hello to him. I couldn't blame her. She had heard all the stories about him, plus she was there during the debacle on our wedding day.

Mom said, "Well these two seem to be hitting it off! Johnny, can you believe those dimples! He's just the cutest boy I've ever seen. No offense, Pauly! Jack, would you like some milk and a couple of Oreos? I'll bring them to you." She turned and left in a hurry. I noticed that Jack had moved to the edge of dad's bed. I was proud of him for not being scared. Dad was still a charmer, even if he wasn't at his best.

Dad asked, "Jack, would you like to come up here and watch the next inning with me? Maybe you'll bring our boys some luck! They need it!"

Before I could even prepare to excuse Jack for

being too shy (which he normally was around people he just met), he was crawling up into the bed and snuggling in under dad's left arm. Again, all I could do was smile. I was amazed at the ease of how my father and son had become friends. I settled into the recliner and looked at them. Dad began to quiz him about what he knew of the Cardinals and the game of baseball. Jack was impressing him with his knowledge. Another flush of pride hit me.

Then, in a moment that should have been singularly satisfying, I felt a pang of jealousy. I was jealous of how loving and gentle dad was being with my son. Why had he reserved this behavior for his grandson? Where was this kind of attention and praise when I was growing up? I hated myself for even having those thoughts, but I couldn't help it. This man was fawning over Jack in a way that I almost never experienced as his son.

Still, Jack was clearly enjoying himself and he was brightening the waning moments of dad's life. I prayed that those negative feelings would drift away and allow me to enjoy a rare moment of peace. Eventually they did, and I was able to appreciate the surreal vision of my past and future snuggling together in dad's bed.

***

When Karen told me she was pregnant in the late spring of 2005 it wasn't a surprise. We had made the decision about six months before to start trying for a baby. But knowing you're trying for a baby and actually knowing one is on the way are very different feelings. I was excited to be starting a new chapter of our life together. But I was equally terrified by the prospect of becoming a father when I had only the example of Johnny Ray to draw from. The questions came quickly: what kind of father would I be? Was I too selfish to be a dad? Would I repeat the pattern of putting myself ahead of my child?

As usual, mom helped to calm my fears. I called her that night and told her she was going to be a grandmother. I cried over the phone as I explained my fears.

She calmly answered, "Pauly, are you listening to me? I want you to hear me. You are an amazing man. You have all of your father's best qualities and none of his flaws. You're a loving husband, you have a great career, and you have a strong faith. There is no doubt in my mind that you'll be a great dad. You are not your father and you never will be."

"But mom, what if I make mistakes? What if I screw this kid up with all my issues?"

"Of course you're going to make mistakes. No parent is perfect…no kid is either. There's going to be days when you feel like you're failing. But that doesn't matter. I think the most important thing you can do for that little boy or girl is just being there. Think about how you felt when you were listening to games with your dad. He wasn't doing anything special, he was just here. He wasn't here nearly enough, but when he was things were good. Just be there with the kid and love them, and they'll think you're the greatest dad in the world!"

Mom is a rock of faith and sound advice. Thank God for her.

When we found out we were having a boy, my fears intensified. I didn't want the ghost of Johnny Ray hovering over my relationship with Jack. The best thing I did was have long talks with Karen about what kind of parents we would be. Our communication is great, and one of the major reasons why our marriage is still going strong. She helped me to use my fears about being a bad father as motivation.

She said, "Think of it this way. You come from a long line of terrible fathers, and your goal is to break that trend. Make it your mission to be better than your father in every way possible. That's a pretty low bar, so it shouldn't be too tough. And then someday, after we've raised Jack into a wonderful and caring man like his dad, he will have children and be a better father than you were. Maybe you can start a new trend in the opposite direction!"

I loved the way she phrased it, and I took her words to heart. I swore I would never make Jack feel abandoned and manipulated the way dad did me. I would make sure that he knew without any doubt that he has a daddy that loves and supports him. And it really was much easier than I had imagined. With my focus on being there as much as possible for Jack and Karen, there was little room for the selfish old me to maneuver. Having a child really does change your life, and in my case it made me a better person.

But the specter of Johnny Ray was never far from the forefront of my mind. Even now, I constantly compare what I say and do with Jack to my experiences with dad. Sometimes I hear his words coming out of my mouth, especially concerning the Cardinals. Most evenings during the season, when we're done with supper and the kitchen is cleaned up, Jack will sit with me in my recliner and watch the games on Fox Sports Midwest. He can recite most of the entire roster and their numbers. And he loves imitating their batting stances when we're playing around in the yard. He mimics Albert's most of the time. God, I hope he can hit like him someday!

***

As I continued to watch the two of them getting to know each other, I noticed that dad would raise his head up every so often and give me a look. I wasn't sure what it was at first, but then I recognized the message. He was thanking me for this time with Jack. I initially thought that my coming home would be a kind of gift to him, but it was Jack's homecoming that was the real prize. He was soaking up every second with the kid because he knew he didn't have many left. It was touching, sad, and maddening all at once. Never had I seen him so engaged and loving toward another person for this long.

I heard Jack say, "Stan Musial? Yeah, daddy says he was the greatest Cardinal ever. But he played a long time ago."

"That's right. I saw him play when I was growing up. He was amazing. He twisted like a corkscrew when he swung, but boy did he hit the ball hard! Have you been to the stadium and seen his statue?" Dad asked.

"No, daddy says we're going to wait until I'm seven and then I can go with him to a game. He says that's when you took him to his first game."

"Oh, I see. Well, I'm sure you'll get to go a lot when you're older. Your daddy will make sure of that!" Dad looked at me as he said this. I know lots of folks who will take babies to the ballpark, and they would say I'm silly to make him wait. But I know how special it was for me, and I want to make sure that when the time comes he will not only enjoy the day but carry it with him for the rest of his life.

Mom came in the room and brought Jack a plate with a few Oreos and a glass of milk. Normally I would object to Jack having sugar this late at night, but there was no use in arguing with mom. She wanted to see the boy smile and enjoy a cookie, and if he stayed up until three a.m. that was Karen and I's problem. Jack twisted the first cookie and ate the half with no cream on it first, just the way I eat them. Mom's face lit up when she saw this.

Then she looked at me. "It's just like having a little Pauly in the house again! I'm so glad you brought him over!"

Should I have brought Jack to his grandparents' house before that night? Probably. I certainly felt that way after seeing how he and dad bonded. I had been too caught up in trying to avoid the confrontation with dad to see how Jack would change the equation. But even if I had disregarded all the baggage of my childhood, I still wouldn't have showed up because of the anger I was holding on to from my wedding day.

That was the final emotional scab that I needed to pick before the night ended. And it was the one that I feared would ruin all the progress we had made during game six. I couldn't bring it up with Jack present, so I told myself that I would let him stick around for one more half inning for dad's sake. Then we would discuss the topic that I had intentionally shied away from: the day I banished dad from my life.

Top of the Eighth

A swirling storm of conflicting emotions made it difficult for me to know what my next move should be. First, there was immense joy and satisfaction as I watched Jack falling in love with his grandfather. Then there was the stabbing sensation of guilt from not allowing Jack to have met him sooner. Finally, there was dread over our impending conversation about my wedding and the knowledge that the World Series was quickly slipping away from the Cardinals.

I needed to get out and reset my thoughts. I stood up and stretched. Mark Rzepczynski, a lefty reliever who came to the Cards in a mid-season trade, was in the game and pitching to Josh Hamilton. If there was any hope for a rally, "Scrabble" would have to hold them at seven. I walked out of the room and toward the front of the house. I heard voices in the living room and found that Karen and Megan had settled in for a long conversation.

"Where's mom?" I asked.

"I think she's in the kitchen. She wanted to give 'us girls' some time to catch up," said Karen. She was perched on the couch and wrapped up in one of mom's many afghan blankets. "How's Jack doing with your dad?"

"I think he's found a new BFF. The kid is snuggled up with him in the bed and they're talking baseball like they've known each other for years. It's one of the best things I've ever seen," I said, grinning and shaking my head. Both women let out a soft "ahh" and then giggled.

"I'm not surprised. You know dad's quite the charmer when he wants to be," Megan said from dad's recliner. She also had a blanket around her legs and her rainbow colored, Wizard of Oz inspired socks were showing.

"Yeah, when he wants to be. Too bad he never wanted to be with us. You know that's going to be a fun conversation…explaining to Jack why he won't be able to visit his grandpa anymore," I said.

"Well, that's a problem for another day. Best to just let him enjoy this time tonight. Best for all of us to do that, actually. We won't get another night like this one," said Megan. I knew she was right. Both Jack and dad deserved this meeting, and I shouldn't ruin it by thinking too far ahead. Sometimes it's best to just stay in the moment.

"Megan, can you do something for me? In a few minutes could you come in there and grab Jack? Just make up some excuse why you need him. I hate to pull him away from dad now that they're hitting it off so well, but we've got something else yet to talk about and Jack can't be in the middle of that. It might go bad, I'm not sure."

"The wedding?" Megan asked, as if she didn't know.

"Yeah. I've been debating whether or not to even bring it up, but I have to."

Karen responded, "I think he'll understand that you need some time alone with your dad. We'll turn the game on for him in here."

I walked to Karen and kissed her forehead. She gave my arm a squeeze, and I instantly gained more strength. As I turned to leave the room, Megan gave me a wink and a sly grin. I was grateful to both of them for being with me.

Megan had obviously made her peace with dad before that night because she was remarkably calm and pleasant. She seemed much more concerned about my emotional state than her own, but then again that's just who she is. Megan, like Karen, is simply a better human being than I am. They're both more generous, loving, and supportive than I'll ever be. Their presence in the house that night was crucial in helping me deal with the meeting with dad. I left the living room with a renewed sense of purpose.

***

The Cardinals beat the Cubs 2-1 in twelve innings on Saturday, July 12th, 1997. Andy Benes, the pride of Central High School in Evansville, pitched nine strong innings but didn't get the win. It was a good day at Wrigley for a team that ended up sputtering to a fourth place finish. Also on that day, Karen and I got married.

Though the day ended with celebration, it was tainted by the poisonous presence of Johnny Ray.

I knew after the night we watched *Field of Dreams* that Karen was the woman I would marry. It still took me another nine months to give her a ring. It was a tiny, pathetic little speck of a stone, but Karen accepted it like it was the Hope Diamond. We stayed engaged for over a year as we both finished our degrees at SIU. She spent her final semester student teaching in a room full of second graders. I spent mine battling in the Missouri Valley Conference. The team didn't fare very well, and frankly, I was tiring of basketball and not at all unhappy when our season ended in March. I was ready to focus on graduating, getting married, and starting a new life in a new place.

Karen and her parents wanted to have the wedding in their hometown of Carmi, Illinois. I was on board with the idea completely, though I knew mom and dad would not approve. Mom had always dreamed of seeing me married by Reverend Marne in our home church in front of Powell's finest. I had no intention of going back home, especially for a wedding. My whole life was wrapped up in Karen and a handful of friends I made in college. Aside from mom and Megan, there was nothing left for me in Evansville.

Mom was finally forced to accept that the wedding would be in Carmi, especially since Karen's parents were paying for the entire event. I never asked mom to help out with expenses because I knew she was in no position to.

In the four years since I left for college, dad's

antics hadn't abated. Mom called me often during those years and kept me updated (the one perk of her job was free phone service). She would tell me how proud dad was of me, but I never heard it from him. In fact, I only saw him twice in person in the four years I spent at Carbondale.

The first happened during my freshman year when mom, dad, and Megan staged a surprise visit to my dorm. We spent the afternoon walking around the campus and generally it was a good day. The second visit came during basketball season of my junior year. They came to watch me play on our home floor, but they left before the game started because dad heard there was bad weather coming and said he didn't want to drive home in a storm. That was also the day they met Karen for the first time.

Karen was cordial to him, but I think mom and dad both sensed a hidden animosity. By then she had learned my history, and wouldn't have faced him at all if I hadn't insisted. I heard from dad directly after he got the news of our engagement later that spring. The phone in my dorm room rang at two in the morning, and when I answered, I was confronted by an irate and very drunk Johnny Ray.

"Boy, you're gonna marry her huh? Well, I didn't think she was very nice. What do you see in this girl?" He was slurring his words worse than I had ever heard.

"That's right, dad. I love her. She's a wonderful person and she'll be a great wife."

"So you're gonna bring her back here right? You're gonna live here with her close to home so you can take care of your mom." I knew why he really wanted me back home. He was counting on getting a piece of the income from the job I would land with my degree.

"Dad, we're going to live near St. Louis. We've already talked about it. There's a lot more job opportunities there for both of us, plus I can see more games. Aren't you happy for me, dad?" There was a long pause.

"You need to get rid of that bitch and get your ass

home! She's got your head all screwed up!" The anger that I should have felt was dwarfed by pure shock. I couldn't believe those words had come out of my father's mouth, even if he was drunk.

"I...I don't know what to say. I'm going to be very happy with Karen, and I'm not coming back home to live. I have to make my own life for myself. Can't you understand that?"

"Yeah, I understand. I understand that you're abandoning us. You're walking away from your own mother. You're leaving us behind for some slut you barely know. I'm telling you now, if you marry this girl you'll be sorry!" By then tears were streaming down my face. I needed to end this immediately or say something I couldn't take back.

"I'm sorry you feel that way, dad. I hope you'll change your mind and come to the wedding. I gotta go." I quickly hung up the phone before he could level any more venom at me.

In the days after, I burned with fury. His words were seared into my brain, but I never told Karen about that conversation. He didn't know her, he was just trying to manipulate me into coming back home. He hadn't prepared himself for the possibility that I wouldn't come back to Evansville when I was done with school. He really thought that I would experience four years of freedom and new people, only to finish and come back to the emotional prison he had waiting for me. I knew that if I did settle back in Evansville, I would never be able to leave.

I spent the remainder of 1996 trying futilely to put that conversation out of my mind. Whether I was hanging out with Karen or listening to the Cardinals, they both kept bringing me back to dad. His voice echoed in my head for months after the night of his rant, and I'm ashamed to admit that they started to work. I began to doubt if Karen was the right woman for me. I battled pangs of guilt

wondering if I really was abandoning my family. For a couple of months during that summer I stayed away from Karen because I told her I needed "time to think." It seemed Carbondale wasn't far enough away from Powell to escape dad's reach.

That summer I spent an inordinate amount of time at Busch Stadium. I decided that the best method for figuring out my life was to become immersed in Cardinal baseball. As it turned out, I picked a hell of a season to do that.

1996 was a pivotal year for my favorite team. A new group of owners led by Bill DeWitt purchased the club from Anheuser-Busch before the season started. That turned out to be a godsend for the fans because the Cardinals had fallen into a rut. The two seasons preceding had been dreadful. The "Whiteyball" era was long gone, and the young talent of the early 90's hadn't panned out as well as hoped. I turned twenty-one in '96 and hadn't seen a great Cardinals team since I was twelve. When I heard the news of the ownership change I was encouraged, and it didn't take long for the improvements to begin.

First, the old artificial turf, so beautiful to me as a child, was replaced by natural grass. While that didn't make the team any better, it certainly made Busch Stadium feel much more like a baseball field.

Those fields built in the '60s and '70s were all identical and lacking in any soul or character. The diamond in St. Louis was the same in Minneapolis, the same in Cincinnati, and the same in Pittsburgh. The trend in recent years toward older looking stadiums built only for baseball is wonderful. Each one has its own quirks and unique features, like Houston's Minute Maid Park, which boasts a hill in deep center field with a flag pole on the playing field. The Green Monster, Chicago's Ivy walls, the Western Metal Supply Company building wedged into San Diego's Petco Park: these are part of what makes it fun to go to the ballpark.

Busch Stadium was still a "cookie cutter" type facility, but at least it finally had a real playing surface as it had when it first opened in 1966. Still, the product on the field was the most important ingredient. The new owners opened up their checkbooks and lured several talented new players to town such as Ron Gant, Gary Gaetti, Andy Benes, Todd Stottlemyre, Dennis Eckersley, and even our old friend Willie McGee.

Just as important, the Cardinals brought in Tony LaRussa from Oakland along with his pitching coach Dave Duncan to lead the team. In one off-season the Cards went from less than mediocre to more than competitive.

With classes out of session, and my forced hiatus from Karen underway, I found no reason why I shouldn't be at the ballpark. Three friends and I would drive over and stay in a cheap place outside the city for a weekend, then buy some bleacher seats and take in a whole series. What we saw that summer was a team that was still gelling and getting used to a new manager, but also winning.

Gant and Gaetti provided some needed power to go with the speed and talent of players like Ray Lankford and Brian Jordan. They got veteran leadership from Ozzie (in his final season) and Willie. Their starting pitching was rock solid, and the bullpen (long a source of anguish in prior seasons) was bolstered by proven winners like Rick Honeycutt and Eckersley.

By the time my senior year of college began in September of '96, I had seen perhaps twenty games in person during that season alone. I had rediscovered my love for Cardinal baseball (if I ever lost it), and in the process I also realized that I was being stupid about Karen. How could I even consider throwing away the best person I had ever met because my drunk father thought it was a good idea?

Karen, being the kind and understanding woman

that she is, took my summer of doubt in stride and welcomed me back without a word. Sometimes I can still keep myself awake at night with terrifying questions: what if she had met someone else during that summer? What if I had lost her because of dad? I'm not sure how my life would have turned out, but there's no doubt I would have become a lesser man. She certainly could have done better than me, but I know I maxed out my luck when I won her.

After the Cardinals clinched the NL Central title I felt a strong urge to call dad. It had been years since we had a good team to discuss and I was eager for his analysis. But every time I came close to picking up the phone, I remembered his slurred insults toward Karen. My pride and my respect for Karen kept me from giving in.

The Cards drew the San Diego Padres in the opening round of the playoffs. They were led by the amazing Tony Gwynn, who looked like he had no business being on the field, but could spray line drives as if at will. I stayed cautiously optimistic about their chances. In the playoffs you need timely hitting, effective pitching, and nerves of steel. The Cards displayed all of those against the Pads. They won the first two games at home 5-4 and then 3-1, and headed to San Diego needing only one more win to take the short series. In game three, Brian Jordan hit a huge late home run and they held on to win 7-5.

That night, once again around 2 a.m., the phone in my room began to ring. I considered not answering it, but the part of me that knew it was dad could no longer be denied. I picked it up, but didn't speak. I could tell it was him even before he began to speak because of his breathing. "Uh, Paul? You there Paul?"

"Yeah, dad. What's up?"

"Well, our boys did it! Back in the LCS again. Braves are some tough hombres but I think we can give 'em a series if we keep getting this kind of pitching."

As always, the state of the Redbirds took

precedence over any family tension. I wanted to believe that he just didn't remember our last discussion, but I couldn't buy it. I had the choice of rehashing his words and starting a fight, or simply humoring with him.

"I think you're right. If we can steal one of the first two games in Atlanta, it could be an interesting series. We're getting clutch performances from a lot of guys right now," I said, deciding that 2 a.m. was too late to engage him on anything other than baseball.

"What do you think about LaRussa? Seems like he changes pitchers too much. I'm not sure if I like him or not," Dad said.

It was true that Tony LaRussa had a different style about him as a person and manager than we were used to. But I didn't care what kind of person he was, he had just led us back to the edge of the Promised Land.

"Well, I don't always agree with his decisions. But the guy went to three straight World Series with Oakland so I think we have to trust him!"

"Hey, if we make it to the World Series are you gonna come back home and watch a game or two with me here?" There was genuine excitement in his voice. This was his way of saying he missed me.

"We'll see, dad. My classes are pretty rough right now, but maybe I can get away. I'll let you know."

We talked for a minute or two longer, with dad giving me the updates on Butch and the gang. Neither of us mentioned Karen. When the call ended, I realized that the empty feeling in my gut was gone. I had satisfied my need to share the Cardinals' success with dad. I slept well after that, but of course I never made it back to watch any games with him. The Braves ensured that I wouldn't have to make that choice.

The NLCS seemed like a bit of a mismatch. The Braves were defending World Series champions and could throw studs like John Smoltz, Tom Glavine, and Greg

Maddux out to pitch every day. The Braves took game one 4-2, but our guys responded with a big outburst the next night. Gary Gaetti smashed a grand slam and the Cards took game two 8-3.

I felt strongly that if the Cards could win two out of their three home games coming up, they would win the series. In game three, Ron Gant hit two home runs and they held off the Braves for a 3-2 win. The next day, the Braves took a 3-0 lead only to see the Cards rally in the seventh and eighth to win 4-3. Suddenly the upstart Cardinals were one win away from meeting the Yankees in the World Series. That's when the proverbial wheels fell off.

The Braves asserted their dominance over the final three games, two of which were horrific blowouts. I was left with the familiar ache from '85 and '87 of getting so close and then seeing it all fall apart. Karen got her first taste of what it was like to be around me after the Cardinals lost a playoff series. I was grumpy for at least a week after, but having her around helped to ease the blow.

For most of my life I had derived a large portion of my happiness from Cardinal baseball. If they lost, I had few other sources of joy to draw from. In '96 it was much different. I had the love of my life with me and a future as a college graduate with means to travel and settle anywhere I wanted. I no longer needed the Cardinals to win, though it still hurt to see them lose (especially in October).

I nearly called dad after the loss, if only to have someone to share the pain with. I knew what he would say. Donovan Osborne wasn't ready to win a game seven. The team looked scared and hesitant while the Braves looked like champs. I decided I didn't need to hear it. The loss was particularly tough to take because it was Ozzie Smith's final game as a player. He and Willie were the last of the players from the teams of my childhood, and his retirement was as much a reminder of the passage of time in my own life as it was his.

My senior year of college flew by and suddenly it was the spring of '97 and we were planning a wedding. My focus was mostly on landing a job to get my career started. I hoped to get something in St. Louis, but I hedged my bets by sending out resumes all over the country. As opposed to the year before, I didn't make it to a single game in '97 because I was so busy. That was probably for the best as the '97 Cards were a disappointment.

Coming off their great run the year before, they stumbled at the start and never seemed to get any momentum going. The only buzz came shortly after we were married when, at the end of July, the Cardinals traded to get Mark McGwire from Oakland. He was an exciting addition but not enough to stem the tide of a tough season.

I talked with dad only once before the wedding. I called their house one evening expecting mom to answer as always, but dad surprised me. We talked baseball and school for a few minutes, and I waited to hear him begin blasting my decision to carry on with the wedding. He never mentioned it, and the conversation was one of the most pleasant we'd had in years. I was encouraged that this meant he had finally accepted the situation and was going to let me live my life.

***

Weeks slipped away with frightening speed and the big day was upon us. Mom, dad, and Megan were to arrive at New Beginnings Baptist Church of Carmi early on that Saturday. Megan was a bridesmaid and was very excited about the job. Mom never quite got past the fact that we weren't marrying in Powell, but we did manage to get Reverend Marne to drive over to do the ceremony.

I was nervous to find out what spirits dad would be in when they showed up. I was standing in the parking lot when I saw mom's Ford station wagon (complete with wood paneling) pull in. I quickly deduced that dad was not among the passengers in the car. Mom was behind the wheel and looked distressed. She parked crooked and took up two spaces, then launched herself out of the vehicle.

"Pauly I'm sorry, but your father won't be coming today. He told me last night that he couldn't do it and he was staying home. He wasn't even around this morning when we left," mom said. She was wearing a flowered dress and, with her haired pinned, I thought she looked every bit the part of the groom's mother. Listening to her words, I found more relief than anger.

"Wow, okay. Well, we'll just carry on without him. At least you two are here. And you both look beautiful!" The more I thought about it, the more I was glad he didn't show. Karen would be relieved as well. I was used to dad not showing up for my events, so I wasn't crushed when I got the news.

The morning progressed and the usual picture taking and milling about proceeded around the church. The wedding was scheduled for one o'clock, with the reception to follow at the local Elks Club lodge. The morning seemed to drag on as my anticipation soared: I couldn't wait to marry Karen and make this new era of my life official.

At around twelve-fifteen, I retreated with my groomsmen (four good friends: two teammates and two guys I had met randomly in classes) to an upstairs classroom for a bit of a pre-wedding pep rally. The guys all gave me advice and we joked about what married life would be like. Then we huddled and the guys prayed for me, which I'll always carry as a highlight from that day.

With about twenty minutes to go before the show would start, we made our way back down to the room from which we would eventually emerge into the sanctuary. Though I knew I had the right woman, and I truly believed it was the right time, the jitters finally hit me. The surreal feeling of knowing your life is about to change hit me fast and hard.

I was lost in my own mind for several minutes,

pondering the past and future. That's when I noticed a murmur coming from inside the sanctuary. I looked up in time to see the door swing open and Johnny Ray walk through. I blinked and did a double-take, but the man really was standing there.

He wasn't dressed for a wedding. He looked like he had come directly from an all-night bar fest to the church. He had managed to pull on some faded grey corduroy pants, but had only one of his white V-neck T-shirts covering his top half. He had managed to attract the attention of everyone sitting in the pews because he entered exactly where my bride would be coming from in a matter of minutes.

"We need to talk," he said, looking at my groomsmen who were probably staring with mouths open. I made it my immediate mission to stay calm above all else. I couldn't let him ruin this day for Karen (or me).

"Yeah, okay. Guys, can you give us a minute?" They responded by marching back up the stairs. Ronnie, my best man and closest friend, shot a look back at me to ask if I was okay. My eyes told him that I could handle it, and he retreated along with the others. I walked past dad and closed the door to the sanctuary. We were alone.

"Paul, you can't marry this girl. She's gonna ruin your life, and you won't even know it until it's too late. I need you at home. Your mom needs you. Your sister needs you. How can you be so selfish when we've been waiting for you for four years?" I could tell he was drunker than usual because he was swaying slightly as he spoke.

"How did you even get here?" I was still grappling with the reality of his presence.

"Don't worry about that." Most likely dad either threatened or paid someone to bring him. Either way, here he was literally standing between me and the altar.

"Dad." I paused for what felt like a long time. I couldn't find the words to respond because I didn't know what I was feeling. It was emotional overload. "We talked about this already, remember? I have to live my life, and I'm sorry if you feel like that's being selfish. Karen is great and you'd know that if you had bothered to spend any time with her."

"Yeah, she's great now. You're just starting out. No kids, no responsibilities. It's all fun right now. Later you'll find out. You'll see who she really is, and you'll regret it. Trust me."

"Trust you? Trust you! Jesus Christ, dad! Look at yourself. You're crashing your son's wedding because you're too fucking selfish to understand that this is my day and my life! I'm never coming home, dad! Never. And you're either going to have to accept that and move on or…" I stopped because I didn't exactly know how to finish the sentence.

Dad's face turned to a sneer. He didn't look anything like the man I had once been so proud to call my father. The man who took me to my first game, who sat with me for hours explaining the game while listening to the Cards on radio, who stood in front of our congregation and professed his faith in Jesus…that man was gone.

Some would say he "lost the battle" with alcoholism, but I believe he just gave up. He was consumed, not so much by his addiction, but with himself. Seeing his face in that moment, I felt both rage and pity. This was the final act of our relationship, played out on his terms in the church I was to be married in.

"Well, that's fine if you don't come back home. You're not welcome in my house anymore. You just wanna walk away and abandon us? Go ahead! As far as I'm concerned I never had a goddamn son! You're dead to me!"

I wanted to punch him. I felt the dam inside of me break and the anger rolled through my body in great waves. I moved to within a foot of his face, daring him to get physical with me.

"I can't believe what a self-serving son of a bitch you are! What did you think was going to happen here? Huh? This is my wedding day. I'm ten minutes away from getting married, and you're here drunk and talking about me coming home? I'm dead to you? Great! I'd rather have no father at all than have the terrible fucking father that you've been! You're a terrible father! Do you hear me?"

I was fully expecting to get smacked or punched in that instant, but nothing happened. In the back of my mind I was aware that everyone sitting in the sanctuary had probably heard every word of this exchange.

Dad's expression changed, as if he had just dropped into his own body and was becoming aware of what had transpired. I immediately felt a twinge of regret. I wasn't lying when I told him he was a terrible father. In fact, I had never spoken truer words about the man in my life. Nevertheless, I wondered if I had gone too far. So much for staying calm.

I could tell he wanted to say more, to keep trying to hurt me because that's all he had left. But he couldn't. My rant had sobered him, and I saw that he was caught up in his own mental battle. Our eyes stayed locked for only a second longer, then he turned slowly and began to walk toward the rear of the church. He was almost staggering, more from what he had just lost than from the effects of the Jack Daniels. More than a small part of me wanted to stop him.

It's one of the biggest "what ifs" of my life. If I had gone to him, told him to wait. If I could have explained my feelings for Karen more eloquently. If he could have seen through the fog of his own making to realize he could still stay and enjoy his son's wedding day. It would have been a long shot, but that moment could have been our turning point. I'll never know, because I let him walk out of the back entrance and out of my life.

I stood in silence for a minute until Ronnie came

flying down the stairs. He asked how I was and I told him I just needed a little time alone. He gave me a pat on the back and then moved back to his post upstairs. Just then Reverend Marne, who knew my father about as well as anyone, walked through the sanctuary door. He looked nearly as shaken as I was.

"Paul, I'm afraid I couldn't help but overhear. Is there anything I can do for you?"

"I just...I just can't believe he did that. I mean, I knew he didn't want me get married. But to come here and say those things to me. On my wedding day. I..."

The emotional toll of the last few minutes finally overtook me, and I grabbed the pastor and sobbed into his shoulder. I cried because there was no taking back some of the things we said. That day, which should have been my best, would be forever stained. Marne, to his credit, didn't try to explain away dad's behavior or quote Bible verses to me. His presence alone was comforting.

Soon word had reached Karen somewhere on the other side of the church. She managed to find her way back to me without being seen by the restless crowd. Marne had left me to my thoughts when she appeared from the very door that dad had left through a few minutes before. She was stunning in her white dress, and my mood immediately shifted. I stood gaping at her as she approached.

"Baby, I just heard what happened. Is he gone? Are you okay?" She had that same look in her eye as the night we watched *Field of Dreams* and I first told her about dad.

"My God, Karen. You're absolutely gorgeous." I truly was swept up by her beauty. It instantly cleared my head and made me remember why I was here. I gave a smile to answer her question as I stroked her cheek. "Seriously. I can't believe how beautiful you are in this dress. How is it that I'm the one who gets to marry you?"

"It's strictly for the money." I laughed out loud. What's amazing about Karen is that her beauty is surpassed by her sense of humor and her good nature. "And, because you're the sweetest and most loving man I've ever met. Are you sure you're okay?"

I was grateful that she had come to see me as soon as she heard and didn't get caught up in the ridiculous tradition of not seeing the bride before the wedding. The real jinx had already left the building.

"Yeah, really. I kind of knew this might happen. He said what he thought he needed to say and I did as well. I don't think we'll be hearing from him anymore, and that's probably for the best."

"That bastard. What kind of man does this? It's amazing that such a good man like you came from a father like him," she said as she straightened up my tie.

"I had a good mom. That helped. Karen, I promise you that I will never act like my father and I will always try to put you first. I've seen enough examples of how not to be a father and husband. I'm never going to be that guy."

"I know you won't. I believe in you." She gave me a long and reassuring kiss, then looked at me with her deep blue eyes.

"What do you say we get married? Right now, like two crazy kids!" I said.

"I'm up for that! Just give me some time to get back to my place. These shoes are a nightmare!"

With that, she turned and moved unsteadily toward the rear exit. She finally got to the door and I was once again alone. I closed my eyes and felt a giant boulder lifted from my soul. I knew I would one day have to come to grips with what happened between dad and I, but that would wait. I was free to enjoy the whole experience of the wedding and reception with (most) of the people I loved. I called for the guys to come down and join me again, and Ronnie went out to signal Marne that the wedding was a go. Minutes later we were walking as a group into the sanctuary and seeing a lot of stunned faces. No one seemed to know how to react to what they had heard and seen.

Then, something remarkable happened. As I led my groomsmen toward the altar from the side door, the crowd broke from dead silence into raucous cheering and applause. So many of the people there knew my father, and they were clapping for me because they understood that I was about to break away to make a better life for me and my new wife. It was an awkward moment, but I managed to crack a smile and wave.

I whispered to Ronnie that this felt like we were in a movie, and he agreed. Once the applause died down, the music began and the ceremony came together without any further roadblocks. At one point, just before Karen came down the aisle, I stole a glance at Megan. She had a smile on her face, but when her eyes met mine her façade melted into tears and I quickly looked away before she got me going again. I didn't dare look at her or mom for the rest of the ceremony.

***

Dad, Jack, and I watched intently as Rzepczynski did exactly what they needed him to do. He induced three weak grounders from Hamilton, Mitch Moreland, and Beltre to keep the deficit at three. Jack had finished off his Oreos and milk and looked like he could easily fall asleep right there next to dad for the entire night. Shortly before the commercials ended, Megan appeared at the door.

"Having fun boys?"

Dad responded, "We're not enjoying the game if that's what you mean. But I think having Jack here is going to help us turn it around."

"I'm sure you're right. But could we borrow him for a few minutes? Mom and I want to get some pictures with him in his cute little outfit," Megan said.

"Good idea. Jack, go with your aunt Megan." I said, perhaps too abruptly.

"But dad, I wanna keep watching the game with

201

grandpa! Can't I stay?"

"I promise you'll get to come back in and watch more with him. But you're needed by the women right now and there's no resisting them. The sooner you go with them the sooner you're done!" I said. He bought my line of thinking and began to climb down from the bed.

Dad added, "I'll save your spot right here, pal!"

Jack took Megan's hand and she led him out of the room, closing the bedroom door as she went. Lance Berkman was just digging in against Derek Holland when I shifted myself to fully face dad in bed. His face told me that he already knew what was coming.

"Time to talk about my wedding day."

Bottom of the Eighth

B
efore I could get the next words out of my mouth, Berkman swung at the first pitch and popped it into right field. Cruz ran toward the line and made the catch, and automatically I saw the scoreboard in my mind: three runs down, five outs to go. We were running out of time.

"What's there to talk about? We both said things we probably didn't mean. That's what happens sometimes in arguments," dad said. I could tell he was on fumes and agitated as I was at the status of the Cardinals.

"It wasn't an argument. You were literally trying to break up my wedding. What was I supposed to say? Thanks dad! So glad you showed up to stop me from marrying the girl of my dreams?"

Before dad could respond our attention was diverted back to the game. Allen Craig, who had entered the game in the seventh inning to replace Holliday (he hurt his hand while getting picked off of third), crushed a low pitch deep to left field. The ball sailed into the crowd, and I instinctively clapped my hands together and let out a "Yeah!" It was only a solo shot, but it got us one run closer and helped to bring the crowd back into the game.

"Man that Craig is a hitter. He's done nothing but good things in this series. I bet he'll be starting at first base if Albert leaves next year," Dad said.

I completely agreed. Craig was young, but clearly not intimidated by the big stage. I was tempted to table the rest of our talk until after the game, but he would never last that long. It was a minor miracle that dad had stayed awake and alert for this long. I had to finish what I started, regardless of what was happening in the game. A DVR box would have been very handy in that moment, but naturally mom and dad didn't want to pay for one.

As if to underscore the importance of what was to

follow, I grabbed the remote control and muted the ball game. Dad sighed and gave me an annoyed look. I ignored it and pressed on.

"Look, I think we can agree that you've made some mistakes in your life. I never asked you for an apology. But my wedding day...that went beyond everything else. You nearly wrecked the biggest day of my life, and I think I deserve an apology." This was a speech I had rehearsed numerous times in the days leading up to game six.

Dad did not respond right away, he was clearly grasping for a strong reply. Finally he spoke, "Paul, you walked out of here after high school and haven't been back until right now. You ran away and left us behind. You never had any intention of coming home did you? I was trying to make you see that there was a family back in Indiana that needed you. But you didn't want to hear it!"

"And what would I have been coming back to? Giving up half my money so you could continue pissing it away? Being a father to Megan when you weren't around? Pretending like mom that everything is fine? I couldn't do it. I'd had enough of that shit for the first eighteen years and I wasn't going back. I didn't abandon this family, you did!" I kept my voice at a reasonable level, though I could feel that old rage creeping up.

"Paul, I may be old and dying, but this is still my house. I won't lay here and be judged by my own son. You're right, I made a lot of mistakes. And God is going to judge me for all of them, but not tonight. If this is all you've got left to say then maybe you should just leave."

"Just apologize! You know you were wrong! You tried to get in my head and make me walk away from everything that was good in my life. I almost did it! That summer before we got married, I actually broke up with her for a while. Thankfully, I came to my senses and she took me back. I know what that was really about. You didn't give a shit about me 'abandoning' the family. You've never done anything that wasn't at least ninety percent about you. Just for once, admit that you were wrong and say you're sorry!" I was consciously muting my rant because I didn't want Jack to get upset.

"So I'm the only selfish one, huh? Bullshit! You've been keeping me away from that sweet grandson of mine since the day he was born. Why? Was it punishment? Is that it? That boy deserved to see his grandfather. Now you bring him here when I'm on the verge of death? Knowing that I'm going to see him once and never again? What kind of man does that?" Dad had developed an amazing ability to deflect blame away from himself. It worked. I struggled to find my next retort.

"Don't try to twist this! You're lucky you're meeting him at all! I brought him here for his sake, not yours! I wanted him to be able to say he got to meet his grandfather before it was too late. I didn't keep him away from you on purpose, it just happened that way because I wasn't ready to face you."

"I don't believe that. You've been trying to punish me for my mistakes ever since you left here. But your mom has suffered more than me! You broke her heart when you moved to St. Louis. She won't say it out loud, but deep down she believes you abandoned her too."

"That's a lie! My God, even now at the end of your life you can't be honest about things! I came here tonight because I thought we could finally put our past to rest and at least part as friends. It looks like you're not going to let that happen, so maybe I should get going," I said. I stood up and moved toward the door. I felt empty, like the whole night had been a failure.

"Fine. Get out. But don't even think about leaving without letting me say goodbye to Jack."

I left the room without another word and slammed the door. For all the good things that had happened that night, it seemed as if nothing had changed. He was the same man he had always been, and apparently not even death was going to budge him. I walked to the kitchen to regroup. The ladies were all in the living room with Jack, and I could hear that they had turned the game on for him. I fully expected one or all of them to come bounding in to find out what was going on. I didn't hear them coming, but I decided to slip out the back door.

The cool darkness of the back yard was comforting. I stood in silence for a long moment. I looked around at the small covered porch and let out a small gasp when I saw that it was exactly the same as I remembered. A small rusting grill sat in the far corner. In the center were two fading lawn chairs separated by a chipped white wicker table. On the table, an ancient black portable GE radio stood as a reminder of so many nights of baseball gone by. It was as if dad had preserved this area like a curator, hoping I would come back and take in another game with him.

I eased into the chair nearest the door, half expecting to be transported by Rod Serling back to my childhood. I knew the station would be set on the game because dad hadn't touched the dial in thirty years. It was like a car stereo with only one preset. I laid my head back and closed my eyes as John Rooney's voice filled the void. The Rangers had just brought in Mike Adams to pitch after Molina singled with two out.

It felt good being back in my chair. I tried to think of all the games that I had attended over the years that dad probably listened to from right here. Missing those porch evenings with dad and the Cardinals had been the toughest part of staying away for all those years.

Adams quickly surrendered hits to Daniel Descalso and John Jay, and suddenly the Cards had the bases loaded. Now we were one swing away from tying or taking the lead, and Rafael Furcal was coming up. Furcal was yet another late arrival to the team. His play at short and at the top of the Cards' lineup had been crucial in getting them into the playoffs.

These situations are what make the game so truly beautiful. So many variables are at play all at once. Mike Shannon likes to say that when the bases are loaded with two outs and the batter has a full count, it's the "prettiest play in the game." That's because the men on base get a running start with the pitch, and there are seemingly infinite possibilities. At that moment, with Furcal digging in with perhaps the season on the line, I was completely lost in the action. My frustration with dad (and with myself) fell away in the drama of late October baseball. All I could see in my mind was that field.

Just like Descalso and Jay, Furcal hacked at the first pitch he saw. The result was anti-climactic, a chopper back to the pitcher for the final out. When I heard the result, a flood of pent up anger came rushing out of me. I let out something between a scream and a howl, a loud and long sound that came from my very core. I didn't care who heard or how it made me look, it just needed to come out. I had an urge to pick up the radio and throw it (I have been known to break a remote control or two in my lowest moments), but thought better of destroying such a relic.

My body lay limp in the tattered lawn chair for another few moments, unable to respond after such a release. Part of me wanted to stay on the porch and continue listening, hoping for a rally like the old days. But there was too much unfinished work remaining. I willed myself to stand up and stretch.

I felt the exhaustion of the night's experience beginning to sink in, and I thought I couldn't imagine how much worse dad was feeling. My mind flashed an update of the Cards' dire situation: two runs down and only three outs left. A new sensation, urgency, began to percolate in my mind. I switched off the radio and, without hesitation, reached down to unplug it from the lone outlet. I wrapped the cord around it and carried it into the house. I wasn't sure what I was going to do with it at the time, but something told me I was going to need it.

I came back inside and found mom sitting at the kitchen table. I pretended not to see her at first and went straight to the sink for a glass of water. She noticed the radio. "A little souvenir?"

I looked down at it and then at her. "More like a talisman. I'm looking for some magic to help our boys."

"Ah. I was afraid you were getting ready to leave us," mom replied.

"Well, it is getting late and I know dad must be exhausted. Maybe I should get going soon."

"Paul, your father hasn't been awake for more than two hours at a time for probably two weeks. He's struggled to carry on even short conversations with me because he loses his breath. The cancer is in his lungs too. When he's awake, he usually shakes with fever and has trouble focusing. Have you seen any of that tonight?"

"No, not really. He's been awake and alert the whole time. He's coughed here and there, but I haven't noticed him struggling to talk or breathe. And his focus has been sharp."

"What do you think that means?" mom asked, her eyes piercing me.

"I…I don't know. He's having a good night?"

"No Paul, he's having a miraculous night. He hasn't looked or acted this well in weeks. You want to know what I think? I think your father has somehow been storing up his energy, waiting for this night. He knew he would only get one shot with you and Jack, and he wanted to make the most of it. He's in more pain than we can probably imagine, and his body is fighting him like crazy. But he's fighting back tonight, Paul. He's fighting back because he loves you and he loves his grandson. He wasn't going to let a disease cheat him out of this night. Do you see what I'm saying?"

I sat silent, wondering at mom's perception. While I never understood why mom stood by him, even after his relapse and fall, I had to respect her love and devotion to him. She knew my father in a way no one else possibly could, and I believed that what she said about him was true.

"But why is he still being so difficult? If he loves me so much, why does he refuse to apologize or even own up to what he's done?"

"He's a flawed man. His first instinct is always to serve and comfort himself. That's why sometimes he lies to himself, because it's too hard to face the truth. But I know he's sorry. I promise you that. He's sorry for a lot of things, and one of the biggest ones is that he drove you away," mom explained while I continued to grip the radio. Her words were both comforting and frustrating at once. If he was so sorry, why couldn't he just drop the act and show it?

"Mom, I don't know what else to say to the man. We've been over a lot of stuff tonight. We've talked more openly and honestly than any other time in my life. But I feel like I've hit a wall. When he says things like I abandoned you guys, I just want to punch him!"

She grinned slightly. "I can't tell you what to do now, Paul. But I do think you need to give him another chance. He has forgiveness from me, from Megan, and of course from Jesus. He still needs it from you. He may not ask for it, but I know he needs it."

With that, mom stood up and gave me a peck on the cheek. She left the room and let me gather myself. I took one deep breath and slowly let it out. Then I moved to the front of the house to collect Jack. He was lying on the couch with his head on Karen's lap. The ninth inning had just started, and Jack was doing his best to fight sleep. He had turned his cap backwards on his head for a rally, just as I had showed him. Karen looked up and flashed her beautiful smile. I returned it half-heartedly and then motioned to Jack.

"Hey buddy! You want to watch the ninth inning with us in grandpa's room?" I asked. Jack's eyes instantly regained their sparkle and he rose up from his comfy post. He looked at his mom and she gave him a nudge. He walked to me and I picked him up. I gave him a big kiss on the cheek and said, "Nice rally cap, pal. Hope it'll work for us now!"

The hallway between the living room and the kitchen seemed very long as I started toward the bedroom with Jack in my arms. I heard mom's words echoing somewhere, and the importance of the next few minutes became plainly apparent to me. I pushed aside the doubt and lingering anger and instead rededicated myself to the belief that this night would turn out as it should.

I turned the knob and pushed open the door. Dad was wiping his mouth with a paper towel. There was blood on it. He had suffered a coughing fit and was still trying to recover. By rights he should have been dead, probably weeks before game six, but his strength and stubbornness had carried him further than most men could stand. I had a moment of admiration for what he was doing. He had been in constant pain all night, and suppressing the vile effects of the cancer that was destroying his body, all presumably because he wanted to see me and my son.

Standing in the bedroom doorway, seeing him struggle to once again compose himself, I made the decision that I wouldn't leave until I was able to forgive him.

Top of the Ninth

Jack was quick to jump back into bed with his grandpa, and his presence seemed to instantly reenergize dad. I took back my chair and tried to focus my attention on the game. Jason Motte was in to pitch for St. Louis. His usual role was to come into the ninth to protect a lead and close out the game. Tonight it was even more important that he post a zero on the scoreboard.

Motte's ascension to the closer role in 2011 helped to stabilize the bullpen and bring some sanity to the end of games. I grew to enjoy watching him pitch during that season because he looked like a guy they had pulled out of the stands. Unlike some pitchers who make it look easy, Motte looks like he is throwing the ball as hard as he possibly can. He does it well: his fastball consistently hits ninety-eight on the gun.

While I wasn't sure where to go next with dad, I knew that having Jack in the room with us would lighten the atmosphere. Dad still couldn't take his eyes off him. I wondered if he was having any flashbacks of me as a young boy. I heard his voice, which was probably at half the strength it had been at the start of the night, speaking to me. "Hey, you ever take this boy to the Fall Festival? I bet he'd love that!"

The West Side Nut Club Fall Festival, known unofficially as the second largest street festival in America (sliding in just behind Mardi Gras), is perhaps the greatest of all Evansville traditions. For any kid living on the west side, the Fall Festival is a rite of passage. It goes Monday through Saturday during the first full week of October each year.

"You know, I'm ashamed to say it, but no he's never been. I guess we missed it by a couple of weeks. That's something to put on the list for next year!"

"That's a must! You gotta get this kid a pronto pup

211

and a funnel cake and then get him on some rides!"

"Maybe not in that order. I don't need him puking everywhere! I've been there. I remember the first time I rode the Bullet. I was probably about fifteen and I got so sick after that I never rode it again."

That image aside, thinking of the festival brought back a lot of good memories. It dawned on me that I hadn't been to the festival since I was a senior in high school. It was yet another sad reminder that I hadn't been home in many years.

The Fall Festival runs along about a mile of Franklin Street, an area that features many classic buildings from the early 1900s, which house lots of small shops, banks, and restaurants. The sidewalks on both sides of the street are covered with hundreds of food booths, nearly all of them representing charities, churches, schools, or clubs. The festival is essentially a celebration of eating. There is almost nothing conceivably edible that isn't sold in at least one booth.

Thinking of the festival brought me back to when I was six, and dad promised to take me for the first time. I sat around all day on that Saturday, waiting for dad to return and take me to what I knew would be the most fun I'd ever had. The day slipped away slowly, and my anticipation turned to bitterness as I realized that dad wasn't going to show up. I cried hard that night alone in my room. I tried to console myself with the knowledge that we could go next year, but somehow I already knew that was a lie. Dad never got around to keeping that promise.

When Jack came along I told myself that I would never allow him to feel that kind of rejection from his father. I truly hope that I never make a promise to him that I can't keep.

***

The old house on Delmar had triggered so many memories, and some of those hurts were still surprisingly raw. I began to mentally berate myself for having kept Jack away from my father and my hometown for this long. Like some of the words we exchanged on my wedding day, keeping Jack away was something I couldn't take back. I tried to focus on the image of the two of them together and feel relief that I hadn't been too late. Jack would remember this night for the rest of his life, and that would have to be enough.

Sometimes I question if I'm fit to be a parent. I have a strong selfish streak, something that apparently is a trait of all the Gibson men. There are times when all Jack wants is for me to spend a few minutes playing with him, and I find excuses why I can't do it. Even when I do spend time with him, sometimes all I can focus on are the issues in my own life. It eats me up inside to know that in some ways I have inherited my father's self-centeredness.

I have nightmares about Jack as a grown man. He comes to visit me, but he doesn't speak. He sits and we watch the Cardinals in silence. When the game is over, he looks at me with an irrepressible sadness and then turns around and leaves. That's a dream I've had several times just in the last year. It's a fairly obvious one to interpret: I'm scared of never connecting with Jack on anything but baseball and thus replicating the failures of my father.

I watched Jack as he fought against sleep while nestled up against his grandpa. Dad was looking at him and smiling. "You know, I forgot what it's like having a young boy around the house. Everything is new and exciting for him. He's completely loving and trusting. I've missed it."

"I think if I told him I was going to leave him here to live with you guys he wouldn't put up a fight! He seems pretty comfortable here."

"Yeah. Looks like Motte is taking care of business. We've got the right guys coming up. It could get interesting," dad said.

Even at the very end of his life he was still capable

of being more optimistic than me. While he saw the potential for a rally, I saw a desperate situation. Texas would be bringing in Neftali Feliz to finish us off and claim their first championship. Feliz had already proven that he could be dominant, and he would be working with at least a two run lead. Still, dad's confidence lifted my spirits.

"It ain't over 'til it's over!" Yogi's words flew out of my mouth reflexively. I was talking about the game, but I quickly noted the aptness of this quote to our evening together. Despite what had been said and done in all the years before and on that night, I was still standing in the box and taking my swings.

Motte was indeed doing just what was needed. He walked Mike Napoli with one out, though no one was complaining about that because he had been pounding the baseball the entire series. Daniel Murphy grounded into a force out, and with two outs I watched Endy Chavez step to the plate. My memory of playoff games past immediately kicked in.

"Endy Chavez. Do you remember what he did to us back in '06 with the Mets?"

Dad's eyes became slits as he concentrated on the question. I was about to give him the answer when his face flashed with recognition. "Game seven, NLCS. He robbed Scott Rolen of a home run! One of the greatest catches I've ever seen!"

I grunted in agreement. "I thought for sure it was gone, and after he caught it I thought we were finished. Tough to come back from a gut punch like that!"

For me it is the greatest catch at least in postseason history, and maybe the best of all time. The Cardinals and Mets were tied 1-1 in the top of the sixth when Rolen blasted a ball toward deep left. Off the bat it looked like a sure home run, but Chavez never gave up on the play. Sprinting toward the fence, Chavez timed his leap perfectly and "snow coned" the ball in the top of his glove. If he tried that jump and catch a hundred more times, he might have made it only once or twice. After he landed, he fired the ball back into the infield and the Mets doubled Scott Spiezio off of first to end the inning. It was perhaps the most dramatic momentum swing I've ever witnessed in a game. "We still won the game...thanks to Yadi!"

"Do you know what I was doing during that game in '06?" I shook my head slowly. "I was sitting at the hospital with Herm and Butch. Herm had a heart attack a few days before that, and he was just out of ICU. I think I nearly gave him another one the way I yelled when Yadi hit that ball out!"

"I never heard about this. Whatever happened to Herm?"

"Well, it wasn't a good ending for him. I'm pretty sure we were the only ones who visited him. I never saw any family come in, and he didn't like to talk about them. He got out of the hospital shortly after that and he seemed fine. About six months later he dropped dead in the shower from another heart attack. No one found him for days."

He trailed off for a moment. I had inadvertently brought up another bad memory for him. Then he continued, "I guess none of us guys were going to live long lives. First Phil, then Herm, Chuck moved away and I heard that he had passed on a couple of years back. After I'm gone, Butch will be the only one of our little gang left! And he was the wildest one of the bunch!" Dad tried to smile, but I could see the hurt on his face. He loved those guys as much as he loved his own family. He actually spent more time with them over the years than with us.

"What was it about those guys? Why did you invest so much of your life in them? I mean, I'm sure they were fun..." I stopped because I couldn't read dad's face. It was contorting in a way that could mean he was angry or just fighting the physical pain of his condition.

"Honestly? I liked being with them because they

were easy. I got to be the leader and they were happy to join in on whatever I had going on. I...I didn't feel like a failure when I was with them. I didn't feel guilty or self-conscious. It was just fun. Then I'd come home and that feeling would go away. I'd walk around here wondering about all the ways I was screwing up as a husband and father. I felt guilty about not spending time with you, but when I did I had a hard time relating. I'm not proud to admit this, but I hated myself when I was here at home. I wanted to be better, but I didn't know how. It was easier to run away and get drunk. The guys helped me to feel good about myself. And they really were good guys."

Dad's sudden burst of honesty caught me off guard. I sat staring at him, stunned by the revelation. Finally, I mustered a response, "I didn't know you felt that way dad. That's actually something I can relate to somewhat. I feel that way with Jack sometimes. It's hard not to feel like I'm failing too."

He stroked Jack's hair gently. Jack had finally given up the battle and was sleeping soundly. "Paul, you're not a failure. You might have days when you're not father of the year, but you love him and I'm sure you're around a lot more than I was. When you were first born, I told myself I wasn't going to be like my dad. He was very cold and distant. He made it clear he didn't give a shit about us kids and that's how it stayed.

"I ended up doing just about the same thing. And then I went and got baptized and they made a big deal out of me turning my life around. The problem was I never really changed. I mean, I believed in the Biblical stuff and I enjoyed Marne's messages. But I was too weak to stay off the booze. And the guys didn't really help much. They were always wanting me to come out and join them. I guess I gave in too easily. Maybe if I had taken the whole thing more seriously. Maybe if I had joined a group or got new friends or something. Maybe I could have been the father you needed," his voice, already badly weakened from exertion, broke completely. I noticed him shaking and thought at first it was his temperature spiking, but then I saw the tears. For only the second time in my life, I saw my father crying.

My own eyes welled up, but I caught myself and fought to hold back the tears. Inside I was elated to see him like this. It was the kind of breakthrough I had been waiting for my entire adult life. Unsure of how to continue, I turned to my fatherly duties. I stood up, wiped my eyes, and moved to scoop up Jack. Dad was still rhythmically stroking his hair with his left hand while covering his face with his right. I wanted badly to comfort my father in that moment, but I had no experience with it. So many years had gone by. So much bad blood had passed between us. I didn't know if it was possible to move past it all.

I slowly reached out my right hand and placed it on his shoulder. His reaction was immediate. His trembling ceased and he rose up slightly. I nearly pulled my hand away, but instead I began patting him tenderly. He took his hand away from his face and turned to look up at me. There was pain in those eyes, but also gratitude. We stayed frozen in that position for several seconds, my patting of his shoulder and upper back feeling more natural with each repetition. I took a deep breath through my nose and released it. We were both frozen; desperate to break through a lifetime of distance, but utterly incapable of finding a way.

Not wanting to let the moment turn more awkward than it already was, I cleared my throat and then spoke. "Well, I probably need to get Jack out of here. He's out and Karen's going to want to get him back to the room and into bed. He's had a big day, I'm sure he's exhausted."

Dad nodded and I nudged Jack to wake him up. Ordinarily I would have let him sleep, but I wanted him to be awake for his last goodbye with grandpa. His eyes flickered open and he looked confused for a moment.

"Jack? You awake buddy? Mom's going to take you back to the hotel now so you can get to bed. You need to say goodbye to your grandpa first, okay?"

He rolled over and then pulled himself up onto his knees. Without a word, Jack flung both his arms around dad's neck and gave him one of those hugs that is so full of love that only a child could produce it. Dad's eyes opened wide with surprise, but then he closed them and returned the hug with as much force as he could without hurting him. Dad released him first and then lowered his head in an attempt to get to Jack's eye level.

He said, "Jack, it was really nice meeting you tonight. Even though you've never seen me before, I've loved you your whole life. You've got a great daddy who loves you very much too. I want you to be a good boy and listen to your dad and mom. They're gonna help you grow up and become a smart and strong man. Can you do that for me, Jack?"

"Yeah grandpa, I can do that. It was nice meeting you too! Can I come over again sometime?" The question nearly brought me to my knees. I bit my lip to keep the tears from starting up. Dad just kept looking into those beautiful young blue eyes.

"You can come and visit here anytime you want. I may not be here next time you come, but you know your grandma would love for you to be here. She'll give you some good things to eat and let you stay up as late as you want!" He gave a quick turn of the head and winked at me. "Now, you go on with your dad and get some sleep. I need to rest too."

Before Jack could question why dad wouldn't be there the next time he came, I grabbed him under both arms and pulled him up into mine. Dad gave Jack one more big smile, then I turned and moved toward the living room. By the time I got him to Karen he was already asleep again.

I laid him back down on the couch. Karen whispered, "Is the game over?"

"Not yet, bottom of the ninth just started and we're down two. Probably be over soon. You going to take him back now?"

"Yes. I'll just say my goodbyes here and take off. Meet you back at the room later?"

"Yeah. Not sure how much longer I'll be. Thanks for everything tonight…for being here and bringing Jack. It helped having you around."

"Don't mention it. I love you. That's what I do!" She patted my cheek and smiled. She has a way of instantly relaxing me.

Walking back to the bedroom, my focus began to shift back to baseball. Dad's confession and Jack's final goodbye had consumed me for the past few minutes. I had to remind myself that the Cardinals season was now on the line. Down two runs with three outs left, I re-entered dad's bedroom, hoping for a rally that not only would keep our season alive, but would keep my last evening with dad from ending.

Bottom of the Ninth

Ryan Theriot, the Cards' sparkplug shortstop, had already begun the inning with a swinging strikeout when I got back to the recliner. I didn't see it, but dad said simply that he was overmatched. Feliz could throw just as hard as Motte, and he was capable of blowing away anyone standing at the plate. My heart began to pound as the magnitude of the situation settled on me. This team had come so far, weathered so many difficulties, it made me sick to think that they were going to fall short now on their own field.

The last time I had that feeling was in 2004, when the Cardinals were swept out of the World Series by the Boston Red Sox. The Cards won a hundred and five games during the regular season and barely survived a seven game war with the Astros.

That was without question the best team St. Louis has had in my lifetime. They boasted the "MV3" combination of Albert Pujols, Scott Rolen, and Jim Edmonds. Not only was their lineup stacked from top to bottom (even more so when they acquired the heavy hitting Larry Walker at the trade deadline), but they also had a defense that rivaled that of the great Whitey teams of the '80s. Rolen was a magician at third base with a rocket arm, and Edmonds was capable of making the most unbelievable acrobatic catches in centerfield.

After they beat Roger Clemens in game seven of the NLCS, I was confident that they had the firepower to take out the Red Sox. Of course, that was the year of destiny for Boston after so many seasons of agony. They came from three games down to win four in a row against the hated Yankees, so I should have known the "baseball gods" were on their side. The vaunted Cardinals lineup faded against unfamiliar pitching, while Boston's bats stayed hot. Game four ended when Edgar Renteria grounded back to the mound.

We had to watch the Red Sox players dance and celebrate on our field. I told myself that when the third out came this time, if we lost, I would quickly leave the room and avoid that painful image.

Next up was Pujols, who had been legendary in game three, but hadn't contributed to the offense since. I pushed away the thought that this was probably his last appearance as a Cardinal. Instead, I focused on willing him to get on base. A home run would be nice, but we needed two runs to tie. We needed a base runner in the worst way, and Albert delivered on the first pitch. He swatted a low delivery into the left-center gap for an easy double.

Now the pressure fell on Lance Berkman to keep the rally going. Berkman had surpassed all our expectations during the season after signing as a free agent. He personified the 2011 Cardinals: tough at-bats, high character, and a penchant for clutch hits. That was a hallmark of Tony LaRussa's teams throughout his time in St. Louis: he counted on his men to grind out wins and stay consistent over a hundred and sixty-two games.

Berkman, a switch hitter, batted left against the right-handed Feliz. Ball one sailed up and in. Lance repeated his trademark of waving the bat over the plate as he waited for the next pitch. This one was way outside for ball two. Feliz snapped at the ball as it came back from the catcher.

"He's rattled! You can see it. I bet he walks him here. No reason to challenge him anyway with first base open," dad said. I hoped he was right. Feliz did look agitated, and Berkman was very good at laying off pitches out of the strike zone.

The third pitch was again well inside and off the plate, and again Feliz snapped at the ball. Perhaps he was stunned at the way Albert had managed to pull a low outside pitch into left field, or maybe the weight of the moment had descended on him. Some athletes seem to be born to handle these pressure-packed situations, while others wilt.

It was still too early to tell if Feliz was going to fold. Ball four was nearly over Berkman's head. A four pitch walk after the Pujols double. I cast a hopeful glance at dad, he looked battered but excited by the turn of events.

Allen Craig marched to the plate with the opportunity to become a World Series hero. He had just hit a home run in the previous inning and was perhaps the most reliable clutch hitter on the team in that series.

"I like Craig in this spot. If Feliz gives him a low pitch to drive, this game could be over in a heartbeat!" I don't normally utter such optimistic comments during games, especially when we're on the losing end of the scoreboard. But of any player, I think most Cardinal fans would have agreed that Craig was their man in this spot. Craig was a rookie, but he wasn't playing like one now.

For the first time in a few innings, dad was sitting straight up in his bed and his focus was like a laser on the screen. We were both hanging on every pitch, just as we once had in both '82 and '85. I could no longer bear to sit as my legs became restless. I stood up and bent toward the screen much like a fielder getting ready for a pitch to be sent home.

Craig took the first two pitches for balls. That was six straight out of the zone for Feliz, who wisely took a moment to go the rosin bag and collect himself. The job of a closer is never easy, but this was magnified to an incredible degree. Feliz was attempting to close out a World Series on the road.

The 2-0 pitch hit the top of the zone for strike one. Craig had yet to take a swing, but on the fourth pitch he unloaded on a fastball and crushed it toward left. I stiffened for a second because the ball was hit hard, but he had swung a fraction of a second too early and pulled it foul into the seats. How close had he come to tying or winning the game?

I stomped my foot when I saw it had gone foul. I heard dad let out a grunt of disappointment. Craig was obviously sitting on the fastball, and had to be upset about pulling the trigger too early. Now I wondered if he was set up for something off-speed. The 2-2 pitch was indeed a breaking ball, and Craig managed to foul it off gamely. I thought to myself that a lot of guys would have struck out on that pitch.

Now what would he throw? Would Feliz back up the slider with another one, or try again to blow him away with his powerful fastball? The pitch was a slider, and Craig found himself frozen. The pitch ended up right over the heart of the plate, but it was good enough to fool Craig and send him back to the dugout.

I cupped my hands over my eyes for a moment after strike three was called. We were now officially down to our final out of the season, and David Freese, a St. Louis area native, was heading for the batter's box. Freese's work in that postseason was already impressive. His bat caught fire against the Brewers and he led a relentless offense that overwhelmed Milwaukee's pitching in the NLCS.

"You can do this, David!" I whispered.

I assumed my standing fielder's position once again in front of the recliner. If the Cardinals' season was to continue, David Freese would have to find a way to get on base or put one over the boards. Feliz started him off with two off-speed pitches, the first was in the dirt off the plate, but the second bent into Napoli's glove for a strike.

The shots of the crowd on TV reflected the same anxiety that Cardinal fans were feeling all over America. I didn't dare move from my position out of pure superstitious fear. In their most desperate moments, true sports fans will usually forego logic in favor of rituals and sacred items.

Feliz began looking in for his next sign, but Napoli

thought better of it and jogged out to discuss it with his pitcher. It's a normal part of the game, but it was an agonizing delay for us. With the game and season hanging in the balance, the last thing fans want is the tension extended. The next pitch finally came, and my heart dropped. Freese swung through a fastball on the outer half of the plate.

The situation could not have grown any direr: two runs down and only one strike left. I stood all the way up and let my hands clasp on top of my head in preparation for what seemed like the inevitable conclusion. Feliz had shown that he could blow a fastball by Freese, and another one was surely coming.

I looked down at dad. He was like a statue, frozen in the same place as he had been for the entire inning. I began trying to ease the sick and painful feeling of losing that we were both experiencing.

"Well, win or lose, it's been a hell of a run. I wouldn't have thought they'd make it this far." Dad didn't move or respond. They were empty words that dissipated instantly.

Freese dug back in and awaited the 1-2 pitch. I fully expected to see David swing through the fastball and Mike Napoli leap into the air to celebrate their final victory. Unlike 2004, there was no shame in losing this series because they had fought hard and lost to a superior opponent.

The pitch came, Freese swung, and the ball hit the bat.

Time seemed to stop just after Freese made contact with the Feliz fastball. My breathing stopped as well. The Rangers were in a "no doubles" defense, which meant that a ball hit to deep right field like this one shouldn't get over the fielder's head. Nelson Cruz was drifting back near the warning track and seemed to have a bead on it. In that second my spirit was torn between exhilaration and despair.

Cruz jumped, and the ball slammed off the Gulf sign and rolled away. I heard myself screaming with joy and at some point I realized I was jumping and doing the windmill with my right arm to tell the runners to head for home. A second later, Freese was on his knees after sliding into third with the biggest hit of his life. Like me, the crowd at Busch Stadium was in hysterics. I heard Joe Buck utter the word "unbelievable" on the broadcast. There was no other way to describe it. No one on either side seemed to be able to comprehend what had just happened. The unthinkable rally had forced the game to a 7-7 tie.

As the replays of Freese's miracle were airing, Megan came jogging into the room with mom just behind her. "What's going on? Did we win?"

"No, but we're tied now. David Freese just pulled our asses out of the fire! One more strike and it would have been over!" My heart was still pounding as I said this. Freese's heroics had literally taken my breath away, and I was barely able to get the words out.

Megan smiled and gave a small clap at this news. "Dad, what do you think about this?"

Dad's stare still had not diverted from the TV. He had a satisfied look on his face, but now it was time to get greedy. One more hit and we're heading to game seven with all the momentum in the world on our side.

"I think we need one more great at-bat and this thing will be over!"

The game nearly ended on the first pitch to Molina. Feliz threw a slider in the dirt that Napoli managed to block. A wild pitch after giving up that hit to Freese might have been the cruelest way a game could be lost. Napoli saved the game, at least temporarily. Molina hit the next pitch toward right field, but Cruz was able to track this one down and send the game to extra innings. I laughed and flopped back into the chair in a state of relief and exhaustion.

"I've never seen a hit like that in my life. One strike away! One strike! That's the beauty of baseball I guess!" I said as the women lost interest and left us alone again.

Dad was shaking his head. "You're absolutely right. I can't think of another hit that was this important, at least not in a World Series. This is crazy."

The sudden burst of adrenaline from Freese's shot helped to rejuvenate both of us. To be pulled from the brink of ultimate defeat and given a reprieve was a rush I hadn't felt in a long time. Dad and I were chatting again about the possibilities in extra innings. Not only had Freese given his teammates another chance at victory, he had given us another chance to end our relationship on good terms. The wave of emotions that hit me after his triple was dizzying. The feeling of futility and loss had been completely eradicated. I was amazed both then and now at how dramatically one pitch in a game can change everything.

Somewhere in that torrent of thought I also felt a bit of sympathy for the Ranger fans who had just seen their team blow a chance to secure a championship. The feeling we had in 1985, when a blown call at first and a couple of well-timed hits had deprived us of a winner, was terrible to experience. But it couldn't have been as tough to take as what their fans had just witnessed. One strike away. It had to be a hard pill to swallow.

I had to admit that if we did end up losing the series I couldn't feel too deprived as a fan. The Cardinals already had ten World Championship banners flying, the last one coming just five years before in '06. The Rangers had been in Texas for forty years and were still waiting for number one. Worse yet, they were coming off a loss in the previous year's World Series to San Francisco. Still, no one can blame a fan for wanting their team to win every year. You have to be greedy, even if your team has been to the mountain top many times. There is no guarantee that they'll ever have another shot.

As the commercials ran and the euphoria started to die down, I refocused my mind on how next to approach dad. Attempting to force an apology out of him again didn't feel like the right move. We'd caught a massive break with Freese's hit, and I didn't think going back into attack mode was wise. For the first time all night, or any other time in my life, I realized that I had said nearly everything I needed to say to him. I decided then to forget about making any more "progress" with him and just let the rest of the evening go where it may. For the rest of the game I would simply be his son and enjoy the game with him.

It also occurred to me that with extra innings approaching, this night may not be ending any time soon. That's another wonderful and unique aspect of baseball: no clock. The game ends when it ends no matter how long it takes. I was reminded of that once in April 2010 when the Cardinals lost to the Mets at home 2-1…in twenty innings.

I had already promised myself that I wouldn't leave until this game was over. I thought of the twenty inning game and shuddered. Neither of us would last that long even if the World Series was hanging in the balance. Extra innings meant extra time with dad, and that was the most important outcome of Freese's hit for me. Most of us don't know how many innings we have left in this life, but that night we all knew that dad was working on his last one. Just how it would end was still unclear to me.

Top of the Tenth

Dad's posture had finally relaxed and he was once again leaning against his pillows that were cushioning the headboard. Freese's lightning bolt had been like a shot of caffeine for him, but I still noticed that his grip on his body was loosening. Sweat beads appeared on his forehead, and his breathing had a distinct wheeze that had not been apparent earlier.

The look on his face as he watched the game was grim determination. He was consciously willing himself to stay awake for the end of the game. He looked like a combination of marathon runner and boxer, both in the midst of their struggle. I wondered if he would still be watching tonight if I hadn't been there. According to mom, he had caught portions of each game but struggled to stay with it for more than an hour. At this point he was well into his fourth hour, which in hindsight seems impossible for a man in his condition.

Mom had been right. There was no other way to explain how he was staying with me through every pitch and play. The amount of energy he was expending just to sit there and focus on the game had to be enormous. Though he hadn't responded in exactly the way I had hoped, he was putting forth much more effort than I would have imagined.

The tenth started with Jason Motte back on the mound for a second inning of work. I immediately sensed trouble because he was used to only going one inning. Motte, like most closers, is a unique breed. Many closers are easily spotted by their outlandish style. Motte, like the 2010 World Series closer Brian Wilson, has a style and look that I would term "lunatic lumberjack." Their personality quirks seem to give them the power to overcome the pressure of the ninth inning. But there is something else that most closers also share: they tend to perform differently when throwing in a non-save situation.

I made this point to dad and he responded, "That is true sometimes, but Motte hasn't thrown that many pitches. Top of the order is coming up for them and he's the best we've got."

Motte seemed to confirm dad's belief in him when he got Ian Kinsler to pop up on the first pitch of the inning. Pujols caught the ball with a flourish. Getting the lead-off man in any inning is crucial, but in this instance it was even more important. There's almost no room for error against the Rangers' thunderous bats. Next up was their shortstop Elvis Andrus. He took a heater from Motte inside for ball one, but lined the next one into centerfield for a single. As Mike Shannon likes to say, "It's never easy!" Motte would have to pitch out of the stretch against the heart of their order.

The reigning MVP of the American League, Josh Hamilton, walked to the plate. He hadn't quite been himself in the series to that point because of a groin injury. But hurt or not, Hamilton was the most dangerous hitter they had. I didn't need to say anything to dad about him, we both knew this was a treacherous spot. Motte tossed the ball to first to keep Andrus close to the bag. Then he brought the first one home to Hamilton.

One only needed to hear the sound off the bat and the groan from the home crowd to know it was trouble. The ninety-eight mile per hour inside pitch was now a missile heading for right-centerfield. Berkman turned and looked up, but there was nothing he could do. The ball was in the seats and Texas was right back in the lead, 9-7.

I lowered my head into my hands and stayed that way for at least a minute. I could hear the frantic shouts of joy from the Texas dugout as Hamilton rounded the bases. I wanted to cuss, or punch the TV, or throw the remote. Instead, I sat still, just staring at the floor and wondering if this is what Oakland fans felt when Kirk Gibson hit his

immortal shot off of Dennis Eckersley in game one of the
'88 series. This was an absolute gut punch, one I feared
even our resilient Redbirds would not recover from.

I finally looked at dad and saw that he too had
turned his eyes downward. At that moment I wanted the
Cardinals to win that game more than any other in my life.
I wanted it for myself, as usual, but even more so I wanted
it for dad. He was struggling so mightily to enjoy one last
game with his son, it would be a shame for it to end in
agonizing defeat.

In terms of watching sports, it was the lowest
moment of my life. We had just witnessed one of the great
rallies in World Series history, and it had been completely
undone in a matter of seconds. The swing in emotion was
too much, and I had to get out and walk around before I
exploded.

"Dad, I gotta get out of here. I'll be back when it's
time for us to bat."

I walked to the kitchen where mom was sitting at
the table and reading. Mom is extremely well read on
Biblical matters, so I wasn't surprised to find her reading a
book by Max Lucado. I thought about going outside again,
but decided instead to go to the refrigerator for comfort. I
rooted around until I found what I was looking for: bologna
and Velveeta. Though these items were normally reserved
for celebrations, I needed them immediately. Mom looked
up as I was preparing my depression sandwich.

"Judging by your face I'd say the game wasn't
going that well."

"Yeah, you'd be right. We're down two again in the
tenth inning. They came back once, but it would be a
miracle for them to do it twice in a row." I spread a
generous amount of Hellmann's on both pieces of wheat
bread and added the main ingredients.

"Well, not to sound corny, but maybe this is a night
for miracles. Think about it. You're here for the first time

in years, you've been talking with your father all evening, and he got to meet his grandson for the first time. This isn't your typical Thursday night in the Gibson house!"

I gulped down my first bite and chased it with a sip of Ski. Mom's words immediately made me feel better. She was absolutely right. I had no business feeling sad about this night. Too much good had happened in the last four hours to let it be spoiled by a game I had no control over. I chuckled and laid the sandwich down.

"Mom, you're an amazing woman. Anyone ever tell you that?"

"Yes, but it never gets old! You know your sister is in the living room watching the game. That's got to be a good omen, right? Didn't you always used to say that Megan never loses at anything?"

"True. Hopefully that applies to games she watches as well. I don't mean to get so down about the game. It's just...I really want to see them win tonight. For dad. I wouldn't have said that at the beginning of the night, but it's true. He's made mistakes and he pisses me off, but he's still my dad and I want him to go out with a winner."

"Paul you may not believe this, but your dad doesn't care who wins this game. He's already had two much bigger victories tonight: you and Jack. Don't get me wrong, he still wants the Cardinals to win. But it won't affect him the way it used to. He doesn't have time to get upset over a game at this stage."

"Does he realize how blessed he's been to have you with him all these years? What would he have done if you had walked out? He'd have been dead within a year, probably." I brought this up intentionally because I still had never heard her talk about dad's "backslide" away from sobriety and the church.

"I believe he does. And you're probably right. I doubt anyone else would have taken care of him."

"He doesn't deserve you and he never did. I hope

you've got some extra crowns or mansions coming your way when you get to heaven. You've earned them," I said.

"How can I make you understand? You're married. You know how you feel about Karen. What if she developed an addiction and slowly got worse over time? What if she refused to change her ways even though it was hurting you and Jack? Would you just leave her? Could you walk away from years of devoting your life to her? I don't think it would be that easy for you.

"I tried to walk away. When I moved us to Pauline's house I didn't think I was coming back here. But I missed him, Pauly. I missed him so much and I felt guilty for leaving because I made a vow. Maybe he didn't deserve us coming back, but I couldn't stay away. I knew if I left him for good that he wouldn't handle it and probably end up drinking himself to death. And when he fell back into his old ways later, I didn't have it in me to try to leave again. I figured having him around some of the time was better than you and Megan having no father at all. I'm sorry if you think that's wrong, but it's too late to change it now."

Mom squeezed my hand to let me know she wasn't scolding me. I do and always will believe she was wrong for staying, especially after the relapse. But everyone has to make their own choices and live with them. I could see that she had made peace with hers.

***

I knew Megan felt the same way as I did, we had discussed it numerous times. But Megan's relationship with dad was much healthier than mine, starting around the time I entered high school. Of course she was the baby and a girl, but her connection with dad developed into more than that. During my college years away from home, she became the focal point of the family. Though dad still wasn't home that often, he was more willing to engage in her life. He attended at least some of her volleyball games in high school, and still brought her to Lamasco's on occasion (dad knew the guys in that place wouldn't dare hit on her).

As she began dating, dad assumed the role of protector and made sure to be home on nights when guys would be coming over. I can't imagine the terror in those young boys' hearts when they saw big Johnny Ray open the door and eye them with something close to disdain. At least one of them decided it wasn't worth it and left before the date even began. Another one brought her home thirty minutes after curfew and got quite a scare. Dad walked outside and made the boy get out of his car and explain why they were late. I don't believe they went out again.

Dad never showed the least concern about who I was dating or what I was doing with them. Mom was always the stickler when it came to my love life. I could have brought home a forty year old cocktail waitress and dad wouldn't have blinked. At least he was consistent in his concern about us drinking. I never tested his warning to me, but Megan did. Once.

It was her senior prom and she swore to mom and dad after she was caught (an anonymous tip from one her "friends" brought the police to the house they were hanging out) that it was a one-time mistake. Dad was so angry at her after that night that he couldn't speak to her for weeks. Megan said when he finally did calm down, all he ever said to her about it was "please don't throw your life away."

The fact that he and Megan have had steady and mostly cordial communication all these years since my wedding hasn't bothered me much. A father and daughter's relationship is completely different from a father and son's. Megan knows I had to get away and stay away from dad in order to keep my sanity. I know she had to stay in touch with dad for much the same reason.

I left mom in the kitchen and decided to check on Megan and the ball game in the living room. I chanced a look at the screen and saw Beltre at the plate with two outs. No further damage had been done, though that was no consolation. Megan was curled up in dad's recliner. She gave me a sympathetic look. "Did you break anything when they hit that last home run?"

"No...I wanted to. I can't believe Motte gave that up," I said.

"How are you doing with dad? Any better?"

"Well, I'm still here. Maybe that's enough at this point. Win or lose, I'm going to be with him when this game ends."

Megan gave an approving nod. "That's all he would want. You're doing a good thing here tonight. I'm proud of you."

"Thanks. You know when I got here tonight I wasn't here for his sake. I came here to settle things and get some closure for myself. But now...now I'm staying for him. I really wanted him to see a winner. Looks unlikely now," I said, motioning toward the TV. Beltre grounded out and the top of the tenth was over. Once again we were three outs from elimination.

I knew it was time for me to get back in the bedroom with dad. Halfway down the darkened hallway, I stopped and bowed my head. For the first and only time in my life, I prayed for the Cardinals to rally. It wasn't a selfish prayer for victory, but for a man who was losing a bit of his life with each pitch. I prayed for runs, and that there would be a game seven. I was overwhelmed with the desire for my father to go out a winner. It felt like there was a lot more at stake in that moment than just a baseball team's season. The entire evening we had spent together, and perhaps our relationship, seemed to be hanging in the balance.

Bottom of the Tenth

Dad was wiping his forehead with a cool rag when I walked in. He was visibly trembling, though just slightly, and I realized that his fever had spiked. How he was still conscious I wasn't sure. He started to speak, but a weak cough came out instead. He wiped his mouth with the rag and I saw more blood. Earlier in the evening it had been easy to ignore the fact that he was literally lying in his death bed because of his energy and sharp look. Now it was impossible not to notice.

Darren Oliver was on the mound for the Rangers in what had to be the most important outing of his very long career. The left-hander had been a Cardinal starter for a couple of years in the late '90s. I was somewhat stunned to see that he was still in the majors. I was more surprised that he was Ron Washington's choice to try to close out the World Series.

I thought, *There's no way Darren Oliver is going to close us out! Not this guy. Not tonight.*

"We've got Descalso leading off. He's a scrapper, but its lefty against lefty," I said just to break the silence. We still hadn't said much of substance since my blow-up earlier.

"Can't believe they took Feliz out of the game. That's a mistake. I think they can get to Oliver here. Descalso's good against lefties," dad said with what voice he had left. Even through the extreme pain, he was still able to muster solid insights on the game. Our season was now in the hands of the bottom of the lineup.

Daniel Descalso's role on the team was utility infielder, but I thought he was more valuable than that title suggests. He personified the guts and determination of that team. Even his bearded face suggested a toughness that was more befitting a soldier in combat than a ballplayer. I like to joke that Descalso looks like a guy you would have seen storming the beaches of Normandy in World War II. In short, he was the ideal man to have leading off when in need of a rally.

True to form, Descalso started fouling off pitches and making Oliver work hard. On the eighth pitch of the at-bat Daniel slapped a solid single into right field. I had to smile because it was a classic Descalso effort. Next up was another lefty swinger: Jon Jay. He'd had a tough series. In fact, his first hit of the series had come in his last at-bat. Representing the tying run, it was crucial that he find a way to get on base. After taking strike one, Jay swung and hit a flare down the left field line. It was a perfectly placed single, and now the second rally that couldn't possibly happen was well underway.

"My God dad, are they going to do this again?"

He flashed a grin. "Never seen anything like this. It's like they're just refusing to lose."

LaRussa originally sent Edwin Jackson, the journeyman pitcher, to the plate. But then he changed his mind and decided to send Kyle Lohse up, presumably because he is the better bunter. With the tying runs on and none out, this bunt would be critical. The Rangers huddled on the mound with their pitching coach, hoping that the baseball gods weren't about to crush their championship dreams yet again. I noticed that dad was still grinning and I gave him an inquisitive look.

"This is taking me back to a game I played in my senior year," he said as Mike Maddux discussed the situation with Oliver and the Rangers infield. "City championship. We were playing Rex Mundi High. We had the best team that year and we all assumed that we'd pound them pretty good. We already had two wins against them in the regular season. But damned if they didn't come out inspired. Somehow they managed to get four off our best pitcher in the sixth inning and put us down 4-2.

"We were down to our last outs in the bottom of the

seventh and it looked like we had just blown our chance. Well, we got a walk and a hit mixed in with a couple of loud outs, and now it was up to me. I knew the pitcher well. Eddie Schroeder. He had a decent fastball, but nothing else really great to speak of. I knew he would try to get ahead with his fastball, and I was on it. I hit a rocket into left-center and it went to the fence. I remember screaming as I was running for our guys on base to get home. They both scored. Jimmy Fendrich on first knew I would kick his ass later if he didn't score! That tied it up and we went to extras."

I listened with rapt attention, not only because every word he spoke was magnified at that late hour, but also because I hadn't heard any of his old baseball stories for years. These were the stuff of legend around Lamasco's bar. The guys would swap hero stories and add a little more embellishment every time they told it. They were like fish stories for guys who never fished.

But when dad told his tales, it was different. There was no need to add fiction because he had done some truly remarkable things on a baseball field. As a kid, I was fascinated by those stories. The other guys talked in hushed tones when they discussed dad's baseball and softball career, because he was the only one of them who was a legitimately great athlete.

"I think I remember this story. Didn't Rex Mundi score again to go ahead?"

"Yeah. Pete Bowling their shortstop, the smallest guy on their team, smacked a ball out of the park and put us down 5-4 in the eighth. Well, we managed to squeeze across a run in the bottom half to keep us alive, but we couldn't finish them off. We put them down 1-2-3 in the ninth, and I knew this was my chance to end it. I didn't normally go up there looking to hit homers, but I did that night! They had some new pitcher in there, a guy I didn't know, but I found out later he was a sophomore. Fendrich worked a two out walk in front of me, so I guess they decided they shouldn't pitch around me. I took a couple from the kid just to see what he had. I decided I'd whack at the next one if he put it over the plate. Well, he tried to throw me a curveball, but it was a lollypop. I crushed it toward left and the only question was if it would stay fair. Think of Carlton Fisk in the '75 Series...not that I was doing that little dance like him, but it was that kind of fly ball."

He stopped and stared at the screen and I realized that the action had started again. Lohse was nearly hit by the first pitch from Oliver, which would have been a nice break if he had been willing to hang in and take one in the ribs. There was no mystery to what Lohse was trying to do. The Rangers had the "wheel play" on, which meant the shortstop Andrus would be running to cover third, while the third baseman would charge hard toward home plate. It would take a very well executed bunt in order to move the runners over.

The next pitch came and Lohse made contact. My eyes flew open wide as I saw the ball go into the air. A bunt in the air is usually disastrous for the team that's batting. The pitcher could catch it on the fly, then spin and nail one of the runners before they could get back to the bag. Even avoiding a double play, normally a bunt in the air doesn't get the runners over.

But the normal rules didn't seem to apply to this game anymore. The night had turned magical, as if the players had fallen into a Twilight Zone episode without realizing it. The bunt, much like Jay's blooper, couldn't have landed in a better spot. When I saw it land to the right of the pitcher's mound, I thought it was going to turn into an infield hit for Lohse. Only an impressive play by Andrus, who had to change direction mid-stride in order to field the ball, kept that from happening. But the job had been done, the tying runs now stood at second and third with only one out.

I slapped my hands onto my knees and grunted. "Good bunt!" said dad.

"Have you ever seen that happen? The ball went over the third baseman's head!"

"Nope." That was all the reaction dad could muster. Both of us were starting to get used to the idea of strange things occurring in this game. The replays confirmed what we already knew: the bunt was just bad enough to be effective.

With the Cardinals sending up Theriot and then Pujols, Ron Washington elected to go with a right-hander. We would be forced to wait again before seeing if our season would continue beyond this inning. I motioned to dad to continue his story.

"Oh, right. Well, I trotted a few steps toward first, watching the ball, and then watching the home plate umpire because it was his call to make. I really wasn't sure what he was going to signal until I saw him put out his right arm…fair ball! I think I jumped in the air, and I remember seeing all my teammates running out toward home plate as I was rounding the bases. I also saw Rex Mundi's coach, an old prick named Blatch, storm out and yell at the umpire. God that was a good moment. Maybe my best. That feeling is hard to describe. You dream about doing it and then when it happens, it doesn't seem real. I guess that's why I always liked telling the story, to remind myself that it actually happened."

Being there with dad as he relived his hero moment was the first time all night that I felt genuinely glad to be there. Never mind the sadness in knowing that his best moment came before I was ever born, or that it came on a baseball field instead of with his family. I was just glad that he had a moment like that to bask in. No matter what happened later in his life, dad could always feel satisfaction in a city championship-winning home run.

"Maybe one of our Redbirds can do a Johnny Ray impression and send us to a game seven!" I said. Dad grinned again and nodded.

Scott Feldman took his warm-up tosses as the Rangers' latest hurler to attempt to lock down a world title. With their closer already vanquished, Texas would need an unlikely hero to get those last two precious outs. Theriot dug in and immediately fell into a 0-2 hole. He managed to foul off a couple of pitches, and then finally put one in play. It was a chopper to Adrian Beltre at third. He made the safe play and threw Theriot out at first as Descalso came home to make the score 9-8. The tying run was still at second, but once again we were one out from defeat.

I was disappointed, but not surprised when the Rangers elected to walk Albert with first base open. If he hit a home run and won the game, how would their manager possibly explain the decision to pitch to the best hitter in baseball? Putting the go-ahead run on base was risky, but both dad and I agreed it was the right call. Now the game would fall into the hands of Lance Berkman, a man who had a career full of successes of every kind except a World Series title.

I caught myself rocking back and forth on the edge of the recliner. I stopped and focused on willing a base hit out of Berkman. The count went to 1-1 and then Feldman unloaded a nasty pitch that dove toward Lance's feet. He swung through it, and for the second time in two innings the Cardinals were one strike from elimination.

I could hear dad's forced breathing get a little faster. We both wanted this so badly, it hurt to even consider the possibility that Berkman would fail. The next pitch flew in and it was well off the plate inside for ball two. Deep down I knew that wishing for two dramatic comebacks in two consecutive innings was a massive long shot. Even in most movies the good guys only get one shot at a rally.

Feldman rocked back and I steeled myself for what

I believed would be the last pitch of our season. I was out of optimism despite the incredible effort our guys were putting forth. I saw Berkman swing and make contact, but the flight of the ball eluded me. I leaned forward, desperately searching with my eyes to see where the ball was headed. Then the camera changed and I heard the crowd react. Feldman's pitch had started inside, but tailed over the plate, and Lance delivered a game-tying hit to centerfield.

"Yeah Lance! Yeah! Holy shit, dad! Do you believe this?" I was bouncing around and nearly giggling with glee. Dad's only reaction was a slow shaking of the head coupled with that satisfied grin. Just for a moment our eyes locked. We were caught up in the game, but there was something else in his eyes. I sensed that he was thankful, not just the game, but for the entire evening. He was struggling to stay with me in that late hour, but I know he wouldn't have wanted to be anywhere else.

As the crowd at Busch and the men of Delmar Avenue celebrated a second amazing rally, Joe Buck broke in with a phrase that perfectly encapsulated the feelings of all Ranger fans: "They just won't go away." I gave a loud laugh when I heard that. LaRussa's "hard nine" philosophy had now extended into extra innings.

Allen Craig bounced out to third a couple of pitches later to end the inning, but I couldn't be upset at this lost opportunity. The Cardinals had just gotten off the mat after two knockout punches and were still standing. Now there was no doubt, something very special was unfolding in St. Louis. All of us in the house felt it, as did everyone waving the towels and screaming their heads off at Busch.

"You up for another inning, dad?" I was half joking. He was holding his own despite the pain and there was no chance he was retiring before seeing this game through.

"Sure. I'm up for three or four more rallies if that's what it takes! God's not going to take me before the end of this game! I don't think he's that cruel!"

"Hey, I've got an idea. Be back in just a minute," I said. From the hallway I could hear mom and Megan laughing in the living room. I jogged in there and saw that even mom had been pulled into watching the game.

"Looks like you're the lucky charm tonight, bro! You're not going anywhere until this game's over!"

"Are you kidding? No one is leaving this house or going to sleep until this game ends! We're in full superstition mode right now. I'm actually headed to the kitchen to grab the old radio that I found out on the porch. I think we need the power of Mike Shannon to pull us through!"

I looked at mom and saw her staring down at the floor. She looked very sad for the first time all evening. She was being such a soldier for all of us that it was easy to sometimes forget that she would soon be losing her husband.

"Mom, you okay?" I asked.

She blinked and then looked up at me from her chair. "Yes, I'm fine. You go on and get back in there. I don't want you guys to miss a minute together."

I gave them both a smile and then returned to my original mission. It seemed silly and juvenile. Why would it matter if we listened to the next inning on radio instead of watching the TV? It probably wouldn't, but that didn't mean we shouldn't try. Maybe there was some magic left in that old radio, which had brought us so many winners during my childhood. Bringing in that radio didn't just feel right, it felt necessary.

As I re-entered the bedroom with the portable under my arm, I stole a glance at dad. For a second he was confused, but then a look of total understanding fell over him. I plugged it in and we heard the crackle followed by the familiar voice of Mike Shannon getting ready to call the eleventh inning. I grabbed the remote and shut off the TV without a word.

We sat, as in olden days, immersed in the sounds of a baseball game. Our last inning together was about to begin.

Top of the Eleventh

The Cardinals turned to Jake Westbrook to get them through a scoreless frame. He had been a reliable fifth starter for them all season, but hadn't seen much action in the playoffs. Facing the likes of Cruz, Napoli, and Murphy, it was clear he had a major challenge ahead of him. Falling behind a third time would be a killer for a team that had been battling all night.

The old GE radio made the game sound like it was being played inside a large tunnel. We had traded stereo sound and high definition images for the tinny emanations of a wind-blasted portable that was older than me. I wouldn't have had it any other way. Sitting with dad with the ball game coming through those old speakers transported me back to the best feelings of my childhood.

"Is it too loud?" I asked. I turned the knob slightly counter-clockwise without waiting for his response. I wanted us to have a chance to talk if the opportunity arose. I began to realize that turning off the TV had deprived us of a convenient focal point. On a darkened porch it's easy to stare out into the yard and never face each other. In a lighted and enclosed bedroom, the lack of a visual stimuli suddenly made things awkward. I tried focusing on the radio, but after a few moments I found myself looking aimlessly around the room. We needed a jumpstart.

"What are you going to miss? When you're gone, I mean." Maybe it was a stupid question, but it was all that came to me. Dad turned his head toward me and I could see that he was taking the question seriously. That was a relief.

"I guess it depends. If your mom's right and I'm going to heaven, then I probably won't miss much. I'll miss her more than anything. You know I wasted a lot of time with the guys, and that was fun. But now I wish I would have stayed home more. I never thought to appreciate things—and people—before they were gone. It took getting cancer to keep me home and now that I'm used to being with her every day, I don't want to go. I don't give a shit about heaven, I just want to hang around here with her for a few more years."

He might have continued but he was hit by a coughing spell that lasted over a minute. With every cough he recoiled from the pain radiating throughout his body. Before that night I was familiar with the term hospice, but experiencing it was heartbreaking. How does it feel knowing that you've been sent home only to wait around for death? I thought he was handling himself remarkably well…dying with dignity if there is such a thing.

"I'll miss you, dad. I know that sounds terrible considering I've been gone for fifteen years, but it's true. I wish I had come over and done this with you years ago. And I wish you'd been there when Jack was born. I'm sorry I wasn't a stronger person, because if I had maybe I would have come around more often. You know it's not like I didn't think about you all these years. I thought about you every day. I even prayed for you sometimes. I wanted to see you, I did. But then the years started to pile up and the thought of facing you again just became this huge event in my mind. I'm sorry it came to this, I really am dad."

My eyes moistened but my body automatically shut down the urge to cry. I still wasn't ready for him to see me vulnerable.

Dad's expression was one of almost total disbelief as he looked into my eyes. I believe he was genuinely surprised to hear those words from me, and I was a little surprised that I was able to get them out. I didn't want to have to be the first one to apologize for the past, but if it helped to get us to some kind of final resolution, and then I was willing to give up some pride.

"Well, I hope you know that I've missed you a lot too. Do you know how many times I've wanted to talk to you during and after ball games? Hell, just about every night of every season! I can't talk with the guys about baseball because they don't get it. They never loved a team the way you and I loved the Cardinals. I even tried talking to Doris about it sometimes, but she couldn't care less! But let me say now, in case I forget later, that I'm really glad to have you here tonight. You're giving them good vibes! And the radio? Great idea! I just wish Jack Buck was still alive to call a game like this!"

My satisfaction with the positive turn in our communication was quickly stifled when I heard Mike Shannon announce that Napoli had singled to center with one out. Even before I could say anything, dad reacted.

"Jesus Christ! Do we have any pitchers that can get that guy out! What's that about five or six times he's been on base tonight? That's ridiculous."

I said nothing, but I couldn't have agreed more. Napoli would absolutely be the MVP of the series if the Rangers ended up winning.

We sat silent for a moment, intent on finding out if Westbrook would be able to keep a lid on the rest of their lineup. Daniel Murphy took a couple of pitches and then mercifully popped the ball into centerfield for the second out. One more out and the Cardinals would finally have a chance to go for the win instead of clawing back from behind. I relaxed a bit.

"Can I ask you a question without you getting mad? I'd like to know why you never came to any of my basketball games. I mean, I know you really wanted me to play baseball and I just wasn't that good at it. But that's no reason to boycott my basketball games! I was good! Our team was good. I looked up into the stands during every game and hoped so badly to see you. I always saw mom and Megan, but never you. How do you think it felt for me to be the only player whose dad wasn't cheering like hell for them? I felt like shit after every game, even when we won, because I wanted you to see. Even when we were barely talking and I hated being around you, I still wanted you to be proud of me because you're my dad."

Dad closed his eyes and started shaking his head. I wasn't sure if he was denying what I had said or if he was trying to clear his own mind so he could respond. His fever had been creeping up all night and at that point was probably making it hard for him to concentrate. He let out a slow breath through his nose and then opened his eyes.

"Paul, I don't know what to tell you. I wanted to be there. I was proud of you. Hell, I bragged to the guys all the time about your stats and your team's record. You guys had one of the best years in the school's history for God's sake! Looking back, I feel stupid about it. You have to understand, I didn't avoid your games because of you. I was just caught up in my own shit."

"I'm supposed to accept that?"

"You're right. I had no good reason for not being there for you. If you would have let me finish I was going to add something. There was another thing keeping me from going into that gym. Everyone in there knew who I was. If I went in there, even sober, I'd have gotten a lot of dirty looks and whispers from the goddamn hypocrites in this town. I wasn't about to go in there and be judged and take the spotlight off of you. I wanted them looking at you and not worrying about me. Does that make sense?"

I had to admit that it did. It still didn't satisfy me, but I could understand. I nodded and looked back at the radio as if to refocus us on the game. With two outs and a runner at first, the pitcher's spot was due up for Texas. Scott Feldman had worked the tenth and was one of their best relievers. A pinch hitter, Yorvit Torrealba, had been standing in the on-deck circle while Murphy was batting.

But it seemed that Ron Washington was having some second thoughts, and Feldman appeared on the field with a bat in his hands. Even without the benefit of the TV we could tell that there was real indecision on the part of the Rangers' management. After a moment in which several players milled about on the field, Washington settled on using Esteban German as a pinch hitter instead of Torrealba.

"He should have stuck with Feldman. He's the best guy they've got left. German's not much of a threat and they don't have a runner in scoring position," dad said.

"He's got a little pop. I just hope Westbrook doesn't make a mistake and groove one."

The first pitch was low and away, but the next one was bounced meekly to Theriot at second. He threw to first and completed a successful mission for Westbrook and the Cards. The score remained tied at nine, and David Freese would be leading off in the bottom half.

"You know, a lot of those Friday night games I did get to hear you on the radio. I always made the bartender turn off the jukebox and turn on their portable so we could hear your games. God you were a great shooter! I don't know where that comes from…maybe your mom's side of the family!" dad said with as much intensity as he could spare.

"Thanks. I spent a lot of afternoons and evenings in the gym working on that. It kept me out of the house and out of trouble I guess. I still say you should have been there, dad. Since when did you give a shit about what people thought about you?"

"Well, that wasn't the whole truth either. I thought about going a few times. Once I was even in the parking lot. But I never went in because I know me. I know I would have gotten mad at one of the refs or maybe the opposing coach or even a player and done something stupid. You saw what I did to those kids teepeeing our yard that time. I didn't want to be the guy who got arrested because he went out on the floor and beat the shit out of a referee! If I had done that, you'd have never lived it down. I got nervous when you played. I wanted you to be great and win every game. Having to watch and not have any control, that was too much to handle," he said.

I sat with my hands folded in front of me and stared straight ahead. I thought his initial answer, when he said he was too into himself, was probably the most honest. But I knew there was more than a hint of truth in his other explanations. I could imagine him shushing the guys at Lamasco's as the announcer called the action of our basketball games on the radio. I could see him cheering loudly whenever he heard "Gibson hits a three-pointer!" I could even picture him buying a round for the entire bar after we won the game.

A warm feeling slowly grew inside of me. I never knew that he kept tabs on my games by listening to them. We hardly ever talked about my games at home, aside from an occasional "go get 'em tonight, Paul!" This wasn't the same intense feeling of pride that a boy gets from hearing his dad cheer for him, but it was satisfying nonetheless.

"I'm glad you were listening. Still wish you would have just shown up though."

"Me too. But that's something you can make right for me. Whatever Jack plays, even if it's soccer, God forbid, you'll be there for every one of them because you're a good father. Hopefully I'll get to see him too from wherever I'll be!"

I smiled and nodded in acknowledgement. My hope was that the baseball gene had simply skipped a generation and that Jack would be a natural hitter like his grandpa. To me, hitting a baseball always felt more like trying to hit a ping pong ball with a wooden spoon. Perhaps Jack would have dad's ability to see the ball where it would be a second before it was actually there. I couldn't wait to find out.

We had cleared another hurdle, both in the game and in our ongoing summit, and now we waited. Win or lose, we needed an outcome soon. The internal dam that dad had constructed in order to experience this night was failing rapidly. His energy, demeanor, and voice were all fading. I estimated that we had perhaps two more innings before he would need to sleep or pass out from exhaustion.

"What do you think here? Can we push one across and call it a night?" I asked, trying not to sound desperate for that run. That's when dad said something I'll never forget. He sounded bold and confident, as if he had already seen this game and was catching the replay.

"David Freese is going to hit a home run."

Bottom of the Eleventh

There are certain moments in every person's life that are unforgettable. There are huge events (like 9/11 or the Kennedy assassination) that are indelibly imprinted on the minds of those who experienced them. But there are other less important but still incredibly memorable events that etch themselves onto the timeline of each life. There are a few that fit that description for me: the first time I met Karen, playing in the state basketball semi-finals (and losing), and my wedding day. The latest occurred on a chilly Thursday night while sitting next to my dying father.

Of course the entire evening was a unique experience that was equally thrilling and wrenching. I have played each conversation, and each inning, over and over again in my mind. The echoes of that night will stay with me for the rest of my life. But one moment must stand alone. Whenever someone mentions game six of the 2011 World Series, a flood of images hits me. But the first one is always the same: David Freese's sweet swing that tied the series and put a perfect cap on perhaps the greatest baseball game ever played.

After dad's matter-of-fact prediction, I was locked in to every word that Mike Shannon uttered. I was simply hoping for a lead-off walk or a bleeder to get the winning run on base. I figured Freese had already used up his magic earlier when he crushed what might have been the series-clinching pitch for the Rangers into right field and extended the game.

This time he faced Mark Lowe, a hard thrower, but not of the caliber of Neftali Feliz. Though I didn't realize it at the time, the Cardinals had already set a record by becoming the first team ever to score runs in the eighth, ninth, and tenth innings of a World Series game. A run in the eleventh would make it a truly historic effort.

The count ran to 3-0. I said something out loud

about taking one and possibly two pitches in this situation. Dad didn't answer, but I hardly noticed. We were both dialed in. A borderline inside pitch was called for strike one. I grimaced, knowing how big a lead-off walk would be. Swing and a foul, and now the count was full. Still, Freese would certainly get a pitch to hit. With no room for error, and a hopeful crowd weighing down on him, Mark Lowe prepared to deliver the payoff pitch.

I closed my eyes and waited. One of the beautiful and unappreciated aspects of baseball is the building of suspense. People complain about the frequent pauses in the game, but sometimes they can add a delicious drama that no other sport can match. It seemed to take forever for Lowe to get a new baseball, get the sign from Napoli, set himself, and throw. First we heard the sound of wood connecting with ball, then the excited description from the "voice of the Cardinals."

"Swing and a high drive to center field!" My eyes opened and I shot out of the chair and onto my feet. "Get up baby! Get up baby! Get up...oh yeah! David Freese has just sent us into game number seven! This series is tied three-three with a walk-off home run here in the bottom of the eleventh..." I launched into the air and let out a banshee-like cry of joy and victory. Half laughing and half screaming, I turned to dad and saw the most satisfied look of anyone I've ever seen. His muted reaction was necessary in his condition, but it conveyed every bit of the same euphoria I was feeling in that moment.

I bounced toward him with a hand raised in offer of a customary high-five. He raised his right hand as far as it would go, and instead of slapping it, I grasped it as if we were about to arm wrestle and held it for a time. I bent to eye level with him and tried not to shout when I said, "How's that for a finish? Oh my God! How did you know, dad? How did you know?"

"I just had a good feeling about him. He's a hell of

a hitter."

I released his hand and moved to turn on the TV for a replay. The picture came on just in time for us to see Freese's teammates pounding on him in front of home plate. Nick Punto was engaging in his tradition of tearing the uniform off of the player who got the winning hit. We both laughed at the sight of grown men dog piling each other and running around like they just won the Little League World Series. They had earned every second of it. The game had gone more than five hours, about four and half of which the Cardinals were hanging by a thread.

We watched the replay over and over. No matter how many times I see it, even now, I get chills watching that ball sail over Josh Hamilton's head and land on the grassy knoll in center field. Joe Buck's line, "We will see you tomorrow night," was a perfect homage to his father who gave the same call on TV in 1991 when Kirby Puckett of the Twins hit a tenth inning homer to send that World Series to a game seven.

Only a handful of men in history have experienced the Roy Hobbs moment that Freese did that night. My favorite baseball movie has always been *The Natural*. I get choked up every time that ball hits the lights, and he's running in slow motion around the bases, and Glenn Close is weeping in the stands. Aside from the absence of sparks showering the field, the Freese home run was every bit as dramatic.

I continued to stand motionless, watching the post-game and trying to process what we had just witnessed. The first and most important consequence was that there would be a game seven tomorrow night. I found the idea of them playing another game less than twenty-four hours after this epic contest to be inconceivable. Both sides would be emotionally drained, but the Cardinals would have all the momentum.

My phone began to vibrate with messages from

friends all over the country. I didn't have to look at the phone to know they were congratulating me. Later that night I found that Facebook and Twitter had also been completely dominated by talk of the game. It made me glad to see that baseball can still bring joy to so many diverse groups of people.

I ran out of the room to find Megan and mom. I had heard Megan let out a scream when she saw Freese's blast clear the wall. She was standing in the middle of the living room with her hands on her head, still staring in disbelief. I heard Jack Buck's voice in my head crying out, "I don't believe what I just saw!"

This would be one that I would be telling my grandkids about many years in the future. You spend your whole life rooting for a team, and most of the time the season ends with disappointment. But once or twice in a lifetime there will be a game or just a moment that makes it all worthwhile.

Megan looked at me with a crazed smile and started laughing as she put her arms around me. She didn't really care about the Cardinals, but I knew she was celebrating because of what the game meant to dad and all of us on that particular evening.

She said, "So, game seven tomorrow night. You coming over?" The question struck me harder than I expected. I realized that I hadn't really considered the possibility of coming back for a game seven. The consummate pessimist within me had made it impossible to plan for any eventuality other than our losing the series. Plus, it had been such a special night and so much good had been accomplished between dad and me. Did I want to risk coming back and ruining that?

I managed a casual response. "We'll see."

Mom had been in the bathroom and now I could hear her talking to dad. She laughed in response to something he said. Megan said, "Crazy how things turn out isn't it? The way dad looked a couple of days ago, I would have never believed he would be able to stay up and watch that whole game with you. He's got to be exhausted."

"Exhausted, but happy!" I replied.

"Did you get to say everything you needed to say?"

"Yes and no. I'd say I got out everything I needed to, but I don't think he did. He's still making excuses for a lot of things. I guess this was never going to turn out exactly the way I hoped. But it could have been much worse. I'm glad we got to do this," I said.

I hated to sound disappointed considering I had just spent more time with my father than I had in the last fifteen years combined. There was one thing that I hadn't heard from him, and I didn't think it was going to happen.

"I've got to see him! I'll bet he's bursting!" she said and slipped out of the room. I was alone in the place where dad and I had watched all those playoff games in the '80s. His black leather chair had been upgraded to a new model, but the rest of the room seemed frozen in time. The royal blue carpeting was badly faded. The never used fireplace surrounded by stark black wood was still the centerpiece of the room. Even the paint-by-numbers replica of The Last Supper that I had done in sixth grade was still hanging over the TV stand.

I suddenly felt a need to sit and I slumped into dad's chair in a heap. The high of seeing our Redbirds pull off a miracle was already starting to wear off. The murmurs from the bedroom between dad, mom, and Megan reminded me that a family, my family, had once lived here together.

Dad's words came back to me. Had I abandoned them? Should I have been stronger and stayed in contact with dad just to make it easier for everyone? I let my head lay back on the cushion and closed my eyes. Before I could stop it, tears were running down my face. I wiped them away hurriedly, half embarrassed. It was as if the emotional barrier I had been fortifying for fifteen years was finally collapsing.

Several minutes passed in silence. I needed this break to collect myself and battle the fatigue that was overtaking me. *Get off your ass and get in there!* I thought. *You'll never get this time back.*

When I got back to the bedroom, Megan was lying next to dad much as Jack had done earlier. Dad looked exultant and used up all at once. It reminded me of times when he was approaching drunkenness but not quite there. In that phase, he would look around with a kind of goofy grin and seem like the happiest man in the bar. If we could have just kept him in that tipsy state he might have been the greatest father ever.

Mom was standing at the foot of the bed when I entered. She came to me and wrapped her arms around my left arm and leaned against me. *This is it,* I thought. *This is the last time I'm going to be with my whole family. This is the last time I'm going to see my father alive.*

The revelation made me shudder, but mom didn't seem to notice. She was soaking in what she also must have known was a fleeting moment.

Megan was whispering something in dad's ear as he continued to smile. When she finished she kissed him on the cheek and got out of the bed.

"Well mom, why don't we step out and let these two dissect that win!"

I gave Megan an appreciative glance and the two of them turned toward the kitchen. I stood a moment longer, then slowly approached him. I forced myself to forget that these would most likely be our last few moments together. I needed all my focus on the present.

Somehow he looked even smaller than when I had arrived just hours earlier. He turned his head to look at me. Having completed his mission, he was nearly swooning with exhaustion. The color in his face was just a shade above white, and his eyes showed deep avenues of red. He looked miserable, but the smile of a victorious man remained in place. If life were more like the movies, he would have died in that very moment with me by his side.

"So it turns out Freese had a little Johnny Ray in him after all!" I said as I turned off the old radio and unplugged it. It wasn't quite an eleventh inning home run ball, but for me it was the best souvenir I could hope for.

"It's just the damnedest thing. Son, I don't know what kind of magic you brought over here tonight, but it worked!" Magic seemed like the only proper term after seeing the guy from St. Louis get two of the most important hits in Cardinals history in a span of three innings.

"I guess no one in St. Louis will be sleeping tonight…I know I won't get any. God, I can't wait to go back and watch the game again at home!"

Seconds passed, I settled back into the recliner next to the bed. I knew I needed to wrap this up. He was spent and I desperately wanted to part ways on a good note. I just wasn't sure how to make it happen.

Finally, as if sensing my struggle, he spoke. "Look, I know you probably need to get going. It's late and you need to get back to that boy of yours. Don't feel like you have to stay on my account."

"Yeah, you're right. It's actually really late. Feels like two in the morning. You need anything before I go?"

He nodded and gestured for me to come closer. I leaned in.

"I…uh…I need to say something before you go. First, for what it's worth, I'm very proud of you. For everything. You're a good husband, good father, educated, good job, and you managed to do all that with me as your dad. Your mom deserves a lot of credit, but so do you."

He paused to catch his breath. The voice was nearly gone, he had preserved just a bit more energy for this moment. Our last shared moment. I felt the tears welling up, but this time I resisted the urge to bite my lip.

He continued, "But more than that, I need to say I'm sorry. You were right about all that stuff you said at your wedding. I was an asshole for most of my life, and I admit that. You didn't deserve a father like me. I was too busy chasing the things that made me happy to notice that I had a great family right here. I can't ever make those things up to you. All I can do is say I'm sorry."

I grabbed his left hand and put it in between both of mine. Single tears streamed down both of his gaunt cheeks. I felt the warmth of my own tears and welcomed them. These were words I had waited a lifetime for. We stayed silent for some time, I can't say how long. I was lost in the wave of relief, joy, and pity welling up from deep inside.

"Thanks for saying that, dad. You don't know how much that means to me. Truly. I'm so glad I got to be with you tonight. I'm sorry I didn't do it sooner." With his eyes closed, dad shook his head as if to dismiss my apology.

"Tonight was perfect. I got to see all the people in the world that I love, and the Cardinals won the craziest game I've ever seen. It couldn't have been better," he choked on the last word and began coughing again. The shockwaves of pain roared through his body and he growled fiercely in defiance of them. It was also my reminder that time was up. I needed to let him rest.

"You're right. Tonight was perfect. And now I'm going to let you try to get some sleep. I'll call tomorrow night and check on you, okay? We can talk strategy for game seven."

His coughing finally ceased and he struggled to regroup and find the ability to speak. "Sounds good. We'll need a big effort from Carp."

I smiled and squeezed his hand. "That's right. Dad? I love you. I hope you know that. Even with all these years that I stayed away, you were always my dad."

Now he smiled and my words seemed to calm him. He squeezed my hand in response with a surprising force.

"Paul...Tiger...I love you too. More than you'll ever realize. Now go. Tell your mom I'm asleep. She worries too much."

I wanted to say so much more. It had taken all evening for us to really open up, and now I had to walk away. I slowly rose and released his hand. I closed my eyes and turned toward the door. I desperately wanted to turn back to him and keep talking, or at least give him a smile. I moved in slow motion, hoping he would stop me. I heard nothing, so I left without looking back. Closing the door behind me, I wiped my eyes and stood silent for a minute as if guarding the door.

I didn't stay long after that. The next few minutes were a blur of hugs, kisses, and goodbyes. I told mom I would call tomorrow and talk with both of them. I was still hopeful that dad and I could share in one more victory, a World Series winner, before he left us. I made sure to take the old radio with me, knowing that I would probably need it to get me through a tense game seven.

Walking to the car, my knees began to weaken and I steadied myself just before falling. It suddenly felt as if my blood sugar level had crashed. I sat in the driver's seat for several minutes in perfect silence. It was impossible to recount all the events of the evening. My mind kept wanting to process all of this new input and put it in instant perspective, though I knew it would take weeks or months for that to happen.

Before long I found myself praying silently as I stared at the steering wheel. It was an unconscious action, like a reflex. The urge to speak to a higher power at that moment was probably stronger than at any time of my life. I'm not sure what all I said or asked for, but the core of my message to God was simply to say thanks. Though I couldn't yet understand all of what we had accomplished that night, I understood that it had been a blessing. I was especially grateful that I hadn't waited too long. I thanked

God for keeping the old man around just long enough to see his son one more time, his grandson for the first time, and a Cardinals win that people will be marveling over for decades.

Finally the chill of the car's interior forced me to turn on the engine. I gave my childhood home one more look before pulling out onto Delmar Avenue and rolling east toward the hotel.

On the radio they were already discussing the preposterous ways in which the Cardinals had fought back and finally prevailed. The "experts" were saying it could be the greatest baseball game ever played. I tend to agree.

The weak feeling left me and I was very much awake when I entered our room on the second floor and found Karen and Jack asleep together on one of the two queen beds. Knowing that I wouldn't be able to sleep just yet, I decided to take a late night walk. Walks have always helped me to think through problems and develop solutions, but that night it was more like a victory lap. The longer I walked through the streets of Evansville, the better I felt about the evening that had passed. I came to the conclusion at some point during the walk that the whole night was meant to be. No need to fight it or find a better explanation, it's just what God wanted for us.

I got back and laid down at around two a.m., but sleep did not find me until probably four. Though I only got perhaps four hours of sleep, I awoke on the Friday morning after game six feeling satisfied and excited about the prospect of another game that night. The sight of the radio taken from dad's porch was a reminder that the events of the previous night had actually happened. I couldn't imagine that dad got much sleep either, and I decided that I wouldn't call their house until later in the day to give them both time to rest.

My mind kept reeling back and forth between pondering my reconnection with dad and the craziness of the game. The Rangers must have been in utter despair after game six. They let the series slip away on a night when the Cardinals committed terrible errors in the field (Freese's drop) and on the bases (Holliday getting picked off third), left eleven men on base, and went only three for twelve with runners in scoring position. Funny how an ugly mess of a game can become an all-time classic thanks to one or two magical moments.

That's also how I view my evening spent with dad. It was ugly and messy at times. The mood kept swinging between hope and despair as our conversation ebbed and flowed. There were times when I wanted to punch him and times I wanted to kiss him. In the end, our last night together was saved by one or two magical moments that didn't have anything to do with baseball. For once, we talked about real life and did it with pure honesty. I left my dad's side feeling that we had broken through the years and the pain and ultimately found common ground. It certainly helped that the Cards won the game.

Though I try not to, I sometimes wonder how our conversation would have ended if Freese had swung through Feliz's 1-2 pitch in the ninth. If we had watched the Rangers jumping around on the turf in St. Louis and popping corks in the locker room, would our last meeting have ended so peacefully? Would our anger and disappointment with our boys on the field have spilled over into our last words to each other? Thankfully, I'll never know.

Karen and I took advantage of a beautiful, crisp autumn day in Evansville and took Jack to the zoo. We also took him to Angel Mounds, an amazing site where native mound builders had a thriving society many hundreds of years ago. I did my best to stay focused on my beautiful son and wife; to appreciate good moments as they occur instead of only savoring them long after they're gone. But I couldn't help revisiting the night before, and in the late afternoon I decided it was time to call and check on the family I left behind fifteen years ago.

As soon as I heard mom's voice, my heart plummeted and a nauseous feeling overtook me.

Epilogue

M om sounded as if she hadn't slept since I last saw her. I'm not sure what I expected to hear, but her words stunned me.

"He's been in and out of consciousness all day. His fever spiked a couple of times earlier and he was pretty confused. He didn't know me for a while. Pauly, I think he's close." She was remarkably composed, though her voice was weak with fatigue. I was unable to answer for a few seconds.

"Do you want me to come over and help? I can be there in an hour."

I heard her banging around in the kitchen, probably holding the phone between her cheek and shoulder. "No, no. I don't think you want to see him like this, and I know he doesn't want you to see him like this. I know this might sound harsh, but you had a good night with him and that should be enough. If you come over now it'll just upset you. Wouldn't you rather remember him as he was last night?"

She made an excellent point. I didn't really want to be there to see the end. I thought about Jack. Would I want him to witness my death, especially if it were a long and unpleasant ordeal such as what dad was experiencing? It was decided: I would not be there when he died.

Mom continued after more clanging. "Besides, Megan is still here and she's helping a lot. You know, she's been here taking care of him off and on for weeks now. She wants to be here, and I think it's fitting that she stays until it's over."

That comment stung, though I don't think it was meant to. Still, I knew she was speaking truth. Megan had been a warrior for mom when I was still hunkered down in my fort trying to gather strength for one night with dad.

"Yeah," I whispered.

Mom detected the sadness (and slight embarrassment) in my tone. "Pauly, what you did last night was exactly what your dad—what we all—needed. I could tell after you left that a huge weight had been lifted off him. I think that's why he's slipping away so quickly now. He can finally go in peace. He accomplished his last goal, and now he can rest. Don't be sad, baby. You did great! And soon he'll be free of that old body and be walking into God's kingdom. That's the picture that keeps me going. Johnny, young and strong like he used to be, walking with Jesus!"

She started to giggle at the image she had created, but it turned into a sob. I sat down and whispered to her that it was okay, that she needed to let it out. She got quiet for a few moments, then regained her composure.

"What you need to do is just enjoy the game tonight with Jack. If he asks about his grandpa, tell him he's going to be flying with the angels pretty soon!" The thought of Johnny Ray with angel wings nearly made me laugh out loud. I knew she was right about Jack…he was my future and I needed to stay with him. The past's final chapter had played out the night before. There was no need for me to backtrack anymore.

Though mom had explicitly stated that I shouldn't be there, I felt a crush of guilt setting in. It felt as if Megan had been in the trenches while I showed up for one night, got the best out of dad, and then ran off to let her clean up the remains. I did my best to push those feelings aside as game seven approached, but it was impossible to completely shake. The usual excitement and nervousness I would have felt for the Cardinals had been dulled by the whirlwind of the last twenty-four hours. The knowledge of dad's imminent demise made it difficult to focus on a game.

The one fact that kept me motivated to root for the Cards, aside from the obvious World Series trophy on the line, was that a loss in game seven would serve to nullify much of the magic that we had just witnessed. Much like Albert's dramatic home run off Brad Lidge in 2005, Freese's game-tying triple and game-winning homer would be relegated to the status of impressive but ultimately futile efforts if they lost game seven.

Win game seven, and the Freese game instantly goes into the pantheon of greatest games and moments in sports history. I also knew that this would be without question the last Cardinals game played during dad's life. How many fans get to leave this life with their team being crowned champion?

I stayed in the hotel room with Karen and Jack that evening, watching the game while lying on the bed nearest the window with Jack right beside me. We ordered a pizza, of which I downed only half a slice before feeling ill, and waited for the contest to begin. To her credit, Karen actually watched most of the game with us and was genuinely cheering. She says her favorite player is Lance Berkman, but only because of his looks. I love him because he stroked a two out, two strike pitch in the tenth inning of game six to keep our season, and my night with dad, from ending too soon.

Fittingly, it would be the hard battling Chris Carpenter, the veteran of so many big games for the Cards over the last few years, taking the ball in game seven. He had just pitched in game five in Texas, giving a solid seven inning performance in which he gave up only two runs. Thanks to a rain-out of game six on Wednesday night, Carp was given the chance to pitch game seven on three days' rest.

This was a risky move by LaRussa because one less day of rest than normal can play havoc with a pitcher's performance. However, I don't believe any Cardinal fan was against the move because Carp is one of the most intense competitors in baseball. He would be great because he had to be, because that's what great pitchers do when their team's season is on the line.

That being said, the game couldn't have started worse. Ian Kinsler lined the second pitch of the game into left field for a single. Mercifully, he got greedy and tried to steal second, but the cannon arm of Yadier Molina nailed him. That play would end up being huge as Carp gave up a walk to Andrus, followed by back-to-back doubles from Hamilton and Young. Before the crowd had settled into its seats, the Rangers already had a 2-0 lead.

I leaned my head back against the headboard and let out a long sigh. This was a worst case scenario: Carp didn't look like himself. All of the momentum and excitement that might have carried over into this game was immediately destroyed. The Rangers made a statement in that first inning: they had forgotten the past and were still determined to win the World Series.

In my mind I heard dad's reassuring voice. "Don't worry, Paul. Carp's a warrior. He'll keep us in the game and the offense will pick him up. It's way too early to give up!"

Thanks dad, you're right, I thought. I began to realize how much I was going to miss him. A pang of regret shot through me, and I had to shut my eyes for a few moments to keep from breaking down.

Carp regrouped after the second double, striking out Beltre and getting Cruz on a groundout. In some ways it was only fitting that the Cardinals fell behind in game seven. An easy win would not have reflected the incredible adversity that they weathered throughout that entire season. One more comeback would be necessary.

Naturally, David Freese once again found himself in a clutch situation in the bottom of the first. After two men were out, Albert walked and Berkman followed with another base on balls. Freese received a well-deserved monstrous ovation as he strolled to the plate. Rarely has any player with as pedestrian a career as Freese been able to transform himself into a postseason legend. How could we as fans possibly ask for anything more than he had already provided?

He worked the count ably against the lefty Harrison, fouling one ninety-six mile-per-hour fastball back to the netting behind home plate. The count went full, which was important because it would give the runners a chance to get a head start. The pitch came, and it was clear immediately that his magic was still very much alive.

Freese hit a bullet into the left-center gap for a game-tying double. I could only shake my head and laugh as the camera showed him standing on second, appearing as cool as he'd ever been. I cannot recall another postseason in which one man was responsible for so many crucial hits in so many games. That's the main reason why he won the Most Valuable Player award in both the NLCS and the World Series in 2011.

With the score back to even, Carpenter returned to the mound and was rejuvenated. He would only give three more hits over his next five innings of work, keeping the Rangers off the scoreboard for the rest of his outing. LaRussa's gamble, the last in an amazing three decades of managing that included countless others, had paid off.

The Cards' MVP runner-up (in my opinion), Allen Craig, delivered a home run in the bottom of the third to put them on top 3-2. Though Freese's hit will rightfully be remembered as the biggest of game six, Craig's homer in the eighth inning of that game should not be forgotten. In fact, Craig had important hits in all four of the Cardinals' home games in the World Series.

I had a strong urge to call dad after Craig's homer, but then I realized that that wasn't an option anymore. Our talks about the state of Cardinal baseball were now history. The revelation washed over me, and I felt a pit growing in my stomach. I looked down at Jack, who was intently focusing on each pitch just the way I used to while sitting next to dad, and my sadness was alleviated. I reminded myself that dad's passing was not a tragedy, that he had been given ample time to live his life. Most of all, his pain would soon be at an end.

With Carp back on track with a lead, I started to believe that the Cardinals were going to pull it off. They only needed a couple of insurance runs to give him some cushion. That crucial moment came in the bottom of the fifth, when they managed to score two runs without getting the ball out of the infield. Craig started the rally with a one out walk against Scott Feldman, followed by Pujols getting hit by a pitch. After a groundout put the runners at second and third, Mr. Freese walked to the plate. The Rangers could have just as easily decided to pitch to him, but with first base open they took no chances. They gave him an intentional pass, which no one could blame Ron Washington for.

The key at-bat would fall to Yadi. Though he was still young and not yet in his prime, Molina was already a playoff hero from years before. With the bases loaded, Molina now stood at the plate with a chance to possibly seal the Cardinals' eleventh championship.

Like the true professional that he is, Molina battled Feldman and eventually worked the count full. One of them would have to give, and no one believed it would be Yadi. The pitch came in and sailed tantalizingly off the outside corner for ball four. Yadi gave a victorious bat flip as he left the batter's box and jogged toward first. Craig came home to score (again) and the lead was 4-2. The walk also drove Feldman from the game. C.J. Wilson, a lefty who was normally a starter, was brought in to stop the bleeding.

Perhaps it was the unusual role that Wilson was playing, or the pressure of a bases loaded situation in the biggest game of the year, but something affected him as he began his first windup. His pitch darted inside toward

Rafael Furcal, who as a switch-hitter was batting from the right side. The ball plunked Furcal squarely on his right hip as he tried to jump away. The crowd roared at the realization of another run scored. Five Cardinals had reached base in the fifth without putting the ball in play. The feeling of certainty began to grow.

Jack wasn't as excited as I was, but he was high-fiving me and probably reacting more to my antics (clapping and talking to the TV are two of my favorite options) than to the game itself. When Molina came up again in the seventh and smacked an RBI base hit to center to make it 6-2, Karen (of all people) jumped off the edge of the other bed and yelled, "That's it! They've got it for sure now!"

At that moment I had never loved her (or wanted her) more. And as much as I desired to say that it wasn't over yet and that we shouldn't start celebrating, I didn't feel my usual sense of foreboding or negativity. Sometimes it's just your year, and with six outs to go I knew it was ours. I didn't say it out loud though, just in case.

After Lance Lynn worked a perfect eighth inning, the feeling of certain victory only intensified. As the Cardinals began taking their swings in the bottom half, I decided to call home. I'm not sure what I was expecting, but my deepest hope was that mom would tell me dad was conscious and catching some of the game. Maybe I would even be able to say a few words to him before the final out was recorded.

The phone rang several times before mom picked up. She sounded better than when we spoke earlier in the day. She seemed rested, even relieved.

"Hi mom. What's the word? How is everyone over there?" I was encouraged by the way she answered, but my hopes diminished quickly when I heard nothing but a long silence following my question. Finally, I couldn't stand it. "Mom? Are you there? What's going on?"

"He's gone. Just a few minutes ago. He was actually awake for a while and I was in there with him. He asked me to come close and I thought maybe he was going to ask me to turn the game on. But instead he asked me for a kiss, and he told me he loved me."

She got quiet again for a few seconds. I was frozen, unable to process this news even though I had known it was coming. No matter how much you think you're emotionally ready for a death in the family, it hits you like an anvil nonetheless. I sat, or rather collapsed, into the only chair in the hotel room. Karen must have seen my face because she immediately came to me and knelt next to the chair.

Mom continued, "He was very calm at the end. He just closed his eyes and that was it. I just thank God it's over. He's with Jesus now and that's what we have to remember. Pauly, are you okay?"

The woman just lost the only man she ever loved after a lifetime together, and she's asking me if I'm okay. I rubbed my forehead and tried to cobble together a few words.

"Uh, yeah mom. I'm glad it's over too. I could tell last night how much pain he was in. How's Megan?" Karen caressed the back of my head and rubbed my leg with her other hand as she attempted to console me.

"Like us, sad but relieved. She's already handling the arrangements on her cell phone. You don't have to worry about us. We're okay. I want you to stay with your family tonight and just be with them. You can come over tomorrow if you like, we'll have to sort through some old pictures and things to get ready for the funeral." Though it was counter to what I felt I should do, I honored her wish and stayed with Jack and Karen.

The more I thought about it, the more I believed that dad would have wanted it this way. I needed to be there with my son when the Cardinals got that final out and celebrated with an entire city. It would be a memory that both of us would hold onto for life. I thought of 1982 and dancing around with dad in our living room after Sutter struck out Thomas. It hurt to know that dad didn't get to see this game, but somehow I knew he would see the end. And wherever he was, hopefully Uncle Phil was there too.

"Well, I'm glad you at least got to talk to him one more time before he went," I said, my voice echoing the numb feeling in my chest.

"Me too. We all got to say goodbye in our own ways. That's the way it should be."

"You're sure you don't want me to come over for a while? I'm more than willing..."

"No! Your place is next to Jack right now. There'll be time for all the other stuff later. Are the Cardinals winning?"

A faint smile crossed my lips. "Yeah, actually they're one inning away from closing it out. You think dad is watching?"

Without any hesitation, mom replied. "You know he is. And he's got the best seat in the house." I love a lot of things about my mother, and her faith is perhaps my favorite. Her confidence came through the phone in a powerful way, and I restrained another urge to cry.

"I love you, mom. And tell Megan I love her too. I'll see you in the morning."

"I love you too. Now go and enjoy your son's first World Series win!"

We hung up and Karen gave me a long hug, perhaps thinking that I would need to cry. I hugged her back, but mercifully my attention was diverted by the sight of Jason Motte delivering his first pitch of the ninth. Jack was sitting Indian style near the edge of the bed with his head resting in his hands. His stare was intense...he knew what was at stake. He had heard me talk enough about World Series of the past to know the significance of the moment. The rabid crowd and camera shots of the players in both dugouts also

271

portrayed this sense of historical importance.

I got up and took my place next to Jack. I rubbed his back with my left hand as if he were a living good luck charm. By now I knew charms weren't necessary. The win was already secure. Though the Cards had a four run lead, and thus it was a "non-save situation," LaRussa was taking no chances by sending out the closer.

On TV they were showing the championship flags waving over Busch Stadium, in anticipation of a new one soon to be posted there. Just then Jack looked over at me and said, "This is it, right dad? If the Cardinals get them out, then it's over? We win the World Series?"

I loved that he was already using "we" to describe the team. I've gotten grief from people in the past for saying "we won" or "we've got a shot," but I don't care. When you're a fan of a team, then it's your team and you've got the right to say "we" whenever you like.

"That's right, buddy! We've got three outs to get, and then we're world champions!"

His eyes got a little wider when I said that. We watched as Motte fired a couple of pitches out of the zone before finding it for strike one with a blistering fastball. Cruz swung on the 2-1 pitch, but he was late and popped it up into center. Jay made the easy play, and the decibel level at Busch edged higher.

Next up was our nemesis, Mike Napoli. It was a relief to know he could hit the ball as far as he wanted to, but it would only count for one. Motte wasn't messing around with any other pitches, he was throwing straight gas every time. The gun was showing ninety-eight consistently.

Napoli put a good swing on one of them, but fouled it straight back. On 2-2, he hit a weak chopper to third where Daniel Descalso was patrolling. His throw to first was pure, and the crowd reached a frantic pitch with one out left to go.

I stood up and prepared for the inevitable

conclusion. Though this finish seemed similar to their game five closeout in 2006, this series had been vastly different. The Tigers had virtually given that series away with their shoddy defense, but this one had been a war. The Rangers were most likely the better team, but the October magic was on our side.

I picked up Jack and stood him on the bed. "Can you believe this? Our boys are going to pull it off!" I just hoped that he would remember and treasure this moment the way I had my first one in '82. My greater hope was that this was only the beginning of a lifetime of good memories for him. He giggled as I poked at his ribs.

For a moment I forgot about the past twenty-four hours and reveled in the joy that was about to explode all over Cardinal Nation. I remembered their tortured regular season that left them ten and a half games behind in the Wild Card race in late August. I thought of the final week when they were still three games behind with only five to play, and the final night when Carpenter (who else?) nailed down the win against Houston. The Cardinals' run to this moment had been an amazing quest.

Karen stood and took her place at Jack's side, at least partially to make sure he didn't fall off the bed. I leaned over and kissed her on the cheek. Never in my life (before or since) have I felt such a confluence of emotions at once. My mind was pulled in several directions, I was celebrating, mourning, and pondering our family's future all at once.

Murphy took the first pitch for a strike, then put a late swing on a fastball. The ball sailed high in the air, but when the camera changed I could see that Allen Craig was drifting back with an eye toward catching it. He reached up as he backpedaled, and the ball dropped into his glove. Craig's arms raised in victory, and the impossible mission was complete.

Though I didn't hear him initially because we were

busy jumping around and shouting like goons, Joe Buck summed up their accomplishment, "What a team, what a ride! The Cardinals are World Champs in 2011!"

The men on the field celebrated with unbridled joy, dog-piling and embracing as the fans showered them with loving cheers. Our own personal celebration finally halted and we watched the scene unfold. I thought of Albert Pujols and Tony LaRussa, two greats who would never again don a Cardinals uniform. I thought of Jack, and how this series would always mean something special to him. Most of all, I thought of dad.

A kind of euphoria spread over me as a mixture of happiness, relief, and simple emotional exhaustion. I decided to take it all in, to soak in an event that would never again be as meaningful or personal as it was on that night. I may see other Cardinals teams win a World Series, but it won't compare to the experience of 2011.

***

We took a late night trip to Steak 'N Shake after the game for a round of milk shakes. At some point during that excursion, as I goofed with Jack and teased Karen, I realized that I felt like a complete man for the first time in my life. No longer would I have to look over my shoulder and fear the specter of the father I left behind. I had finally faced and forgiven him, and in doing so, I received a kind of atonement.

There are times when I think of our evening together and wish we had both said and done more to bridge the gap. Sometimes I'll feel the old guilt and berate myself for having waited so long. For the most part though, when I think of game six, I feel satisfaction. It's the kind that comes from having endured a rite of passage. More than that, it's the knowledge that I did the right thing for myself and my family.

We spent most of the weekend at the old house, prepping for dad's funeral on Monday. It was cathartic to rummage through old photos and memories. Jack took the news of his grandpa's death surprisingly well. Perhaps even at a young age, he could sense that dad didn't have long.

At the funeral there was a large crowd, but few tears. I recognized nearly all the faces that I encountered. Each of them had their own unique stories about how dad had either made them laugh, helped them out, pissed them off, or all of those. It was clear that dad's legacy in Powell would live on long after that day.

Butch gave me a monstrous hug and told me again and again how proud my dad, he, and all the rest of their gang were of me. His positive spirit and funny stories buoyed me through a hectic and trying day. Butch realized that he was lucky to still be among the living considering the lifestyle that they embodied for so long. He was being incredibly strong on a day when his lifelong best friend was being buried. He understood, as we all did, that dad was better off.

Talking with the people of Powell, I realized that every one of them believed that dad was their true friend. Softball buddies, drinking buddies, folks he had delivered to…they all felt the loss. Of course, none of them could know the pain and frustration of living with Johnny Ray. All they knew was that the unofficial "mayor" of Powell was dead, and respect must be paid.

Mom spent the day being consoled by her many church friends and, of course, Megan and Karen. I was proud to see both of them rally around her. It seemed that everyone had a well-defined role at the funeral except me. Megan insisted on keeping Jack around her and the other ladies. I can't imagine how many times his cheeks got pinched. I was left to bounce from one guest to the next, each of them eager to tell me a Johnny Ray story. The whole experience was dizzying, and soon I found myself back at mom's house on Tuesday morning.

I decided to stay in town one more day while Karen

took Jack home so he wouldn't miss another day of school. Megan also stuck around, and the three of us struggled to know what to do now that the funeral was behind us. I puttered around for most of the day finding odd cleaning or repair jobs to pass the time. Mostly I just wanted to be near mom in case she needed to talk or just cry.

As I was digging around in a closet trying to find a couple of light bulbs, mom tapped me on the shoulder and motioned for me to come with her. She had tears in her eyes, but I said nothing and followed her toward their bedroom. She silently entered the room and grabbed an envelope that was laying at the foot of the bed. Turning slowly, she looked it over and then handed it to me.

"I found this just now as I was digging through your dad's sock drawer. Apparently he buried it so I wouldn't find it until after he was gone. He was..." She cut herself off as tears began to roll down both her cheeks.

I looked at front of the envelope. It read, "For Jack on his birthday" in dad's familiar handwriting. It was a little shakier than usual, having been written when he was probably in immense pain at some point in the last few weeks. I tore it open, feeling a lump growing in my throat. I decided to stay strong in mom's presence.

I found a folded piece of notebook paper, but with something tucked inside of it. I unfolded the page and let the contents slide into my hand. It took a few seconds for me to comprehend what I was looking at, but when I did I could no longer contain the tears. His gift was simple and wonderful: two vouchers good for any Cardinals home game in 2012. Jack's first live Cardinals game would be provided by the same man who took me to my first.

The letter was brief but powerful. "Paul: Take Jack to a game on me. I hope you enjoy it as much as I did with you. I wish I could be there. I love you both very much. Dad." I stood staring at the letter, re-reading it several times before handing it to mom. She wiped more tears away as she looked at the vouchers and letter.

Neither of us was sure of how dad had pulled this off without mom knowing about it. I decided he must have used Butch to order the vouchers or buy them online and then sneak them into the house. No matter how, it was a perfect gesture. I couldn't wait to get home and tell Jack that his grandpa had gotten him a ticket to Busch Stadium.

Mom broke the silence. "Oh Johnny..." She was shaking her head and still looking at the letter. I smiled and gave her a long hug. We were both grateful for one more Johnny Ray story to tell.

I waited until summer to make use of dad's gift. In June we made the drive into downtown St. Louis and I witnessed Jack marveling over the new Busch Stadium the way I had over the old one. They played the Royals in an inter-league game that was very entertaining. The Cards jumped out to a 6-1 lead, only to fall behind 7-6 in the seventh. Thanks to huge performances from Holliday and Molina, the Cards came back and won 10-7.

On our way out of the stadium, with Jack proudly toting the hat, shirt, and baseball cards I bought for him in the team store, I made sure to stop at the statue of Stan Musial. I read the quote on the base to him and then said, "You know, my dad showed me this exact same statue when he took me to my first game at the old stadium."

Jack's reply was priceless. "Wow! That statue must be really old!"

My only reaction was to laugh and agree. I laughed because that's what you do when faced with the brutal honesty of a child. But I also laughed because I knew, someday, he would be having the same conversation with his son.

The End

About the Author:

Chad A. Cain is a high school history teacher and a lifelong member of Cardinal Nation. He resides in Mount Vernon, Indiana with his wife. One Night In October is his first published novel. Check out chadacain.com for more information.

www.ingramcontent.com/pod-product-compliance
Lightning Source LLC
Chambersburg PA
CBHW060009100426
42740CB00010B/1446